Alexandros Massavetas

going back to CONSTANTINOPLE

Istanbul

a city of absences

ATHENS NEWS

ISBN 978-960-89200-2-7

Published by Athens News
3, Christou Lada Str.
Athens 102 37
www.athensnews.gr

Publisher's Preface

Entering the aircraft hangar-sized church of Hagia Sophia in Istanbul, it is impossible not to feel something of the awe of a congregant of the sixth century. Gone are the millions of gold leaf-covered tesserae that made the dome above the nave appear to glow like an eternal sunset, and the incantation of Orthodox liturgy has not been heard since Mehmet II rode into the church five and a half centuries ago to claim it for Islam. Yet the architecture of empire, even naked, is unmistakeable.

Greeks have an ongoing obsession with Istanbul, or, as it was known to Westerners until well into the 1930s, Constantinople. It is the city that connects them to their illustrious ancient past. After suffering defeat at the hands of the Romans in 146 BC, the Greeks eventually got something of their own back. They dominated the Roman Empire culturally, and finally took over governance of its eastern half with the founding of Constantinople in 330. It was a Greek emperor who institutionalised Christianity as a state religion and built its first monuments across the eastern Mediterranean. That empire lasted for more than a thousand years, and marked the last period when Greeks would write the headlines of history.

Four catastrophic dates linger in the memory of the modern Greeks: 1204, when the Venetians and French of the Fourth Crusade sacked the city; 1453, when it fell for the last time to the Selçuk Turks; 1821, when the Phanariot Greeks, who had managed to earn a place in the new Ottoman order as translators and governors, were punished for the revolution that broke out in mainland Greece; and 1955, when a state-condoned pogrom marked the beginning of the end for the residual Greek community.

Not surprisingly, most Greek histories of Constantinople dwell on past glory and devote little space to the city of today. Alex Massavetas, a polyglot Athenian with a love of the East, has set out to strike a balance. He guides us through such diverse monuments as the massive Theodosian Walls in which Kurds and Gypsies squat with their sheep today, and the fine Rustem Paşa mosque, perhaps the most tile-ornamented religious building in all Islam. He visits tradesmen whose purpose-built arcade has been in continuous use for three and a half centuries, and chances upon Ethiopian Monophysite Christians wailing their worship before a bewildered Armenian patriarchate.

All these ethnic groups along with Russian 'Natashas', self-flagellating Iranian Shiites, Jews, Catholics, Bulgarians and others make up the complex society of Istanbul today. Neighbourhoods once famous for middle-class Greeks are now bohemian districts favoured by prostitutes and gays, while what to Byzantine Greeks was the far-flung Pera now has some of the city's prime real estate.

What makes this book such a pleasure to read is not just that it is an education refreshingly ordered by the author's itineraries rather than the history books; it is that the author leaves himself open to the human encounters that reveal hidden corners of the city and its life.

Going back to Constantinople is required reading for anyone planning to visit The City, but that does not prevent it from being an unsurpassed pleasure for those staying home.

John Psaropoulos
Editor
Athens News

Two horses lead a phaeton through
the dense pine forests of Prinkipo (Büyükada)
as part of the island's Grand Tour

To my "other half", my better half,
for being exactly that.
And for colouring each corner
of this beautiful city, our home,
with a memory of tenderness

Table of Contents

A city of absences 10

part one: two feet in Europe

The historic peninsula of Constantinople

Around the Hippodrome: the heart of two Empires 18
Past and present along the Marmara shore 34
Merchant districts of old: commerce alla Turca 48
Chasing Byzantine glory in districts derelict 64
Phanari: phantoms of aristocrats and gloomy dereliction 80
Awakening schoolbook memories: a walk by the Land Walls 102
Imperial district turned slum: Blachernae 118

The old "New Town": the Pera shore

Galata: the "stranger in town" 136
Where buildings are the narrators:
Pera, the Paris on the Bosphorus 156
Tarlabaşı and Tatavla: from "Little Greece" to ghetto 180
Istanbul's Jews: the "Minority of the State"? 200
The hidden face of the metropolis: Istanbul's Hebraica 210
Would-be conquerors turn refugees:
Russians in Constantinople 228

part two: Asia and the outskirts

Old districts of the Asian shore: glimpsing Europe from "across" 246

An Empress' diadem: the Bosphorus 260

The Princes' Islands: people, stories and feasts in an idyllic refuge 276

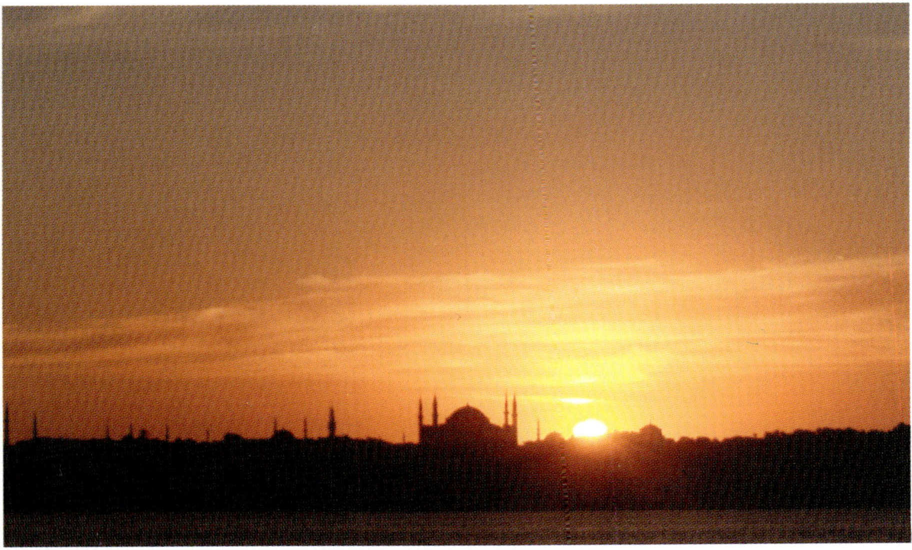

A city of absences

"I have come to stay and I will stay, whatever it takes," I wrote to a friend on July 19, 2003. Four days earlier I had arrived from Athens with a one-way ticket and a huge suitcase, containing all the perceived necessities for my migration. My words betrayed my state of mind at the time: determination and optimism as strong as they were unjustified by the circumstances. I had arrived in a city where I knew nobody, in a country whose language I ignored, where no person or job awaited me. I found myself in a room – a filthy hole, rather – in the Pera district of Tünel. It was a wet and hot afternoon. When the ventilator exploded, scattering pieces of itself all over me just as I had dozed off, I smiled. I chose to interpret this as a sign that things would look up.

This took a while. I had no plan whatsoever, having just abandoned a promising (some still insist) legal career for the uncertain. And I had done so without second thoughts, even though my starting base was now the enormous suitcase and some savings. An irrational passion kept me moving, telling me I was on the right track, and nothing could get in the way of my enthusiasm. *Your home is here now.* The city, in which I had first found myself by accident, had cast an unexpected and irrevocable spell upon me. From setting foot in it until I settled there, my foremost preoccupation was how to spend time in Istanbul – not as a short-term visitor but as a resident. Moving to the city that fascinated me became an obsession that few in my immediate environment could understand. Perhaps because they didn't know the city, or didn't know it well enough. Perhaps because they didn't know me.

There was the obvious question, which I myself had asked many times. Why Istanbul? What is so special about this city, why did it manage to enslave me in a way no other place ever did? What was it that made me feel, at my first ever glimpse of Pera, that *here* was my home? What hid behind my feeling of homesickness and deprivation during the periods that I was away from *my city*, as I had proclaimed her? I wasn't born or raised in Istanbul; personal memories did not tie me to the place.

So what was it that made me identify with it? Now, after three years of living in the city, I think I know the answer to these questions.

Istanbul has a peculiar sort of magic, which no other city radiates. This magic does not derive solely from the unparalleled natural beauty its complex topography produces: on the junction of Europe and Asia, Istanbul sits on a series of hills, on three chunks of land divided by different seas. The city is not limited to its unrivalled collection of monuments, which give Istanbul an idiosyncrasy of its own. Istanbul enchants because it perplexes. It will perplex the outsider as it often perplexes its residents, for it defies categorisation and stereotypes. Istanbul is not a European city, even if two-thirds of it is built on European soil; at the same time it is not the East that orientalists fantasise about. Or maybe it is both. It is a fascinating mixture of people who live shockingly different lifestyles and of monuments to a thrilling variety of nations and periods. Istanbul, or Constantinople, as the city was officially named from its foundation until the 1930s, is a microcosm of the world and its history. Confronting Istanbul necessarily means confronting oneself.

The magic I spoke of does not emanate solely, or even mostly, from its kaleidoscope of images and cultural perspectives. It stems from a profound schism. The visitor with some knowledge and sensitivity will realise immediately that its present life has little, if anything, in common with the silent world of its buildings. A huge gap has separated the two. The contrast is so sharp that many have spoken of a "schizophrenic" city. Istanbul's historic quarters are mostly inhabited by squatters from Anatolia, who have little knowledge or appreciation of their material surroundings. These buildings, their forms and ornaments, are very eloquent in their silence, although they must seem irrelevant to those who now live in them. They cry out for you to know that they were once inhabited by diverse others, others who are now scattered to the four corners of the earth. Istanbul is a city of absences. Its crumbling old houses, its churches and synagogues remain as the memories of those who have left. In shaping its visual aesthetics, its absences are more important than its presences, if may I paraphrase Azar Nafisi's pronouncement on Tehran. There is a very heavy silence over much of Istanbul. Its buildings beg for attention, eager to reveal a world of secrets.

Constantinople (and thus I refer to the Ottoman capital) suffered much in becoming Istanbul. A multi-ethnic imperial capital became the largest city of a nation state, and in the process lost, slowly but steadily, its multi-national and multi-lingual character. Ottoman Constantinople fell victim to the destructive force of nationalism. Its fate is not unique, as it befell every urban centre in the Levant.

The twentieth century was a cursed century; it annihilated the Levant's multi-ethnic metropolises and thus robbed them of their soul and their beauty. Once the *Barcelona of the East*, the *Madre de Israel*, Salonica is now a Christian and Greek-speaking concrete mass; its large Jewish community was depleted by the Shoah and Judeo-Spanish is no longer spoken in its streets. The Ottoman fountains stand in its Upper Town irrelevant to their surroundings, in quarters whose Muslims were evicted to Turkey in the 1923 Exchange of Populations. Writer Mark Mazower has rightly called Salonica a *city of ghosts*, but the term is equally appropriate for Belle Époque Smyrna with its Greek majority, which disappeared in the flames and massacres of nationalist struggle. And for Cairo and Alexandria, where "foreign" merchants and artisans were ousted and their place taken by destitute fellaheen, much more foreign to those cities' memories than the fleeing Europeans. But the destruction was not only limited to the Levant. Have not the towns of Transylvania and Silesia lost much of their soul with the eviction of their Germans?

What is unique in Istanbul is that the city may have lost its non-Muslim inhabitants, but has retained their architectural legacy almost intact. Other cities that suffered a similar ravaging of their character have become dull, provincial. Istanbul hasn't. There is an energy about it, an aura of faded grandeur, a potential that refuses to die. Istanbul has become ethnographically, linguistically and culturally poorer, it has ceased to be a microcosm of the world, but nobody could reasonably dismiss it as boring. Istanbul simply changed name and character, and, after a long period of stagnation, is looking to the future confidently, aspiring to become what it was for millennia: a world city.

This is what has fascinated me here from the start: the constant bombardment of my senses by messages sent from a silent world. In Istanbul, the buildings talk. And they have endless stories to tell. For three years I have been living on two different levels. My personal circumstances were happy, as luck blessed me with a loving partner and a circle of dear friends. At the same time I have entered a dream world, attempting to peep into and live the lives of others who lived in the very same streets where I live, work, party, stroll and do my shopping. Those others have left long ago, and this "other" life of mine is a pursuit of ghosts and visions. These happy three years have taught me much and changed me immensely.

This book has no academic pretensions whatsoever, nor is it a travel guide providing practical information. It is a personal account of what I have learned and discovered over the last three years. In a series of journeys through time and space it aims to unearth the city's memories and help the traveller come to terms with the schism that reigns over much of the city. While trying to convey some of Istanbul's magic, it also attempts the difficult task of connecting past and present. It is first and foremost about nostalgia, and in this sense follows a trend prevalent among the remnants of Istanbul's old Turkish middle class. After years of silence, a nostalgic longing for the once multi-lingual and multi-ethnic city with its refined urban life permeates certain circles, and comes as a belated vindication to all those who were forced to leave against their will. My nostalgia focuses on Istanbul's non-Muslim communities, which constituted more than 40 percent of the Ottoman city's population and much of its character.

Since this travelogue centres on memory and history, it inevitably moves through the city's historic quarters and has a limited scope. Most of the areas described are those that the minorities abandoned, and most are now settled by destitute migrants. This should not mislead the reader into any stereotyped images of "Turks". Turkey is a pluralistic society of extreme, even shocking, diversity of lifestyles and attitudes. Most of the areas where westernised, secular and affluent Turkish middle-class people live lack history and monuments. They are essentially modern boroughs and are outside this book's scope. At some point I would like to write about life in the modern metropolis that Istanbul has become – about the sushi parties in my Pera home, my outings with Turkish friends in the upmarket cafés of Nişantaşi, my experience of Istanbul's anarchist, hip and modern art scenes, and my life with a Turkish partner. But all this is left for the future.

I would like to thank all those who have walked beside me these last wonderful three years, making Istanbul a much-cherished home and refuge. Keeping the chronological order of your appearance in my life, Amalia, Sinem, Defne, Sophia, Leyla, Cihan, Nancy, Nursel, Burcu, Serdar, Şule, Christiane, Solita, Antonis, Demetres, Stella, Harry, Memo. I would like you to know that you are much-beloved companions in a beautiful journey.

Special thanks to Akylas Milas for encouraging me to go forward with a book on Istanbul and to Cihan, Solita, Demetres, Antonis and Christiane for reading the drafts and giving me their feedback. I am also grateful to the young and enthusiastic editor of the *Athens News*, John Psaropoulos. I will never forget that he was the first person to publish my articles and give me a chance to write.

Finally, I have no words to express my gratitude to my beloved parents, who constantly support me even though they are continually freaked out by my choices – moving to Istanbul being the best example.

Galatasaray, Pera (Beyoğlu), October 2006

PART ONE

two feet in Europe

The historic peninsula of Constantinople

The Neo-Byzantine Haghia Kyriake rises over Belle Époque *appartements* in Kumkapı

Around the Hippodrome: the heart of two Empires

Haghia Sophia, the "Great Church" of the Byzantines, is still the symbol of the city, transformed into a museum by Atatürk

I find myself having difficulty explaining to visiting friends how, after three years in Istanbul, I still feel a stranger when visiting parts of the Old City, as if I am entering an exotic and unfamiliar wonderland. I live, work and go out and about on the Pera shore, north of the Golden Horn, the channel splitting European Istanbul in two. Most of my friends live in my immediate vicinity, where city life centres.

As many Istanbulites, I often get a chance to marvel at the Old City skyline. Its domes and minarets appear spectacularly lit at night from the terraces and verandas of Pera bars, or as a grey parade of imposing, bizarre silhouettes from the decks of ferries. For the past year I have had the luxury of having Haghia Sophia framed by my window. Like most locals, I am more familiar with the wondrous spectacle at a distance, rather than with the chaos of its twisting and winding, steep alleys. My pilgrimages south of the channel almost always have a specific aim: to visit some monument; to photograph a neighbourhood; to hunt down a forgotten chapel. The Old City isn't part of my daily life.

Yet I know it far better than any of my Turkish friends, Istanbulites by birth, who hardly ever venture into its quarters. In today's gigantic metropolis the inhabitants of the districts north of the Golden Horn, along the Bosphorus and the Asian shore of the Marmara, have no contact with the impoverished and pious groups who dwell in the derelict quarters of the Old City. The Marmara and the Golden Horn embrace the Old City "like a dark blue garland", as a Turkish song goes. Containing the city's Byzantine ruins and most of its Ottoman monuments, the Old City is the domain of immigrants from the Anatolian countryside.

The Walled City, as the peninsula is also known, was the heart of Constantinople, both Byzantine and Ottoman. Here was the "Polis" of the Greeks, renamed Istanbul by its new rulers. (The name, a corruption of the Greek words Is tin Polin – "in the city" – was initially confined to the peninsula and did not become official for the city as a whole until 1930. Ottoman documents mostly used Konstandiniyye.) Galata, across the Golden Horn, was a separate town under both rules, whilst Pera evolved to challenge the quaint Ottoman capital in every sense. To both Byzantines and Ottoman Turks, the Pera shore was the opposite, faraway shore, viewed suspiciously and with bewilderment from within Constantinople's lofty walls.

Nowadays it's the Old City that bewilders, no more a part of city life but rather an open-air museum whose exhibits are scattered amidst slums. It makes headlines whenever grand restoration projects and art exhibitions are discussed, or when the unpleasant social realities of its conservative quarters make their way to the television screens. The heart of city life is Pera, renamed Beyoğlu, whilst the "opposite shore" is now the string of residential quarters in Asia. Life has moved away from the ancient nucleus.

Sultanahmet is the Old City's most visited corner – the only one many visitors ever come to know. In the daytime, the area around Haghia Sophia and the mosques can be off-putting, with its crowds of photograph-thirsty tourists and insistent touts. Yet at night it radiates magic. A serene neighbourhood spreads under beautifully lit minarets. The air seems heavy with the memories and legends of seventeen centuries.

Haghia Sophia, Istanbul's most famous Byzantine building, is still the city's emblem. Commissioned by Emperor Justinian to replace an older church – burnt in the 532 Nika revolt

Anatolians in front of the obelisk of Theodosius on the Hippodrome

– and inaugurated in 537, Haghia Sophia is one of the few buildings of its age and size still standing. Its peculiar domed figure, that many mosques tried to imitate, knows no rivals. The church was not consecrated to a saint called Sophia, as might be thought, but to the Holy (Haghia) Wisdom (Sophia), meaning God's wisdom. For almost a millennium, it was Christendom's greatest church.

It is difficult to try to visualise what the exterior must have originally looked like. To do so, one must ignore the minarets, the huge buttresses – added by Ottoman architect Sinan to enhance the building's stability – and the series of domed Ottoman tombs and kiosks surrounding it. Only the upper half can be said to have escaped much transformation.

Looking at Haghia Sophia from a distance and standing in front of it convey very different feelings. In the distance the church appears elegant, if bizarre, crowned by the most impressive of Istanbul's domes. "A building which crowns the whole country," wrote Procopius, Justinian's courtly historian. Indeed, the colossal church was a show of power by Justinian, who had just survived the Nika uprising and was determined to resurrect the Roman Empire to its former glory. The church was intended to inspire awe in those approaching by sea.

A closer look reveals a clumsy titan whose façades are concealed behind colossal buttresses. Yet even if one ignores later additions, one cannot speak of elegance. "This Church, doubtlessly the most beautiful building in the world after St Peter, rises frustratingly heavy from the outside," judged French botanist Pitton de Tournefort in 1700. A devout Catholic, he rushed to defend the aesthetic primacy of the Vatican's Great Church.

"It is as if the entire burdensome weight of more than 1,400 years of history has been rendered visible," wrote John Ash, a contemporary British poet and Istanbul resident.

The explanation of this visual disappointment is that the exterior was intended as a mere shell to host the otherworldly effect of the interior. It is a basic rule in Byzantine architecture that a building's exterior should be modest; it's the interior that counts. The building is like a human being neglecting his or her looks in order to cultivate the mind and soul. Haghia Sophia was no exception.

The beauty of its interior was legendary, and it amazed travellers. The huge dome, symbolising God embracing the world, seems to float on air. It is supported by four immense pillars, hidden in the building's interior walls, and buttressed by two semidomes. "From the lightness of the whole building, it does not appear to rest on a solid foundation, but to cover the place beneath as though it were suspended from heaven by a golden chain. All these parts surprisingly joined to one another in the air, suspended from one another, and resting only on the one next to them, form one admirably harmonious whole," wrote Procopius.

The building's architects, Anthemius of Tralleis and Isidorus of Miletus, carried out an experiment of three-dimensional geometry, and the sensation of air and space achieved by them is still present 15 centuries later. A row of 40 windows at the base of the dome lets the sunlight in and makes the dome appear to rise over a wreath of light. Against such a setting,

Christ Pantocrator, mosaic over the Imperial Gate, Inner Narthex, Haghia Sophia

Pantocrator flanked by Empress Zoe
and Emperor Constantine Monomachus

Mosaic of the Deesis, galleries
of Haghia Sophia

the legend goes, the envoys of Vladimir, king of Kiev, thought they had been transported to heaven, and proposed their country's adoption of the Orthodox faith.

The heavenly sensation they experienced is long gone. Thirty million tesserae, covered in gold leaf, covered the upper part of the church, above the marble revetments, producing a bright golden glow. Gold in Orthodox theology stands for purity and truth. The tesserae have mostly disappeared. The church's mosaics were covered in lime or excised after the conquering Turks converted it into a mosque, and few survive. Most remnants of the Christian religion, such as the crosses once inscribed on the marble slabs of the gallery, have been vandalised. Four immense wooden plaques with Koranic verses have been attached to the base of the dome. The immense space reminds more of a corpse than of the rhapsody of visual sensations it once was.

Some outstanding mosaics nevertheless survive. Their vivid colours and intensity of expression do much to overturn perceptions of Byzantine art as overtly stylised and detached from the material world. The mosaic of the Pantocrator greets the visitor over the Imperial Gate leading from the inner narthex to the nave. That of the Platytera (Madonna with Child) in the apse, unveiled on Easter Sunday 846, was praised for its naturalism by the scholarly Patriarch Photius. More are found in the galleries, a section reserved for women when the building functioned as church. The lifelike expression of

Jesus in the Deesis (early fourteenth century) is striking. The mosaic of Empress Zoe and her last husband Constantine Monomachus beside an enthroned Christ, and that of John II and his Hungarian wife Irene are also moving in their details – the melancholic face of John and the high cheekbones of the blonde empress, betraying her Hungarian descent.

Haghia Sophia's most famous and symbolic mosaic is found above the door leading from the narthex to the exit: Constantine the Great is depicted offering his city to the enthroned Virgin, while Justinian is offering her Haghia Sophia. This late-tenth-century work best represents the Byzantine intellectual order: the Great Church is the crown of the city, itself the crown of an empire dedicated to, and thereby protected by, the Virgin. One of the city's epithets was, "protected by God". Until the first sack of Constantinople by the Crusaders in 1204, nobody seriously challenged the idea that Constantinople was protected by the Mother of God and was meant to reign over a blessed realm until the end of the world.

Haghia Sophia excites very passionate feelings to very different groups. For Greeks it is a focal point of collective reference. It personifies the Byzantine Empire and nostalgia for it, as well as representing a painful part of Greek history and identity: Haghia Sophia lies outside Greek territory, as does the capital of the medieval Greek empire. Greek national consciousness has vested the Great Church, as Byzantines called it, with unparalleled drama. Haghia Sophia is much more evocative in the soul of the average Greek than even the Parthenon, and excites much stronger feelings.

Conversely, for Turkish nationalism the conversion of the Great Church to a mosque is the epitome of the 1453 "Conquest of Istanbul", which continues to play an important role in Turkish identity. Unlike the formation of the secular republic, hailed by Kemalists but deeply – if silently – resented by Islamists, the Conquest is a source of pride for all nationalists. In the metro station at Taksim, one is greeted by a tiled depiction of the Conquest. The "Istanbul Conquest Society" placed plaques on all Byzantine and Genoese buildings, noting when the particular spot fell to the conquering army. On the wall immediately exiting Haghia Sophia, a plaque is inscribed with a prophecy attributed to the prophet Muhammad: "Konstandiniyye shall certainly be conquered. What a nice statesman will the one who conquers it be, his army what a glorious army."

In the past it was often alleged by foreign writers that the authorities' treatment of the monument was indicative of a deep complex. For decades, a colossal tower of scaffolding has been "abandoned" in the nave, right under the dome, obscuring a great part of the latter and making it impossible to admire the wonderful effect of space. Rarely is there any work carried out or any workers around. Many people question why the scaffolding was put there in the first place. For years, Haghia Sophia was left in the dark at night, whilst neighbouring Sultanahmet mosque and Topkapı Palace were brightly illuminated. Things are changing, though, and for the last two years the church has joined the pantheon of artistically lit silhouettes that illuminate Istanbul at night.

Ataturk turned Haghia Sophia into a museum in 1935; its new use epitomised the new republic's secular ideals. Yet the church continues to stir controversy. Amplifiers have been placed in one of the minarets, broadcasting the Islamic call to prayer, after insistent demands by the resurgent Islamic movement. A former archaeologist told me: "I would very much like to see those ugly wooden panels with the Koranic verses go, but no one would dare remove them. The protests of the nationalists and the religious would be tremendous." The Islamists are actively campaigning to have the building reconsecrated as a mosque, and have occasionally staged demonstrations in front of it. It is indicative of Haghia Sophia's ability to arouse strong feelings that many of the mosques Turkish immigrants founded in Germany and Holland are named after Byzantium's Great Church.

Behind the church run the walls of the Byzantine acropolis, encircling the triangle of land now occupied by Topkapı Palace. Separating the church and the walls is Soğuk Çeşme Sokağı, a cobbled street lined with eighteenth-century wooden Ottoman houses, restored by Turkey's Touring and Automobile Club. They were garishly restored, and their brightly painted wood shines like plastic in the sunlight. These wooden constructions with the projected covered balconies are called *konak*, and are the archetypal dwelling of Ottoman Constantinople.

Until the 1930s most of Istanbul was made of wood, with the stone silhouettes of mosques, palaces and churches standing out. Wood building was adopted in fear of earthquakes then abandoned in fear of fire. A terrible earthquake struck on September 10, 1509, accompanied by tsunamis in the Marmara, which struck the city. Calculated at 7.4 on the Richter scale by researchers, the earthquake left 6,000 dead and panicked the inhabitants so much that they named it "Little Doomsday". Stone was abandoned for wood in the rebuilding process. Wood was not only favoured for its earthquake resilience, but it was cheaply obtained from the thick forests surrounding the city, and wooden homes had the capacity to remain cool in summer and warm in winter.

Constantinople thus became the picturesque city of ornately carved wood that many travellers described in awe. But wooden buildings and congestion predictably resulted in fires consuming entire neighbourhoods at regular intervals. It has been claimed that no city has suffered as many fires as Constantinople. After the mid nineteenth century, konaks were gradually replaced by stone constructions, better protected against the flames and better suited to the modern ways. Very few konaks survive today – 1 percent of an original 150,000.

Behind the acropolis walls and inside the Topkapı Palace compound lies Haghia Eirene, one of the oldest churches in the city. Together with Haghia Sophia, the two constituted the Great Church. The previous church, dating from the time of Constantine, was burnt during the Nika revolt, the current one was rebuilt by Justinian. Eirene, here again, is not the name of a saint, but is used literally as the word "peace": the church was consecrated to the Divine Peace.

Haghia Eirene escaped conversion to a mosque because it found itself within the Walls of Topkapı Palace. Instead it was used as an armoury for the Janissaries, and later it hosted Constantinople's first military museum. Haghia Eirene is normally closed in the mornings; in order to visit one must obtain permission from the Haghia Sophia Museum. Because of its excellent acoustics, it is now being used as a venue for concerts. The best moment to admire it is during such a concert, when the artistically lit interior provides a deeply atmospheric setting.

Despite losing its decoration of marble revetments and mosaics, Haghia Eirene retains its structural elements intact. Its interior is an elegant synthesis of curves and superimposing volumes. It is the only Byzantine church surviving in town to have a synthronon at the base of the apse – six tiers of seats for the clergy. In the semi-dome over the apse there is a mosaic depicting a cross on a golden background. The mosaic is thought to originate from the terrible crisis of Iconoclasm, which engulfed the Byzantine Empire in the eighth and ninth centuries, when the depiction of figures was prohibited and many works of art were destroyed.

Admittedly the Byzantine city's most bizarre relics are the cisterns – massive underground water reservoirs. The bigger appear as sunken, dark palaces. These were public works with no artistic pretensions whatsoever. They were not meant to be seen by the public, but merely existed to serve its needs. Nevertheless, their forest of columns, their silent darkness, the carvings and sculptures they sometimes contain and their vaulted roofs have traditionally placed them high on visitors' checklists of the city's curiosities.

The largest and most impressive, the Basilica Cistern (called Yerebatan Saray – Sunken Palace – in Turkish) hides a few yards from Haghia Sophia. The French adventurer Pierre Gilles claims to have "discovered" it around 1550, and writes of an abundance of fish inside it. The cistern drew many visitors in the nineteenth century, at a time when water still covered a considerable portion of the columns. Travellers at the time entered the cistern by paying a fee to the owners of the houses built above the monument, and toured inside using a boat.

Much has changed since: the Istanbul Metropolitan Municipality demolished all later buildings raised above the monument, removed most of the water and mud, raised wooden platforms for visitors to walk along, introduced lighting and created an underground café in a corner. Gone are the days when visitors could admire the solemn spectacle of the columns reflected on the water in absolute silence.

I usually visit the cistern early in the morning or late in the evening on weekdays, when massive crowds are least likely to appear. Water still drops from the roof, producing a sound I define as the absolute tranquilliser. The rows of 336 columns, which support brick vaults, are artistically lit. The cistern is a sensation. The columns, all different from one another, were carried from ancient temples or disused churches and palaces. Some ancient temple must have been the former residence of the marble head of the Medusa, used as a pedestal for one of the pillars at one extremity of the cistern.

If Haghia Sophia was the crown of the Byzantine city, its heart was the Hippodrome. Now a long square in front of Sultanahmet mosque, the Hippodrome was not simply an entertainment arena. It was where all civil ceremonies were held, as well as the stage of all political dramas. It was first erected by Septimius Severus, before ancient Byzantium was renamed Constantinople and became the Roman capital. Constantine extended the Hippodrome, inspired by Rome's Circus Maximus, so that it could accommodate 100,000 people. Its north-eastern end bordered Haghia Sophia and the Mese, Byzantine Constantinople's main thoroughfare; its south-western end formed a semi-circle, the Sphendone. Since the 480m-long Hippodrome was constructed on hilly ground, massive stone supports were erected to raise the level on the south-western end.

Not much of the Hippodrome survives; most information comes from the descriptions and, even more so, the engravings of travellers. On its north-eastern side, a triumphal arched entrance led from the Mese to the Hippodrome. At the top of the Hippodrome's outer wall ran a colonnade with an epistyle. The em-

The beautifully illuminated Basi ica Cistern

peror attended the spectacles and addressed the people from his throne at the imperial enclosure, the Kathisma, situated at the centre of the Hippodrome's eastern side. The Kathisma was connected with the Great Palace and Haghia Sophia through private passages, which ensured that the emperor was able to move between this triangle of political and religious power unobserved by the people. A row of statues and pillars was laid out on the symmetry axis running down the middle of the Hippodrome, while statues ornamented its walls.

Besides carriage races, shows involving exotic animals, dances and acrobat performances took place in the Hippodrome. Moreover, the arena was the epicentre of all the pompous fanfare, directly inherited from Roman custom. In the early Byzantine years, emperors were crowned in the borough of Hebdomon (Septiumum), seven miles from Constantinople. They then entered the city in triumphal procession, proceeded down the Mese and, through the Hippodrome, entered the Great Palace. The people assembled along the Mese and inside the Hippodrome to acclaim the emperor. Exactly the same course was taken by triumphal processions after military victories. When emperors started to be crowned in Haghia Sophia rather than at Hebdomon, they used their passages to appear before the crowds in the Hippodrome.

But what registered this arena in history was, more than anything, the blood spilt here during the revolts marking both Byzantine and Ottoman histories. Byzantium had inherited the vulgar popular culture of Rome. Chariot races were often followed by clashes between rival teams. Huge amounts were betted on the races. The spectacle aroused the masses and induced the members of the athletic unions to such violence that Procopius speaks of a "disease of the mind". Races gave the masses the opportunity to chant slogans and voice their political and other demands.

The most famous riot was the Nika revolt of January 532, essentially an eruption of civic disorder joining the Hippodrome's two largest clubs, the Blues and the Greens. The clubs, which opposed Justinian's fiscal and legal policies, asked for the removal of a number of government officials, rioted during a race and surrounded the Great Palace. The rioters set fire to the city and destroyed many buildings. The emperor was besieged in the palace for days, and even contemplated fleeing. He was restrained by his wife Theodora, who famously said: "For one who has been Emperor it is unendurable to become fugitive. May I never see the day when they will not address me as Empress. The purple imperial robe is a good shroud." For five days the city burnt at the mercy of the rioters, whose slogan "Nika!" ("Victory!") named the revolt. Yet Justinian's generals Belissarius and Mundus managed to surround them in the Hippodrome and killed more than 30,000, crushing the revolt.

The chariot race frenzy subsided in mid-Byzantine times; the Hippodrome was mostly used for ceremonies, even though the imperial residence was moved to the Blachernae region. The arena suffered terribly during the sack of 1204, when many of its bronze and other statues were melted down by the Crusaders or sent to Italy. Four horse statues now decorate the façade of the Cathedral of San Marco in Venice. Travellers to the late-Byzantine city found and sketched the Hippodrome in ruins. The colonnade survived over the semi-circular Sphendone until the Ottomans used the columns as building material in 1550. The Sultanahmet mosque was later built on the very stalls.

During Ottoman times, the Hippodrome (renamed At Meydanı or Horse Square) was used for official ceremonies, such as circumcisions of the sultan's sons, Ramadan celebrations and processions of all sorts. It was often the scene of rioting by the Janissaries, the elite military corps constituted from children seized from the empire's Christians as "tax" and raised as Muslims. The Janissaries often rose against the sultans or demanded the execution of government officials who did not enjoy their favour. In 1826, troops of Mahmut II, a sultan remembered as a reformist, surrounded the Janissaries in the Hippodrome and slew more than 10,000, hunting down the rest all over Constantinople.

Three of the Hippodrome's original ornaments survive. The obelisk of Tuthmosis III, carried over from Egypt by Theodosius in 390, is considered Istanbul's most ancient monument. It broke down during shipment to Constantinople and only its top third survived. The Serpentine column, representing three snakes twisted with one another, commemorates the victory of the allied Greek cities over the Persians in Plateae in 479 BC and was carried over from Delphi by Constantine. Less interesting is a pillar thought to date from Constantine's time, but restored and coated in bronze by Constantine Porphyrogennetus. The foundations of all three stand on lower ground in today's square, earth having accumulated over the centuries.

Constantinople's Great Palace was a "forbidden city" of its time. It is described by travellers as a city in its own right, a walled enclosure stretching from the Hippodrome to the Marmara and covering a vast area of 100,000 square metres. The Great Palace was actually a complex of palaces, churches and other buildings, loosely organised in a terrace and garden setting. It fell into disrepair from the eleventh century onwards; the Byzantine Comneni dynasty, unable to finance its upkeep, moved to the Blachernae Palace near the Golden Horn and used the Great Palace occasionally for ceremonies. Pillaged during the Latin conquest of 1204, the palace is depicted as a number of churches set amongst impressive ruins by visitors to Constantinople during the Palaeologi dynasty.

The Russian Anonymous, a traveller who visited in 1389-91, mentions statues of stone eagles and stone rams, whose horns were broken by the Crusaders, scattered around together with smashed columns. He also mentions jasper cisterns and conduits. It is believed that many of the remains of the complex are buried under the

Boy and puppy, mosaic from the Great Palace

Detail, mosaic from the Great Palace

Sultanahmet mosque, and under modern buildings in the area. An underground cistern is incorporated in the Nakkaş Art Gallery, a four-floor concrete building opposite the Sphendone, and is used as an exhibition centre. A Byzantine chapel has also been unearthed nearby and can be accessed through a shop.

The main remnants of the Great Palace are some fragments of mosaics exhibited in situ in the purpose-built Museum of the Great Palace Mosaics. In it are exhibited mosaic pieces and capitals excavated from nearby areas as well. The mosaics, dated somewhere around 450, are very revealing of artistic currents prevalent in early Byzantine years. They belong to the Graeco-Roman tradition and are in fact undistinguishable from Hellenistic mosaics unearthed all over the Eastern Mediterranean. The fragments depict pastoral and occasionally violent scenes: a lion with wings, a lion devouring a horse, peasants heading to the market, a donkey fed by a child, dancers and mythological figures.

This is the most appropriate awakening for those under the influence of the stereotype portraying Byzantium as an austere theocracy. The aesthetics of antiquity existed alongside the new Christian art, and occasionally the two commingled to produce works of the highest quality. Whilst the masses lived in barbarous ignorance, preoccupied with the chariot races and the often bloody religious disputes, the emperors and the nobility lived in opulence and refinement, in surroundings where the aesthetics

Hunting scene, mosaic from the Great Palace

and learning of the Graeco-Roman world were perpetuated. Religious fervour had no place in these circles, which would habitually invoke religion for purposes purely political.

A similar detachment from Islam marked the private life of Ottoman rulers: many sultans forbade their Muslim subjects to consume alcohol, only to die of cirrhosis themselves. "It is curious that among all of Europe's royal families, it has been the dynasty reigning over a people for whom drinking is a sin that has produced the greatest number of drunkards," wrote Italian traveller and journalist Edmondo d'Amicis in his book *Constantinople*.

Past and present along the Marmara shore

Covered and uncovered coquetterie, two sisters outside a Kumkapı hairdresser

It is not only foreign visitors who rarely venture into the districts along the Old City's Marmara coastline. The region remains terra incognita for most Istanbulites as well. I relied on medieval travelogues and the memoirs of Constantinopolitan Greeks to plan my reconnaissance visit to the area. On every subsequent visit I was accompanied by Turkish friends. All of them were unaware of, and bewildered by, the plethora of monuments and the colourful human mosaic that enrich this corner – so close to, and at the same time so far from, the crowds of Sultanahmet.

Byzantine relics, Ottoman konaks and eclectic Belle Époque apartments litter the area. There are no hotels or gentrification projects in the sleepy quarters bordering Constantinople's sea walls. Once affluent Greek and Armenian boroughs are now home to Anatolian peasants,

Crypt, possibly a chapel, of the Bucoleon Palace, now a garbage dump

gypsies and economic migrants from Ethiopia and Armenia. What strikes the eye is the contrast between the silent world of the refined European architecture and the Anatolian crowds, whose attire and manners are markedly Eastern and un-urban.

The coastal avenue, laid out in the 1950s in front of the ruins of the sea walls, is a favourite hangout on sunny days for thousands of Anatolians, who stand around chatting and hold vast barbecues in parks and promenades. Stewing meat alfresco seems to be a favourite pastime here. A stroll down the avenue on a Sunday morning would fascinate any sociologist.

Young boys swimming in their underwear on the Marmara shore. Proper swimwear is a luxury

Extended families are grouped around a mangal (Turkish barbecue). Most women are veiled. The scene is almost invariably the same among the many hundreds of families down the shore: Men grill the meat and watch over the mangal. Women prepare salads, boil tea over gas fires or chat in small groups. Loud children chase each other and flood the basketball and football courts. During summer, the boys swim in the polluted Marmara, most in their white underwear. The wet cloth reveals every detail of their anatomy, something that interestingly enough doesn't seem to scandalise the veiled girls who sit in groups at close distance. It's all lively, cheerful and loud. If you stand out as a foreigner, you will probably be offered some tea or meat.

Young couples are often spotted strolling on the seafront holding hands or sitting on the rocks and contemplating the Princes' Islands and the Asian shore in the distance. It was around here that I first saw a veiled girl kissing her boyfriend in public. I was amazed only because I was new to Istanbul at the time, unfamiliar with the inherent contradictions of a society that many of its members describe as schizophrenic.

The Marmara sea walls ran from the Acropolis (Seraglio) to the Marble Tower, where they joined the land walls, a total of 8,260 metres pierced by five doors and containing 188 towers. A first section up to the Samatya quarter was built by Constantine, the rest added by Arcadius and Theodosius. Until the 1950s, the walls stood on the very shoreline, an awesome sight immortalised in many photographs. Now the avenue and a wide promenade have cut them off from the water.

Easy prey to the waves, the towers often succumbed to their violent attacks during storms. Countless inscriptions honour the emperors who repaired them, after waves and earthquakes tore them down. One such, of Basileios (867-886), reads: "I, the devout King Basileios, rebuilt from the very foundations the present tower that the fierce and prolonged tremor of the waves brought down." Similar inscriptions on many towers prove that the Marmara walls were regularly repaired until the Conquest.

Sections survive here and there, but large portions were demolished in the 1860s – the railway lines pierced them in eight different places. Some sections have been reconstructed without much skill, and have a fake, Disneylandish air. Here and there one spots the marble frames of a gate that's now built-in.

Houses have been built against the walls, both in Ottoman times and much later. Sometimes the walls serve as their back wall; in other cases the upper part of the structure projects over them. In the summer months, homeless people often find refuge inside the ruined towers. Zinc shelters have been set up in some of the latter.

A short walk after the Ahırkapı Lighthouse stand the ruins of Bucoleon Palace, the sole surviving section of the immense Mega Palation. Bucoleon was a complex of several palaces by the water and had a private port; both were sheltered from the wrath of the Marmara by a breakwater, whose remains were visible until the laying out of the avenue. It was often referred to by foreign travellers as "the House of Justinian".

The palace was built by Theodosius and extended under Justinian. The shell of a long hall survives, with impressive marble window frames. It probably dates from the period of Theofilos (829-842) or Nikephoros Phocas (963-969). Dilapidated houses lean against it. Prevailing opinion holds that it was named after the statues of an ox and lion (*bous kai leon* in Ancient Greek) that adorned the port's quay. Anna Comneni testifies so in the *Alexiad*, a work composed about the reign of her father Alexius I. According to the text, the statue depicted a lion overcoming a bull.

Guillhaume de Tyr, the Catholic bishop of the city of Tyre in Phoenicia, today's Lebanon, accompanying the Crusader King of Jerusalem to Constantinople, writes that marble stairs flanked by statues of lions and marble columns led from the sea to the palace. Only the emperor would use them to enter when he arrived from the sea. According to Guillhaume, the palace was rich in stones, silken drapes and tapestries of fabulous wealth.

Many visitors who arrived shortly before the

Fourth Crusade used the name Bucoleon to refer to the entire Mega Palation, most of which was not in use any more because of the emperors' inability to finance its upkeep. Like all other Constantinopolitan palaces, Bucoleon was brutally plundered during the Crusaders' seizure of Constantinople in 1204 and never used again; the imperial family confined itself in the Blachernae after Constantinople's liberation in 1261.

The palace was in good condition until the 1870s, when its western façade was demolished during the laying out of the railroad. According to the travellers' narratives, it was adorned with a covered balcony typical of the Byzantine style (and similar, I suppose, to the one found in the façade of the Porphyrogennetus Palace in the Blachernae) and the statues of two sitting lions. Today railway lines pass where Bucoleon's main hall once stood.

During a visit, I noticed an opening in one of the brick walls adjacent to the hall with the large windows. I entered and found myself in what may have been a palatial chapel. Crosses are inscribed on the capitals of the six marble columns, which separate the room into three parts, like aisles. The recess on one wall must have been an apse. The roof is vaulted; elegant brick arches join the columns.

The space is tiny. Could it have been a cistern? Probably half the columns' height is now underground. It is in an appalling state, and I had to walk on a thick pile of garbage in order to make my way round: tires, mattresses, blankets paper, nylon, everything you wouldn't want to see inside a thousand-year-old building. There was a smell of urine. The columns are covered with a thick layer of dust. Only the dim light penetrating from the holes in the roof delineates the peculiar ionic capitals, their tiny volutes and the crosses carved on their friezes.

Coming out of the chapel/crypt, I carefully climbed the wall and reached what I suppose was the upper floor of a palace hall. Here I was greeted by two squatters. "We had nowhere else to go," they said, as if compelled to explain. They came from a small village on the border with Iran. The hall's roof is missing, and only part of the walls are standing. The bases of large brick arches are clearly visible; a few had survived intact. On the floor, amidst the grass and debris of centuries of neglect, I noticed a column of black and green marble.

With difficulty, I crossed to the hall with the windowed façade, where a row of arches support a vaulted roof. Here and there, rays of sunlight penetrate through holes in the roof. Through the windows the Asian coast and the Princes' Islands opposite can be admired. On one end of the hall stands a warehouse, where wood is stored. Here and there someone had arranged piles of branches, possibly to use for winter. Quite a miserable end for an ancient imperial residence.

Further west, a small gate leads to the Justinian church of the Christian saints of Sergiüs and Bacchus, presently the mosque of "Little Saint Sophia". The name comes from a perceived resemblance to the Great Church. Justinian had it built immediately after his accession to the throne. A legend claims he owed his life to the two saints: accused of plotting against his uncle, Emperor Justinus, young Justinian was about to be executed when Sergius appeared in his uncle's dream to testify in his favour. He erected the church in gratitude in 527-36. Together with Haghia Eirene, it is one of the rare examples of early Justinian architecture.

Converted into a mosque in the late fifteenth century, its mosaics and frescoes have vanished, replaced with the whitewashing and dull floral patterns of Ottoman mosque aesthetics. The dome has been considerably altered, while a minaret and portico have been added. Nothing much Byzantine remains in the exterior, and nothing betrays that the building was once a church. The nave has an octagonal shape and two floors; the capitals on the first bear the monogram of Justinian, while both Justinian and Theodora are named as founders in a long Greek inscription along the marble frieze separating the floors. Extensive restoration works began in 2005, which were dismissed as "destruction" in the press. Whether this is true or not, the sad truth is that not much has survived to be restored.

The tranquil neighbourhood conserves some old wooden konaks, many decaying. It is sad to see these elegant structures, with their intricately carved friezes and railings, rot and collapse. And it's hard, looking at the concrete mass around, to imagine what Ottoman Constantinople once looked like.

Towards the coast, one enters scenic Kadırga. The neighbourhood's name derives from the Turkish word for galley, in turn coming from the Greek word *κάτεργα* (forced labour). In Byzantine times, this was a port for galleys, called Limen Sophion or Limen Exo Neoriou. It remained so even after the city's fall. The construction of the Ottoman arsenal in the northern shore of the Golden Horn led to the abandonment of this port, described by Pierre Gilles, visiting in the 1550s, as fortified and land-filled. The French visitor claims the Turks named the port so because remains of sunken galleys were unearthed there. Land continued to fill in over the centuries and today a square marks the site of the port, and a neighbourhood stretches out where once there was open sea.

Streets around Kadırga Square are lined their

Killing time over tea, Kadırga males

entire length by caringly restored konaks, a revealing sight for those who didn't see Istanbul 40 years ago and a nostalgic one for those who did. The district is like a snapshot from the past. Despite the restorations, one cannot talk of gentrification: the inhabitants are still Anatolian immigrants and gypsies, who have set up an introvert community, much like an Anatolian village.

Neighbouring Kumkapı, with its characteristic Belle Époque houses, is a former Christian district still hosting the Armenian Patriarchate and a couple of impressive Greek churches. Its Greek name, Kontoskali (small port), reminds of the one opened here in 1263 by Michael Palaeologos. The district's Turkish name derives from one of the gates on the sea walls, the now disappeared Porta Kontoskaliou, which they renamed Kumkapı (Gate of the Sand).

Ottoman Kumkapı was renowned as a seaside quarter of Christian fishermen and boatmen, with one of the capital's most famous fish markets and innumerable fish taverns where wine was served. It was also renowned as the centre of the capital's Armenian community. Until the 1850s, Armenians were the vast majority and accounts of the district centre on them.

Armenian collective memory is traumatised by the massacres of the 1890s and the 1915 genocide. This tragic turn extinguished memories of centuries of almost absolute integration into Ottoman society. Politically passive, industrious and conservative, Armenians – unlike Greeks – willingly accepted both Turkish rule and Turkish customs. Many foreigners speak of a calm, pious and hard-working people, whose love for money and individualism hindered the pursuit of any 'national' goal. All agree on their conservatism, manifested in their strict marriage custom and observation of fasts, and speak of their adoption of Turkish mores. Turks referred to the Armenians as "The Faithful Nation" to emphasise that, unlike other Christians, they had never rebelled.

Nineteenth-century Greek businessman Andreas Syngros described his visit in 1850 to a family of rich Kumkapı Armenians. "Armenian notables of the time lived alla Turca... Their women went out of the house veiled, always in carriages and never on foot... Their dress, excluding that of the young and most reformed, was similar to that of Muslim women. Only their footwear distinguished them – Muslims wore yellow, Armenians black shoes... Their mores were a mixture of Ottoman and Christian... Their residences were divided in harems and selâmlıks, men other than close relatives banned from the former. Yet non-Armenian Christians and male servants and teachers were not covered by the ban.

"The reason [for the ban] was that... the future husband mustn't see his wife before the wedding; hence the priest's question, "Blind or lame, do you accept her?" Surely, this strict rule was not followed by the reformed. Yet in the family I visited men and women still dined and entertained their friends separately. There were no street names or numbers in Kumkapı, and we spent an hour and a half to locate the house."

He describes a huge konak where pianos were the only "European" furniture. Only the youngest women wore European dress, the rest were draped in Ottoman clothing. Everybody spoke Turkish, in which Armenians were

always fluent. Ottoman Greeks, by contrast, didn't speak Turkish unless originating from villages in inner Anatolia or involved in commerce and administration. Syngros finishes his account by narrating how one of the Armenian girls made advances towards him and used her French teacher to mediate...

The reforms of 1839 and 1856 created new economic opportunities for non-Muslims, and Kumkapı quickly transformed from a periphery of timber houses and antiquated mores to a refined Old City district rivalling the area of Phanari. Grand multi-storey apartments were the dwellings of a Greek and Armenian middle class inspired by and trying to mimic the "Levantine" lifestyle of their Pera compatriots. Many of the Armenian goldsmiths based in the Grand Bazaar resided here.

The moving of the Armenian Patriarchate from Samatya to Kumkapı in 1641 increased the district's importance for the Armenians. The Patriarchate is still housed on Şarapnel Sokak. On one side of the street is the Patriarchal residence, an elegant konak of impressive size. On the other side a high wall surrounds the Patriarchal church of Surp Asdvadzadzin (the Virgin), whose gorgeous bell tower – mimicking the medieval Armenian line – is a Kumkapı landmark.

No "indigenous" Armenians remain in Kumkapı. The community, generally of good economic standing (the poorest emigrated long ago), has left for better boroughs. "All of our kind have emigrated to Yeşilköy, Bakırköy, Pangaltı and the Bosphorus. Only Kurdish-Armenians remain here," a lady at the Patriarchal church commented. "Kurdish Armenians? Armenians from Anatolian villages," she said. "They're not like us, they are not urban. They don't know our customs and they are not refined." Similar contempt was reserved for Armenian migrants from the Republic of Armenia. "The neighbouring streets are full of them," she said, as if talking of an epidemic.

Her words reminded me of similar contempt aired by Constantinopolitans for other Greeks. The others are always seen as less urban and less refined than those in the Polis – as Greeks have always referred to the city with the largest Greek population from its inception as Second Rome to the 1920s. The identity of local Greeks has always rested first and foremost on their qualities as "inhabitants of the Polis" and their upbringing in a cosmopolitan environment and a heritage heavy with the weight of two empires.

Some claim that the Armenian newcomers, drawn by economic necessity to a country fiercely hostile to the one they come from, greatly outnumber the 60,000 local Armenians. In the streets of Kumkapı it is easy to spot those newcomers. They usually go about in large groups, speaking in the harsh tones of Eastern Armenian. The women are particularly noticeable, their hair brightly dyed and their makeup and clothes too "advanced" for the borough's conservative Muslims. Even more significantly, golden teeth are visible when they smile. They go about confidently and lack the passivity typical of their neighbours, the Anatolian village women.

Most of the Armenian migrants are women, who work in Istanbul as maids and as carers to elderly Turks. Chatting with them one invariably hears the same comments: Making a living in Armenia is impossible, there is no work and no means to guarantee one's subsistence, the country is corrupt and there's little hope on the horizon. As for their existence in Turkey, it is temporary; they dream of making some money which would help them move further west. Few ever talk of returning to Armenia.

An even more unexpected crowd is drawn to Kumkapı by the presence of the Armenian Patriarchate. In the nearby streets one notices groups of Africans. They are usually very tall, have delicate facial features and wear crosses. They are Istanbul's Ethiopians. Monophysite Christians themselves, they consider the Armenian Patriarchate their alma mater in exile.

I will never forget my surprise when I entered Surp Asdvadzadzin one evening and noticed a row of shoes left on the doorstep. Inside, a group of Ethiopian girls, most veiled in transparent cloth, were sitting on the floor murmuring prayers. I approached and sat on a chair behind them. After a short while, they started chanting and clapping their hands. They had beautiful voices whose tone somehow reminded me of American spirituals. Yet the rhythm of their chants was fast and they were incessantly clapping.

At one moment they suddenly stood up. The eldest started to recite prayers. When she finished, they crossed themselves, knelt on the floor and performed prostrations, as Muslims do. When they stood up again, they started chanting and clapping even more fervently; at times they were shouting and palpitating their tongues to produce cries like the Bedouins.

The guardian of the church, a middle-aged Armenian, was shocked. "This is a shrine," he said. "If you want to shout and sing go to the room next door. The church is reserved for prayer." "But they *are* praying," I said, explaining that this was their rite. Remarking how nice their voices were, I urged him to sit and listen. When the girls finished they showed us their prayer books and Bible, written in the ornate Amharic alphabet. Every time I have been to the Armenian Patriarchate since, I always meet

Ethiopian faithful, but I have never witnessed such ecstatic chanting again.

At the centre of Kumkapı, towards the shore, spreads Kumkapı Square, filled with overpriced eateries attracting a tourist crowd that doesn't seem to bother about the prices, the bad food, the kitsch neon lights. Kumkapı was once famous for its fish taverns, where live Turkish music was played. The establishments were all run by Greeks and Armenians; good food left Kumkapı when they did.

Two Greek churches, among Istanbul's grandest, remain from the once affluent Greek community of Kontoskali. The first, Haghia Kyriake, is the work of famous late-nineteenth-century Constantinopolitan architect Pericles Fotiades. Its massive dome, the largest of any Greek church in town, is seen from miles away. Haghia Kyriake stands on elevated ground, above a row of shops. It's an interesting neo-Byzantine affair. Opposite stands the former Greek school, a beautiful but crumbling edifice that closed in the 1970s. I once picked up two fragments from the fallen bricks piled up in the dilapidated interior. They were inscribed *Guichard Frères, Marseilles.* The school's austere Athenian-style neoclassicism was built with bricks from France.

Even more impressive for its unusual line is the second Greek parish of Panaghia Elpida, whose extravagant marble façade blends neoclassicism and rococo. These are the temples of a confident bourgeoisie, strengthened by the reforms of the 1850s. Religious freedom encouraged the rising mercantile class to erect magnificent cathedrals, reflecting its newfound confidence. The tradition of tiny inconspicuous shrines, hidden behind massive walls, representative of the years of fear and persecution, was abandoned. Now the Greek elite was set to demonstrate its status, wealth and refined aesthetics and to impress. To do so, it mixed daringly the forms familiar from its national past with styles its members admired in the European capitals. Both churches are guarded by families of Orthodox Christians from Antioch on the Syrian border as there are no Greeks left in Kumkapı.

The alleys around the two churches contain some of the loveliest Belle Époque row houses and apartment buildings in Istanbul. Some are vast eclectic and Art Nouveau extravaganzas, covering entire blocks, and date from the early 1900s. The majority, three- and four-storey row houses with narrow façades and the bay windows typical of the vernacular style, date from the 1870s and 1880s. It was while admiring their finishings one summer afternoon that I noticed a flock of pigeons flying in cyclical formation. Nothing unusual in that, since pigeons and seagulls, symbols of Istanbul, are to be seen every-

Neo-Byzantine Haghia Kyriake, Kumkapı

With its eclectic line verging on rococo, Panaghia Elpida is the only church of this style in town

where. Yet those particular ones did deserve some attention: they were bright pink!

Asking a man in a small workshop, I found out that the pigeons had been painted by local children, who use them for pigeon races. He led me to the top of the old Greek building, where two teenagers had camped on the terrace. They were training their pigeons and marking them, painting some pink or green with spray and attaching wrought iron talismans on others. They pointed to other children on neighbouring rooftops, busy with their own pigeons. It was as if a city of teenage roof-dwellers had sprung up over the neighbourhood, shouting at one another from a distance as their performing pets competed in the sky, and oblivious of the bustle of the streets below.

Back on the ground, other groups of children were noisily running around and veiled women were trying to wipe the streets, where vendors were selling anything from clothes and kitchen utensils to firewood. Rows of drying laundry stretched over the alleys of Kumkapı, a sight common in many other Istanbul districts. Its children will try hard to get the attention of a foreigner, a rare sight in this area, running around and shouting hello. If you brave it in one of the smoky coffee shops, where an exclusively male and idle clientele plays cards or backgammon, you are guaranteed curious and amazed stares. If you are a lone woman though, you'd better steer clear.

Merchant districts of old: commerce alla Turca

Colourful kitchenware in one of the hans selling household goods

For more than a millennium, the southern shore of the Golden Horn, from its mouth to the second bridge, has comprised merchant districts. The crowded alleys of Sirkeci and Eminönü and the steep slopes between the water and Constantinople's second hill are full of impressive Ottoman hans (caravanserais) – vast buildings with an inner court housing dozens of shops and workshops, of tiny mosques, eclectic mansions and thousands of shops, which haven't been set up for, nor pander to the whims of, mass tourism. Surrounding the burlesque show of the Grand Bazaar, largely sacificed to the latter, you will meet the modest merchant tucked away in the hans following a centuries-old tradition.

The area is home to an impressive architectural medley ranging from early post-Byzantine to elaborate Art Nouveau, the result of a long history and the meeting of races and cultures.

Still visible on some buildings are signs in Greek, Armenian, French and Hebrew. Against this background goods are bought and sold at a slow pace and haggling done over a (tulip-shaped) glass of tea. It's a fascinating experience, although a hard one for the non-Turkish speaker.

Eminönü, dominated by the exquisite Yeni Camii, stretches from the mouth of the Golden Horn to the Galata Bridge. In Byzantine times, there were two commercial ports here. From early times, the shore was inhabited by Jews, many of whom were from the Karaite sect. A number of these moved to the coast opposite when Galata became Constantinople's main commercial port, and Galata's coastal zone of Karaköy is named after them.

The Eminönü area was also home to many Italians from the twelfth century onwards, when Emperor Manuel Kantakuzenos granted Genoa, Pisa, Amalfi and Venice commercial privileges. Later, citizens of Ragusa, Provence and the Iberian and German kingdoms joined in, and a Franciscan church was built by the shore. Byzantine Constantinople, like the Ottoman capital succeeding it, sheltered all races of the Mediterranean, Europe and the Middle East.

Constantinople remained a ghost of its former self, never recovering from the savage pillaging during its 1204 sack by the Crusaders. Immediately after its liberation in 1261 Catholics were banned form the Walled City and confined to Galata, which developed into an independent Genoese commercial port. Commerce was practically confined there until the Ottoman conquest. The Conqueror, Mehmet II, brought Jews from Edirne, north-west Turkey, to settle in Eminönü, which became a major Jewish outpost.

The Conqueror himself inaugurated the Grand Bazaar, and commerce in the Old City was revived. The entire stretch of hilly land from the Golden Horn to the Bazaar was gradually filled with hans. The district's new name, Eminönü, means "in front of the customs", since the Ottoman custom houses were situated by the port. Most visitors to Ottoman Constantinople overlooked these districts, limiting themselves to the Grand Bazaar and the Spice Market. Similarly, most visitors today ignore these delightful backstreets, unaware of how much they are missing.

I normally start my walks at Sirkeci, on the foot of the first hill. Its focal point is the bizarre Sirkeci train station, a building that played an important role in the city's recent history. The station marked the end of the journey on the Orient Express, the luxury train linking Constantinople with Vienna and Paris, and was the first sight of Constantinople for those early tourists flocking here before the Great War. They travelled in utter luxury, in coaches with Persian carpets, silken sheets and gas-lit chandeliers.

Greek actress Eleni Halkoussi, who was born in Istanbul, said that Sirkeci station linked Constantinople with "those mythical capitals, Berlin, Vienna, Paris". It was the capital's link to the outside world. Yet as much as Europe was the dream of Constantinople's non-Muslims, for Europeans the dream was Constantinople. The Ottoman capital personified the myth of the Orient, "nurtured by hours of reading and childhood fairytales", as the Italian traveller Edmondo d'Amicis wrote.

The station's style serves this myth well. In order to impress on foreign arrivals that they were now in the Orient, German architect August Jasmund designed an extravagant building, drawing inspiration from the Ottoman, Seljuk and Moorish traditions. At the same time, the station, illuminated with gas and heated by huge stoves carried from Austria, epitomised modern comforts. Nevertheless, most travellers in their memoirs first describe their shock at being accosted by a multitude of people shouting out in all tongues the moment they set foot on the platform.

Trains from Sirkeci also ran to Constantinople's once distant outskirts on the Thracian plane by the Marmara coast. The city started to expand and the remote villages of San Stefano and Makrohori (the present Yeşilköy and Bakırköy) turned into fashionable suburbs, attracting a non-Muslim commercial bourgeoisie eager to flee the crowded downtown. Eleni Halkoussi, who was born in Makrohori, wrote: "On December 6, 1870, the railway line connecting Makrohori to Sirkeci – in 36 minutes! – was inaugurated. Every now and again they brought over new coaches, with unbelievable comforts and European luxury. This train, with frequent connections, took men to their jobs downtown, women to the Pera department stores and children to the Greek Schools of Pera and Fanari." Despite European luxury, train carriages contained separate compartments for men and women. After all, this was the Ottoman Empire.

For Constantinopolitan Greeks, Sirkeci stands for tragedy. It was from here that many of the 15,000 Greek passport holders expelled in 1964 had to board a train on a one-way trip to Athens or Salonica, allowed only a few kilograms of clothes and other necessities as their fortunes were confiscated.

Sirkeci is the starting point for my excursions to Eptapyrgion (Yedi Kule) Fortress, San Stefano or Makrohori. The rails run along the shore and the journey offers scenic views of the Byzantine walls and the bell towers of the formerly Christian quarters of Kumkapı and Samatya. I've always been the only foreigner on coach.

pp 52-53: View of the Büyük Yeni Han, the han district and the Nur-u-Osmaniye mosque from the roof of the Büyük Valide Han

The streets leading from the station towards Yeni Camii and the Spice Market are where the Old City's economic heart beats. Eminönü became Galata's Ottoman rival, the "Oriental" answer to Italian commerce. Here Jews erected Constantinople's first "apartment buildings" (land had once again become scarce, the result of the massive forced resettlement which formed part of the Conqueror's plan to repopulate the now Ottoman capital). Normal buildings at the time stretched up to three or four floors, but the Jews erected wooden constructions with six or seven floors, which were lived in by extended families. Those buildings were known as "Jeweries" and were expropriated in 1591 for the Yeni Camii to be built on their site. The Jews were moved to Hasköy, on the channel's opposite shore.

Not much is left from the oriental past apart from the Yeni Camii and the Spice Market. The backstreets were completely redesigned in the late nineteenth century, at the time when the empire was making a desperate attempt at modernisation. What changed Eminönü forever was the construction of a floating wooden bridge joining it to Galata in 1845. The Galata Bridge united, for the first time, the city's two economic centres. The ways of the European expatriates and the local Christians and Jews mimicking them reached the dormant Old City, and it is not an exaggeration to say that it was a gap of centuries, not merely two shores, that was bridged.

The incessant movement between the two shores brought western capitalism to the Old City, where a pre-capitalist ethos was prevalent. At the same time, the administrative reforms of 1839 and 1856, known as Tanzimat, created new economic opportunities for non-Muslims. Many of the later Greek capitalists such as Andreas Syngros started their commercial life as apprentices to a trader in one of the area's hans.

For centuries before the arrival of European ways, commerce in the Old City evolved around the hans. A han is at the same time a warehouse, a point of wholesale distribution and a hostel for the itinerant trader. Traditionally, it consists of a number of cells arranged around a large courtyard, at the centre of which stands a mescid (small mosque). All amenities necessary for travellers were provided, including accommodation, food and stables for horses and camels. Hans were usually administered by religious foundations and their services provided free of charge; each merchant was expected to make a donation, according to his means. Stables and warehouses were on the ground floor, kitchens and dormitories on the floors above.

It is often said that a bazaar (çarşı in Turkish) was in a sense the oriental predecessor of the modern mall: vendors of a vast array of goods were assembled in a confined space, where consumers would be able to satisfy all their basic needs. The complex, which was usually covered, ensured buyers and sellers met unhindered by adverse weather conditions. In the han, on the other hand, only one type of goods was usually sold, normally to wholesalers who would distribute them to retailers in the bazaars. Some hans were destined to service traders and visitors from other countries, and functioned as distant predecessors of embassies.

Hans in the traditional sense ceased to be built by the end of the nineteenth century, with the steady development of the railway. The modernisation of trade transformed the han into the "passage", the commercial arcade (still named 'han' by many Turks). The passage was not a place to host traders, much less their animals. It didn't specialise in one type of goods, but, much like the modern mall, catered to a wide variety of needs. On the architectural side, the "passages" of Belle Époque Constantinople no longer bore an oriental style, but conformed to the stylistic fashions in Europe and rivalled similar establishments in the grand European capitals.

Some fine "passages" and other impressive public buildings, in exuberantly eclectic or Art Nouveau styles, are grouped in Eminönü's backstreets. Although they are of the same style and beauty as the buildings of Pera and Galata, they have failed to draw as much attention. Huge, gorgeous and decaying, the "passages" are still used mainly to house shops or branches of banks. My favourite is the Art Nouveau Vlora han opposite the grand Post Office; its façades are decorated with stylised roses and leaves.

The district also houses peculiar buildings in the style known as the First National Movement, a nationalist reaction to eclecticism and Art Nouveau internationalism. The historicist movement aims to revive "national tradition" and create a purist architecture reflecting a newfound sense of national identity. It incorporates elements from the Seljuk and early Ottoman tradition – decorative tiles, domes, pointed windows – on a mass of Doric austerity. This virile austerity reminds of similar trends in Mussolini's Italy and reflects the modernistic militarism of the regime established by the Committee of Union and Progress ("Young Turks"). Turkish nationalism developed as a highly militaristic movement and created a highly militaristic nation state.

After the proclamation of the Republic in 1923, this purist architecture became the new state's 'official style". One of the best examples in Eminönü is the vast Dördüncü Vakıf han behind Yeni Camii, built by Kemaleddin Bey in 1911-1926 as an office complex. Its twin domes with the intricate frieze are more like a spartan version of Mamluk Cairo than reminiscent of anything Ottoman. The momentous Central Post Office (1909) by Vedat Tek nearby boasts twin domes, and despite its decorative tiles it is huge and sombre, the antithesis of Art Nouveau merriness.

Another Eminönü landmark is the Germanya Han on the corner of Sultanhamam and Postane Streets. In these Art Nouveau headquarters, built for the Deutsche Orient Bank, August Jasmund – the architect of Sirkeci Station – this time paid homage not to the myth of the Orient, but to that of German imperial might.

The grand silhouettes cry out that the neighbourhood has seen much better days. The city's commercial centre has moved north and today's Eminönü is like an open-air market for cheap buys. In business hours, streams of people and vehicles make walking difficult. But before sunset and after dusk, the deserted neighbourhood turns into a surreal setting where massive, bizarre silhouettes contrast against the red or dark sky. Only the cries of seagulls upset the silence.

Ottoman imperial mosques, even those of the much-venerated Sinan, have never managed to win me over. Their exteriors do impress with their sheer volume and peculiar form, their large cupolas resting on semidomes and their pencil-like minarets towering elegantly over the city. The mosques of the Old City, seen together lit at night, form a glorious cityscape. Nevertheless, their outline is so similar that it becomes hard for the non-experienced eye to distinguish between one mosque and another. They all appear as failed attempts to repeat the experiment of Haghia Sophia. Their profusion of semidomes and tiny pepper-pot domes surrounding the cupola and the hundreds of windows in the tympana make up a silhouette bizarre and imposing, but not graceful.

The Ottomans erected thousands of mosques over their vast realm, which look like degenerate photocopies of a Byzantine blueprint. If one has marvelled at the carvings of the Fatimid and Mameluk masterpieces of Cairo, glimpsed the tiled cupolas of Isfahan and Samarkand or studied the sombre magnificence of Anatolia's Seljuk mosques, one is doomed to dismiss the Ottoman ones as bastardised Byzantinism, as did William Dalrymple.

The mosques' interiors are, with few exceptions, even more disappointing. The exuberant laces of floral motifs carved on the stucco, which decorate the mosques of Cairo and Central Asia, are absent here. So are the gilded carvings and reds and greens associated with the magic of Islamic decoration. So is the ornate sophistication of the Byzantine archetype, its splendour of colour, material and form. There is a barbaric cacophony of colour, since

Alley between Ottoman hans housing textile shops, Tahtakale

KADİM
TEKSTİL
Fo Baran
ÖZERLER
BÜYÜK TİCARET HAN
Zeki
Şapka
DÖNMEZ ŞAPKA
İMALAT TOPTAN SATIŞ
TEL: 527 22 35
Yaşar
BÜYÜK YENİ HAN

the tones of the tiles almost never match those of the woodcarvings in the balustrades or the floral garlands of the ceiling.

Having said this, I should add that Yeni Camii is the only one of Istanbul's imperial mosques that can make me sit for hours, absorbed in the contemplation of its elegant symphony of curves. The main relic of pre-modernisation Eminönü is an Istanbul landmark, whose cupola and minarets dominate the Old City skyline seen from the channel, immediately capturing the visitor's attention. It was rightly said that its construction, on the site of the Jewish quarter, aimed to show off Ottoman power to visiting foreigners – something of an Ottoman answer to Haghia Sophia.

It's not only the sheer size of the seventeenth-century building that impresses, but also its graceful curves. In front of the mosque is a vast courtyard whose cloister is crowned by small domes. At the centre of the court, which opens to Eminönü Square, stands an elegant fountain for ablutions.

Yeni Camii combines with the domes and minarets of nearby Rüstem Paşa and of the Suleimaniye, on the Third Hill above, to draw a dream-like perspective depicted on the engravings of travellers and immortalised on thousands of photographs. One of Istanbul's most representative images is the grey tableau created on one of those dark, overcast winter days. The grey stone masses of the mosques reflect on the grey-black waters of the channel, all against a grey sky filled with clouds of noisy seagulls. Melancholy is at the core of Istanbul's soul, and few sights can be as utterly melancholic as this combination of natural and man-made greyness.

The cloister of the Yeni Camii is often my refuge from the rain or the madding crowds of the nearby markets. Many marvel at the clouds of pigeons flying over the square and mosque. They inhabit the courtyard and some even fly inside the building. Its interior is disappointing, the sole decoration being some pretty Iznik tiles on the lower zones of the walls. The dull floral designs hardly conceal the nakedness of the huge dome and semidomes, towering oppressively over a bare vastness.

Eminönü Square is a broad open space now, but things were very different some years ago. A cordon of shops surrounded the mosque and the square was a narrow, overcrowded corridor. In engravings and photographs, one sees wooden building cramped on the very waterfront behind rows of boats. The boats disappeared as soon as the bridge made the transport of goods by land much easier, while the picturesque wooden and stone buildings fell prey to a perverse notion of urban planning in the 1950s.

Nowadays, the mosque stands in a sterilised environment, isolated, presiding over an expanse of emptiness. The cleared square is scarred by tramlines and ugly underpasses, whilst rows of buses and minibuses queue by the shore. Eminönü is a transport hub: buses and ferries depart from here for all over the city.

Of the vast complex of foundations belonging to Yeni Camii, only the Mısır Çarşı ("Egyptian Market"), better known as the Spice Market, survives. An attractive stone and brick Ottoman building, it comprises about a hundred shops, whose rents are used to fund the mosque's upkeep – a system common in Ottoman lands. This was one of Istanbul's specialist markets, initially selling only spices brought over from Egypt (hence the name). Today, few shops specialise in spices; the market remains a food market, while all kinds of shops line the surrounding streets. It's in Mısır Çarşı that one can find some of Istanbul's best cheese pastırma (pastrami) and spices, and I have to admit the place is one of my regular pilgrimages.

Even more exciting than the Bazaar itself is the narrow alley right opposite Yeni Camii, named Çiçek Pasajı ("Flower Market"). All sorts of flowers and clay pots are sold there, but so are chicks, baby ducks and geese, parrots, canaries, fish for aquaria and even leeches in bottles – still used as a traditional remedy for various diseases.

Lost in the tortuous and crowded streets behind the Spice Market is one of Istanbul's hidden treasures, Rüstem Paşa mosque, commissioned by the namesake vizier, son-in-law of Suleiman the Magnificent. The mosque's ordinary, almost dull, exterior shelters the loveliest mosque interior in Istanbul. It is situated behind a courtyard on elevated ground, on top of a dozen shops in the Tahtakale neighbourhood. The neighbourhood is still a busy market district, as it was at the time of the construction of the mosque, which was intended as a market mosque to service the merchants and their clients.

Rüstem Paşa is famous as "the most ornamented Ottoman mosque". The percentage of tiled surface on its walls is the highest of all Istanbul mosques. Its tiles are considered the best produced by the factories of Iznik (ancient Nicaea), the city that excelled in tile production in mid Ottoman times. So high was the demand for tiles during the mosque's construction in 1651 that the Iznik ateliers couldn't cope and Rüstem Paşa had to open another workshop in Kütahya, central Anatolia. The tiles depict carnations, tulips and pomegranate flowers in all sorts of patterns. Their blues, greens and tomato reds are radiant despite their age.

Behind the mosque stretches Tahtakale, ascending the Second Hill to the Grand Bazaar. The area hosted a fish and a spice market during Byzantine times. Unlike Eminönü, Tahtakale

EFES

conserves many Ottoman structures and is the most interesting – albeit less visited – of the market districts. Its steep ascents are named after the goods sold or made in the shops and workshops along them. Its main street, Uzun Çarşı, has been a commercial street since Byzantine times, then named Makros Emvolos. Tahtakale is pure han territory: here are preserved Istanbul's largest and most impressive Ottoman hans, still crowded with shops, workshops and warehouses. The foundations and even parts of many are Byzantine.

Up the Tahtakale Hill runs one of Istanbul's most interesting streets, Çakmaçılar Yokuşu. It has some of the city's oldest hans, important relics of mid Ottoman civil architecture. The most spectacular architecturally is Büyük Yeni Han, a stone and brick building of the eighteenth century, attributed to an Armenian architect. The vast complex is skilfully adapted to the steep inclination of the ground; it consists of many contingent segments at different levels. The upper floors slightly project, resting on elegant stone corbels. At a distance, the building gives the impression of waves. It's a favourite layout for Bauhaus and International Style architects, but it was quite radical for its time.

The lines of stone and brick on the façade and the blind brick arches above the windows are direct imports from the Byzantine school. The similarity with the Porphyrogennetus Palace (Tekfur Sarayı), the nobles' houses in Phanari and the so-called "Genoese" buildings in Galata's Perşembe Pazarı proves that these buildings are products of the same style, a local style that transcends both centuries and ethnic groups and is peculiar to the city.

It is now accepted that Ottoman civil architecture was simply a continuation of the late-Byzantine style, which itself bore Italian influences. In the few stone constructions they erected (most of Ottoman Constantinople was wooden), the Ottomans copied the works of the Byzantines. Given that nothing but the walls and the two palaces remain from Byzantine Constantinople's secular buildings, one can get an insight into what the Byzantine capital must have looked like from studying these Ottoman structures.

The Büyük Yeni Han's interior involves three arcaded floors revolving round an inner court. The rooms behind the arcades were used either as lodgings for the traders or storage rooms for their wares; now they've been taken up by small ateliers, mainly coppersmiths and textile workers. They are tiny and many resemble cells rather than workplaces. On the southeast corner of the façade, a ruined pigeonhouse is visible, one of the few such surviving in Istanbul.

The Büyük Valide Han opposite Büyük Yeni

Welder at work in a Tahtakale han

Coating copperware

Tailors

is Istanbul's oldest and largest. It's also decaying, unfortunately. Built in 1623-1640, some parts are considerably older, such as the Byzantine Tower at the back end of the complex. Behind the elegant façade with the grilled windows are three courtyards surrounded by wings in various degrees of preservation. The han has always been administered by the Bektaşî (part of the Alevites – a Muslim heretical sect). In the large central courtyard stands an Alevite temple (*cem evi* in Turkish) also used by Istanbul's small Shiite community, originating mainly from Iran. In the past, curious crowds would come to see the rather repulsive Shiite commemoration of their holy month of Muharrem, when men would whip and knife themselves and parade covered in blood. These customs were judged barbaric and prohibited during the first years of the Republic.

Even today, some of the workers in the han's 210 rooms are Iranian. The rooms in the upper floors are occupied by workshops of textile workers, coppersmiths and welders. There is an air of timelessness and otherworldliness in the long, dark corridors, where everything is decaying and covered in dust.

The back part of the han, dominated by the Byzantine Tower of Eirene, is the oldest. This section is named Sağır han – han of the deaf. The function of the tower is not known, but it is alleged that it once guarded a monastery. At its base, a couple of eccentric Iranian traders

Shoe manufacturer

Anything can be sold on the street

sell Anatolian woollen blankets, kilims and other curiosities. It was in this part of the building that an Armenian from Sevasteia (Sivas) called Apkar founded Constantinople's first Armenian press in 1567, having carried the Armenian characters from Venice.

The attraction here is definitely the roof, a concoction of small domes and chimneys. Their silhouettes draw surreal lines against the sky, like fairytale figures. You should brave your fear of heights (if you have one) and ask the han's guardian, a friendly middle-aged shopkeeper, to lead you up there. From the top you have one of Istanbul's best bird's-eye views. Right below you can get a glimpse of gorgeous Büyük Yeni Han, against the background of the massive Grand Bazaar and the Nuruosmaniye Mosque. In the north spread Eminönü and Galata, the bridge joining them and the Golden Horn, while the huge Süleymaniye towers over the hills in the south.

The market districts are one of my favourite hangouts, although I rarely – if ever – shop for anything but antiques. I love the architecture, the pandemonium of the streets, the exotic timelessness of courtyards and corridors. I like to chat with the elderly shopkeepers and young Kurdish workers who always offer tea. And the rooftop of the Büyük Valide Han is one of my city secrets. To that spot, offering a full panorama of one of the world's greatest cities, I would take my friends to picnic on a sunny day.

Chasing Byzantine glory in districts derelict

"Oh, land of Byzantium, oh, you thrice-blessed city, eye of the Earth, jewel of the universe, star shining afar, beacon of the nether world..."

Niketas Khoniates

Since its foundation on the site of ancient Byzantium in 330 AD and until its first sack by the armies of the Fourth Crusade in 1204, Constantinople was the most magnificent city in Christendom. It was a legend, the envy of the world, provoking the stupefied amazement of foreign visitors. Guillhaume de Tyr called it Constanti*noble*, a very deliberate alteration. Named Tsarigrad (City of Caesars) by the Slavs and Miklagard (City of Enchantment) by the Vikings, Constantinople had created and promoted its own myth. Greeks called it Basilis (City of Kings) or simply The City, confident that no other like it had existed or would ever exist.

Greeks regard Byzantine Constantinople as Greek. Indeed, the Empire, Romanía, shrank after the seventh century to lands where people were Greek-speaking and Christian Orthodox. Nevertheless, its capital, notwithstanding its

The elegant symmetry of the façade of eleventh-century Haghioi Theodoroi (Kilise Camii) in Vefa

Greek majority, had always been a world city, grouping people of all known races and creeds, a city where every known language was represented – something like the London of today. The Imperial Guard contained Celts, Vikings, Avars, Christened Turks and their descendants; Armenians and Georgians ascended to the throne; princesses from all over Europe married into the Palace; Russians and other Slavs poured in, either as merchants or as monks; there was a vibrant Jewish community; Italian merchants settled, founding Catholic churches and Franciscan monasteries; there was even a mosque for "Saracen" traders from the Arabian lands and Central Asia. Constantinople's linguistic Babel amazed travellers of the time, wherever they came from.

Even more so its treasures left them with their mouths open in amazement, an amazement that vividly surfaces in their writings. "The Greek inhabitants are very rich in gold and precious stones, and they go clothed in garments of silk with gold embroidery, and they ride horses, and look like princes," wrote Benjamin of Tudela, the twelfth-century Spanish-Jewish traveller, adding that "Wealth like that of Constantinople is not to found in the whole world." Accounts of Constantinople's legendary riches provoked the reveries and tantalised the senses of leaders and adventurers all over the world. As the pursuit of a mythical El Dorado would later lead conquistadores to the depths of the wilderness, the much more tangible riches of the City of Cities would bring an impressively long list of prospective conquerors before its walls. The Byzantine capital became the most coveted city in history.

Constantinople's fate always reminds me of the ancient Greek notion of hubris (arrogance): one should never boast and should take the utmost care not to cross certain limits. Any excess may offend the Gods and provoke a ruthless reaction. Was the accumulation of such great wealth, such exquisite art and so resplendent a culture hubris? Did it provoke divine retaliation? Reflecting on how a series of accumulated tragedies succeeded in almost erasing Constantinople's legend from the memory of mankind, one is tempted to suppose it did.

Very little is left of what was once the greatest city under the sun; even those sparse leftovers have been disfigured beyond recognition. Byzantine ruins may span modern Istanbul, but their number is small and their deformation irreparable. And if Haghia Sophia, Constantinople's Great Church, remains Istanbul's foremost monument, it is also Constantinople's much-defaced memorial, its state probably the most dramatic testimony of the Byzantine capital's ruin.

Constantinople's death was slow and agonising, a two-centuries-long decay. Greeks lamented its loss with threnodies, which still haunt their collective memory. Normally, they put the blame for its destruction on the Turks, who conquered Constantinople and, in their zeal to Islamise and Turkify it, strived to erase its Christian and Greek past. It is of course true that Turks demolished many monuments, appropriated the churches, excised their decoration and plundered many treasures. But what people normally overlook is that Constantinople's greatest destruction, the beginning of its end, was performed in 1204, by "very Christian" hands.

In his *De la Conqueste de Constantinople*, Geoffroy de Villehardouin, leader of the Fourth Crusade, describes the Crusaders' impressions on their first glimpse of the city: "All who had never seen it before would fix their eyes on the city of Constantinople, which appeared the noblest in the Universe. Seeing the lofty walls and mighty towers surrounding it, the splendid palaces and towering churches, which seemed innumerable, the city's immense dimensions, denoting it was the queen of the Earth, they could scarcely believe their senses."

Geoffroy narrates how the Crusaders set fire to Constantinople during the siege. Huge conflagrations consumed more than a third of the city, churches and palaces burnt to the ground "and in the end more houses burnt than those contained in three of the most populous cities of France". The Crusaders capitalised on a dynastic feud to sack and mercilessly plunder a city where treasures from all over the world had accumulated over nine centuries. The booty was considered the greatest ever seen.

"How shall I begin to narrate the deeds of those abominable men," starts a narration of the lootings by Greek historian Niketas Khoniates. "Alas, the images, which ought to have been adored, were trodden under foot...! They snatched the precious reliquaries, thrust their ornaments into their bosoms and used the broken remnants for pans and drinking cups."

He laments the pillage of Haghia Sophia. "The sacred altar, formed of all kinds of precious materials and admired by the whole world, was broken into bits and distributed among the soldiers, as was all the other sacred wealth of so great and infinite splendour." Mules entered the church to carry the booty; those who slipped on the marble floors were slain on the spot. A whore was made to dance on the patriarchal throne. To prepare the reader for the accounts of rapes and killings, Khoniates argues that those who attacked God with such ferocity would not have spared humans.

Monk Gunther de Pairis narrates how his abbot, Martin, raided Orthodox churches to remove holy relics from "the hands of the heretic

Greeks", not hesitating to threaten the priests with death, should they not hand him their treasures. He wrapped the pillage in his robes…

Crusaders looted the palaces of Bucoleon and Blachernae before the startled eyes of European princesses married to Comneni emperors and residing there. "Of the treasures there I cannot speak; their value was inestimable," Geoffroy de Villehardouin writes.

Gold-bound gospels, beautifully illuminated manuscripts, gold chalices with precious stones, onyx triptychs and gold icons adorn churches, museums and private collections all over Europe, where they were carried off to as booty. The four bronze horses of the Hippodrome ended up on the façade of St Mark's Cathedral in Venice; many of Constantinople's most precious icons on its Pala d'Oro (iconostasis). The decorated pillars of the enormous basilica of St Polyteuctus, a sixth-century extravagance of sculpted marble, were also carried off to Italy. Christian relics and ancient pagan statues were melted, their precious metals reused.

Constantinople never recovered. Liberated in 1261, it lived on past glories until the Fall. Drawings by fourteenth- and fifteenth-century travellers depict most of it in ruins. "Constantinople consists of villages and there's much more country than inhabited space within its walls," wrote French traveller Bertrandon de la Broquière in 1432. Turks completed its obliteration by the gradual demolition or deformation of its churches.

The surviving churches are merely the shells of what once were elegant exteriors with curves and intricate brickwork. Interiors, impressive syntheses of curves, are violated bare carcasses, stripped of all ornaments. Fabulous mosaics and frescoes were excised, and exquisite marble carvings smashed whenever figures were depicted. Thus dictated the newcomers' religion…

To understand the magnitude of the destruction one should take into account that in Byzantine architecture exteriors were simple and modest, at times even neglected for the sake of splendid interiors. This particularly holds true for churches, where outer simplicity and inner splendour have theological foundations, the building paralleled to a person who should be "modest in appearance and rich inside". The mystifying interior of The Saviour in Chora (now Kariye Museum) best illustrates how much was lost. Chora, a small monastic church, the only one to have retained much of its ornamentation, is the last glimpse of a world of magic, wonder and awe.

Constantinople's surviving churches are of medium or small size. The existence of two immense cathedrals, Haghia Sophia and the Holy

Apostles, made large structures unnecessary. Furthermore, the Byzantine Greeks preferred moderate-sized, communal monastic churches. The focus was never on size, but on the effect interior decoration would produce on the faithful. A dozen churches survive, scattered over the Old City's conservative quarters. Few have been listed on tourist guides, hardly any are ever visited by foreigners who are not specialists. Most are bypassed by people who ignore their importance, at times unaware that the building was once a church.

Constantinople wasn't simply replete with churches. Modelled on Rome, it was a city of large squares decorated with huge pillars and obelisks, as dominant as churches in the cityscape. The pillars, often topped with statues, greatly impressed travellers and feature in their sketches. The Column of Justinian, depicting a triumphant emperor on horseback in front of Haghia Sophia, did not survive. Neither did the one of Theodosius in Constantinople's largest square. Yet a few others have survived, the most important being the oldest of them all – the Column of Constantine. Known in Turkish as Çemberlitaş and situated by the tramline on Divan Yolu (the Byzantine Mese), a short walk from Sultanahmet, it is of a characteristic black colour. The large pillar, of seven separate porphyry drums resting on a base and pedestal, was erected by Constantine at the centre of the main square that he laid out for his new capital, the Forum of Constantine.

The founder was depicted as Apollo – holding a cross in the left hand and a lance in the right – in a gilded statue upon the capital. Statue and capital collapsed during a storm in 1106, killing many passers-by, and Emperor Manuel Comnenus placed a large bronze cross in their stead. Termed "the column with the cross" by foreign travellers, it appears in their drawings of Constantinople. The Ottomans removed the cross and tied the column, considered one of Constantinople's talismans, with iron rings to ensure its stability. Presently 35 metres high, it is the only remainder of the Forum. I normally catch a glimpse of the column whilst heading from Sultanahmet to the tea houses and nargile (water-pipe) cafés hidden away in tree-shaded courts, further down Divan Yolu.

A second forum was laid out to the west by Theodosius I, imitating Trajan's Forum in Rome; its site is presently occupied by Beyazid Square. Known as Forum Tauri and inaugurated in 393, it became Constantinople's largest square. It had a triumphal arch on each side, a basilica and in the centre there is a gigantic column with spiral reliefs commemorating Theodosius' victory over the Ostrogoths. Topped by Theodosius' equestrian statue, the column had disappeared

Pantocrator surrounded by Prophets, mosaic in the dome of the pareclession of the Pammakaristos

Mosaics of saints in the funerary pareclession of the Pammakaristos

by the late fifteenth century; it survives in travellers' drawings, and in a painting by Bellini. The Crusaders had previously melted the bronze statues ornamenting the Forum.

The square's only remnants are parts of the Tetrapylon, a ceremonial arch over the Mese supported on eight huge columns with Corinthian capitals. Their shafts were decorated with reliefs resembling the "eyes" on a peacock's tail – a typical early Byzantine design. Parts of those shafts are scattered by the tramlines; segments of the spiral column depicting marching soldiers are incorporated in the façade of the Beyazid Hammam.

Lâleli, a bit further down, was once a respectable borough reserved for the Muslim bureaucracy. It now epitomises the unrespectable and mischievous. Until a disastrous fire in 1911, Lâleli and its surroundings were a forest of wooden konaks. From the 1950s, concrete boxes effaced all elegance, whilst huge avenues with overpasses added hugely to the surrounding ugliness. A spectacular social degradation followed. As pogroms and discrimination forced Greeks out, middle-class Turks occupied their former Pera and Bosphorus homes, leaving the Old City to the Anatolian newcomers, who brought their village ways along.

In the early 1980s, the so-called trunk trade arrived. Istanbul was flooded by women from the Soviet bloc countries in search of cheap buys. They arrived with large travel trunks to fill

Theotokos Kyriotissa (Kalenderhane Camii) is one of the few Byzantine churches to preserve its coloured marble revetments

with goods unavailable at home – anything from make-up and hair dyes to detergent. Lâleli was then described as "a free zone where people converse in Kurdish or Russian and the official currency is the dollar", and as "a black market paradise".

Trunk traders were followed, after communism's demise, by a tide of prostitutes. These Eastern Europeans, fair, tall and appealing to Turkish male fantasies, are collectively known as "Natashas". Natashas made Lâleli and neighbouring Aksaray their terrain. The cheap hotels they and their clients patronise mushroom, and at night time the lights of sleazy bars illuminate backstreets. Shops selling cheap goods, especially textiles, leather products and underwear are everywhere, as are signs in Russian. A mixture of Slavic girls, gigolos and Anatolian pimps tout their services.

Lost amidst this third wordliness is a Byzantine monument that guides never mention and travellers never visit: the Myrelaion monastery (known to Turks as Bodrum Camii), built by Emperor Romanos Lekapenos in the tenth century. Romanos built a private palace with a nunnery adjacent. The nunnery's church was used as his family's burial place. Romanos, his wife and children were laid to rest in a crypt under it, as were many members of the Macedonian and Comneni dynasties.

The church was burnt and the palace destroyed in that dreadful year of 1204. The Ottomans used the church as a warehouse and later converted it to a mosque. The crypt containing the imperial tombs was turned into a distillery – hence the Turkish name of the mosque, "mosque of the cellar". Church and crypt were burnt again in 1911. Restored in 1988, the church was reconsecrated as mosque; remains of the palace were unearthed nearby.

Cruciform Myrelaion has a striking exterior, articulated by alternating cylindrical brick buttresses. The brickwork is simple, without the intricate dichromatic patterns of other buildings. Nothing survives inside. The crypt under the church is of the same size; its vaulted roof is supported by four columns topped with Corinthian capitals. Pierre Gilles, visiting in the mid sixteenth century, wrote that Myrelaion stood on a hill. Today the area is quite flat, another case where the city's topography has changed dramatically over the centuries.

North of Lâleli stretch the much more scenic and well-preserved Kalenderhane and Saraçhane districts. Through them runs for some 625 metres the aqueduct of Emperor Valens. Built around 375 AD, it was still in use well into the nineteenth century. Its markedly Roman aspect contrasts with the konaks leaning against it in the Kalenderhane end. Behind them stands a twelfth-century church, known since its conversion as Kalenderhane Camii, its Greek name sometimes given as Theotokos Akataleptos, sometimes as Theotokos Kyriotissa. It is a cruciform basilica whose asymmetrical, irregular elements belong to different styles and periods. Yet they combine to form an elegant synthesis of curves.

What makes the church remarkable is the interior, which – unusually – has preserved its marble revetments intact. Coating the walls with coloured marble was typical in Byzantine art. Red, green and grey panels covered two-thirds of the walls' height, frescoes and mosaics the rest. The latter are now lost; small fragments unearthed during restoration work are kept in the Archaeological Museum. Among them is a fresco of St Francis of Assisi drawn during the Crusader occupation, the oldest extant image of the saint.

The imam is friendly, eager to show visitors around. His hobby is the internet. He complains that the structure, upkept with parish contributions, is in need of restoration. "Water comes down the roof," he said, pointing at cracks in the dampened paint. "This is a work of art, but nobody seems to care."

A short walk north, just below the huge Süleymaniye mosque, lies Vefa. This quiet, introvert and conservative neighbourhood occupies the western slope of the third and highest of the seven hills of Constantinople. During Byzantine times, the area – near the central avenue of the Mese – was inhabited by the wealthy, who erected mansions with views over the Golden Horn below. Yet it was so savagely plundered by the Crusaders that it was deserted and became monastic territory. After the Fall, important Muslim institutions settled here, giving Vefa an air of piety (the See of the Mufti of Istanbul is here). Vefa was otherwise famous for its great number of libraries. Deadly fires may have wiped out libraries, fountains and Muslim cleric schools, but Vefa is one of the few Old City districts to have escaped "modernisation".

At its heart stands a superb Byzantine relic, eleventh-century Haghioi Theodoroi, the church of a now disappeared monastery. Converted to a mosque, it is known as Kilise Camii. The façade of the outer narthex is stunning, one of the most elaborate of any Byzantine building in town. On the upper part, mullioned windows fill blind arches drawn on the brickwork; below and sixth-century columns with massive capitals separate two other sets of mullioned windows that frame the main door. Those windows rest on large marble shafts, from whose intricate carvings the sign of the cross has been excised.

In one of the domes over the outer narthex, traces of well-preserved mosaics depicting the Virgin surrounded by prophets were uncovered. Since the church continues to serve as a mosque the frescoes were zealously whitewashed in the 1970s as they "scandalised" the faithful. The vaulted catacombs under the narthex were once imperial tombs.

During my first visit I had managed to find the caretaker. He showed me around and, upon learning I was Greek, asked me to read him the inscription on a stone unearthed in the garden at the back of the church. "It's a lovely monument, yet we very rarely receive foreigners," he said. I was the first Greek visitor he had met to that day. "I don't understand. Wasn't it the Greeks who built this? Why aren't they interested in coming?" he asked. I wasn't surprised. Greeks rarely seem to visit the less conspicuous remains of a culture they arrogantly remind everyone that they are the descendants of.

In all my subsequent visits, the church has been locked. Yet a group of extremely noisy children, aged between six and ten and living in the immediate vicinity, always manages to open it for me. The little boys, in the conviction that I am a historian, a professor or something else glamorously unfamiliar, race each other to climb the outer narthex wall, jump inside the church through the windows and open the main door. Almost always an elder parish member follows, minutes later, to drive them out as they run about chasing one another and screaming.

Characterless Atatürk Boulevard, running under the very arches of the Valens Aqueduct, separates Vefa from the fourth hill of Constantinople, where, after Haghia Sophia, the largest surviving Byzantine church stands. The monastic complex of Christ Pantocrator consists of three adjacent chapels; their five domes dominate the Old City skyline from the Golden Horn.

The monastery was built in an excellent position enjoying marvellous vistas over the channel and the Pera shore. It was one of Byzantium's largest and better organised monastic complexes, founded by John Comnenus (1118-1143) and his Hungarian wife Eirene, the couple depicted in the famous mosaic of the Haghia Sophia gallery. Prior to building operations, the hill was levelled and some buttressing made at the slopes; a retaining wall with 12 blind arches survives, visible from Atatürk Boulevard.

First was built the northern church, dedicated to Christ "Pantocrator" ("The Omnipotent") in 1118-1124. The largest of the three, it was richly decorated with mosaics and rare marbles. An opus sectile (mosaic from coloured marble inlay) on the floor depicted mythological scenes. According to Russian notable Steven

Children in front of the apse of the Monastery of Constantine Lips (Fenarî İsa Camii) in Vatan Avenue

of Novgorod visiting in 1348-9, its exterior walls were also decorated with mosaic, which "shines like the sun". The fabulous iconostasis of the church, made of solid gold and containing cloisonné icons of gold and precious stones, was dismantled by the Crusaders. The icons were taken to Venice, and now form the centrepiece of St Mark's Cathedral's famous Pala d'Oro. Pantocrator's holy vessels are also in the St Mark's collection.

A second church, dedicated to Panaghia Eleousa (Virgin of Mercy), was soon added to the south; the space between the two was later transformed into a burial chapel dedicated to the Archangel Michael – an imperial mausoleum where both founders John and Eirene, as subsequent emperors of the Comneni line (a total of 12), were laid to rest. The Crusaders desecrated their graves, stripping the bodies of their precious garments.

A centre of Orthodox veneration, the monastery was under the direct authority of the emperors throughout the Byzantine period. More than 700 monks resided here until the Latin occupation. The Pantocrator also included a hospice for the aged, a hostel for travellers, baths, a hospital, a medical school and a library. On the eve of the Fall it became the centre of opposition to the movement for church union. Among those associated with the anti-unionist cause was Gennadius Scholarius, a Pantocrator monk, who famously pronounced, "To the Catholic mitre, I would prefer the Muslim turban," implying that Turkish rule would be better than that of the Catholics. The historian Phrantzes reports that just before the Fall the people gathered to ask Gennadius: "What are we to do?"

The Conqueror, well informed of Constantinople's politics, raised Gennadius to the patriarchal throne; he also turned the complex into a mosque in 1462, renaming it Zeyrek Camii. Its altar, iconostasis and portable icons were removed, although the mosaics and frescoes were, oddly, left uncovered until they were excised sometime in the eighteenth century.

Ongoing restoration of the exterior began in 1998 and has uncovered the intricate Byzantine brickwork. The interior's state is appalling. Only some fragments of the opus sectile remain, as well as the massive marble frames of the door leading from the outer narthex to the church. Panaghia Eleousa is used as a mosque; the chapel and the Pantocrator are abandoned, covered in the waste and feathers of pigeons flying in from the broken windows.

The surrounding neighbourhood is also known as Zeyrek and is one of the most run-down districts of the city, renowned for the conservatism of its inhabitants. I know the dis-

The Church of Christ Pantepoptes (now Eski İmaret Camii) hides away in the backstreets of the Zeyrek district

trict well, since my friend Cihan gave English lessons to primary school students at the Education Volunteers' Association, housed in an old wooden house opposite the Byzantine church. His students' parents came from the East or the Black Sea region, and often had eight or ten children.

I was present in some of the classes. In one, Cihan was trying to teach children basic words on countries and government. "So… Can you tell me what kind of government Japan has?" he asked, awaiting of course to be told that Japan had an emperor. "Infidel government," a boy jumped in. Cihan was taken aback, but he corrected him. He pressed on: "Now, can you tell me what kind of government England has?" "They are infidels too," another boy said. Explaining that they shouldn't use this word was a challenge: my atheist friend had to deal with boys who were woken before sunrise by their parents to perform their ritual prayers.

Zeyrek is one of the few areas in Istanbul that somewhat preserves the air of the Ottoman city: narrow alleys lined with wooden konaks with the characteristic covered balconies (cumba). The 525 konaks listed, most in dire need of restoration, were the main reason for Zeyrek's inclusion on the Unesco Wold Heritage List. A stroll around is a mini seminar in late Ottoman architecture. The wooden houses usually have three storeys, a narrow façade and a small garden at the back. As this was a Muslim neighbourhood the windows have wooden grills, sheltering Muslim women from the indiscreet looks of male passers by.

Restoration poses grave problems. The konaks' present tenants live in dire poverty. The district is the first port of call in Istanbul for Anatolian immigrants, who stay here temporarily until they secure a job and then move to the slums of the periphery. Any realistic solution for the houses' long-term preservation entails the removal of the present inhabitants, who cannot undertake their costly upkeep. In fact, even the most essential repairs are neglected: different waves of newcomers use the konaks as temporary habitation until they collapse. Another problem is the difficulty in adapting konaks to modern facilities: they were built for a totally different way of life.

The monastery of Constantine Lips, situated on busy Vatan Avenue in the Fatih district, is at some distance from the other Byzantine monuments, but is easily reached by the tramway. Its architectural details and exquisite line make the visit worth the effort. The complex stands two metres below street level, the result of earth accumulated over eleven centuries. Its striking exterior is crowned by three peculiar domes. The eastern façade, an array of six apses, is strikingly beautiful. Along a marble cornice runs an inscription honouring Constantine Lips, its founder and an admiral in the court of Emperor Leon the Wise. The elegance of the brickwork reminds me of the Greek expression, likening Byzantine churches to embroidery.

The complex consists of two churches and a burial chapel, surrounded on two sides by an L-shaped outer narthex. The northern church, dedicated to the Virgin Panakhrantos (All Immaculate), was built by Constantine Lips in 907 AD. He chose an idyllic site by the Lykos stream, which ran along present Vatan Caddesi to the Marmara. It is a three-aisle basilica. Around the main dome are arranged four chapels, a unique feature in Byzantine architecture. What makes the interior exceptional is the plasticity of its line, all curves and superimposed volumes, which gives an air of lightness. A frieze runs along the walls, decorated with palmettes and crosses. The dome rests on a badly damage cornice, where figures of the Byzantine two-headed eagle are still visible.

The southern church dates from the late thirteenth century and was built by Theodora, wife of thirteenth-century emperor Michael Paleologos, who dedicated it to St John the Baptist. Theodora attached to it a burial chapel, now incorporated in the narthex, built in the fourteenth century. The foundress and her daughter Eudokia were followed by a long line of royal deceased, including a Russian princess. Twenty-two sarcophagi, shattered by treasure hunters, were unearthed. An unusual icon of Haghia Euphemia, of coloured stone inlay, was also found and is on display in the archaeological museum. The monastery was converted into a dervish lodge after the Conquest. Falling prey to a number of fires, it was restored in 1967 and consecrated as Fenarî isa Camii.

I often retread these footsteps, as I also visit the land walls and the Blachernae quarter. Every time, my eye grasps a little detail that had escaped it before, on every walk I meet someone with his or her own story to tell. Catching a glimpse of Byzantine glory needs a lot of mental work – drawing inferences and invoking images from the few decaying vestiges scattered in today's megalopolis. And a lot of travelling: one will find in Ravenna, Venice and the oldest churches of Rome more remnants of Byzantium than in its former capital.

Constantinople was far too unlucky compared with other famed cities of its time; posterity was too cruel on the empire and its capital, offered to the protection of the Virgin. Its tragic fall and disintegration makes its legend even more powerful.

Phanari: phantoms of aristocrats and gloomy dereliction

Schoolchildren in street of Lower Phanari (Fener), with typical row-houses in the background

The first reaction of Greek visitors to Phanari, whether they had known this old Greek quarter 40 years ago or not, is shock at its dereliction. Amphitheatrically stretching from the channel up the steep slopes of the fifth hill, Phanari is associated in the Greek mind with distinction. The presence of the Ecumenical Patriarchate and Greek aristocracy made it the heart of Hellenism for 250 years. Walking its tortuous ascents today it is hard to recall a past of magnificence. The area looks "as if plague walked through", Greek writer Kostas Stamatopoulos wrote, voicing the horror of many visitors.

Phanari means lighthouse in medieval Greek. The largest lighthouse on the Golden Horn stood here. In Byzantine times, the area was named Petrion and hosted merchants from Genoa and Venice. It was only after the fall of

Constantinople that it became a Greek haven. Mehmet the Conqueror was a builder as much as a conqueror. He immediately set out to rebuild and repopulate what had become a ghost city. In an important move, he appointed Gennadius, the Pantocrator monk renowned for his opposition to the papacy, to the patriarchal throne.

The latter had been vacant for two years before the Fall, clergy and laity split over the issue of union with Rome – supported by some as a desperate attempt to secure help from the West, vehemently repudiated by others who couldn't forget or forgive the sack of the city in 1204. Familiar with these disputes, Mehmet was anxious to reinstate the Orthodox Church, seen as the pillar of Greek identity. He wished to ensure the clergy's cooperation in legitimising his rule over the Greeks. Mehmet granted Gennadius and his successors all the privileges recognised by the Greek emperors.

Mehmet understood that the return of the Greeks was necessary for his new capital to achieve the status of "world metropolis" that Constantinople had enjoyed before 1204. Greeks were well educated and able in government, trade and the arts. Mehmet called them back promising not to discriminate against their religion, returned properties to their owners, freed prisoners and granted tax exemptions. His policies bore fruit as 5,000 Greeks arrived by September 1453. But Mehmet didn't stop there. He embarked on an ambitious repopulation programme, dragging Muslims and non-Muslims from all over his realm to Constantinople.

His rehabilitation policy produced a fragmented city, like a collection of villages. Neighbourhoods were often settled by ethnic kin from the same region. Greeks settled in Phanari, Galata and the Bosphorus, Jews in Balat and Eminönü, Turks from Cappadocia in Aksaray, and Black Sea Turks in Çarşamba. The inhabitants of those enclaves coexisted at a distance without intermingling, and each enclave developed as an introvert microcosm. Ottoman Constantinople preserved this fragmentation to the very end.

Greeks continued to arrive all through the Ottoman period, induced by job opportunities and the tax privileges reserved for the capital's residents. Most importantly, Constantinople's Christians were exempt from the child tax, whereby a number of male Christian children were collected to become Janissaries.

The Phanariote élite would later claim descent from Byzantine nobility. Yet most Byzantine nobles had fled to the West or the Italian dominions of the Levant. The Phanariote houses all made their fortunes in commerce. Even those sporting illustrious names like Comneni and Palaeologi had no relation with the namesake dynasties.

It has been rightly said that after the conquest, the Ecumenical Patriarch replaced the Emperor as leader of the Greek nation, and a "Greek Orthodox ecclesiastic state" was born. In the Ottoman system, a "nation" ("millet") was defined as a confessional group. Four such were recognised: the "Roman" (Greek Orthodox), Armenian, Jewish and Muslim. The Ecumenical Patriarchate settled around 1600 in Phanari, hence the "unofficial Greek capital".

But the golden age of Phanari was a product of far more secular considerations. By the seventeenth century, the empire had reached its apogee, becoming one of the world's largest states. As the impetus for conquest dropped, the state desperately needed diplomatic representation, particularly in Europe. Turks weren't versed in Western etiquette or languages; they traditionally studied Arabic, necessitated by Islam, and Persian, language of courtly literature and poetry. The language factor turned to the advantage of Phanari aristocrats, who were educated, well-mannered and well-travelled. Many had studied in Italy, Paris or Vienna and were not only fluent in several European languages, but also familiar with the European ways. They were the obvious choice.

They were first employed as translators (dragomans) to the Porte. This was a key post, since dragomans influenced the formation of foreign policy. Entrenched in that position from 1699 to 1821, the Phanariotes penetrated the foreign ministry ranks, using their abilities to ascend. The highest appointment they could achieve was that of Governor (Ospodar) to the semi-autonomous principalities of Wallachia and Moldova (the present Romania), known as the "Danubian Principalities". The post was reserved for Phanariotes from 1711 all the way to the Greek Revolution in 1821.

It appears odd that the Ottoman state's foreign policy was largely left in the hands of Greeks, who also joined diplomatic missions abroad and drafted treaties. What the Ottoman state expected in return was loyalty and the collection of as much revenue as possible for its treasury. The Phanariotes paid huge amounts to purchase the office, providing the Porte another source of revenue.

Phanariote ospodars were generally loyal; they themselves were part of the system and were dependent on it for their advancement. If many were slandered for treason and executed it was usually the result of bitter rivalry. There was the ruthless competition for the post, considered a goldmine, between various dynasties and between members of the same family.

The Great School resembles an Anglo-Saxon college building

These rivalries brought the worst out in the Phanariotes. Their behaviour reminds one of the ruthlessness of their Byzantine ancestors who coveted the imperial throne. At the same time, Sultans were always suspicious of men becoming too powerful and coveted their riches. They would seize the smallest opportunity to have them executed and confiscate their estates. This was an end met by many Phanariotes, as well as many grand viziers.

Wanting to exploit their short period (never more than three years) in office and to compensate for the huge amounts paid for their appointment, Phanariote ospodars drained the local population. Their rule was hugely unpopular. Acting as viceroys, they established sumptuous courts in Bucharest and Lassi, capitals of Wallachia and Moldova respectively. They did not intermingle with locals, but formed a Greek entourage, introduced the Greek language and manners and mimicked the Byzantine etiquette. Some ospodars were Hellenised Romanians and Bulgarians. For the Phanariotes, "Greek" was defined as a Byzantine identity, based on education and religious affiliation rather than race.

The Phanariotes did much to promote education and culture, both in Constantinople and the principalities. They established schools and promoted the classics and the sciences. Many were doctors and lawyers by education and quite a few were versed in philosophy. European writers speak favourably of the sumptuous life behind the modest façades of their mansions. The plays of Aeschylus, Molière and Goldoni were acted in Phanari salons. Phanariote women became famous for their learning and grace; many, like Roxane Scarlatou-Mavrocordatou, organised philosophical and literary circles, and others wrote poetry and patronised the arts.

In 1701, the French traveller Pitton de Tournefort was deeply impressed by Alexandros Mavrocordatos, to whom he was introduced by the French ambassador to Constantinople. Mavrocordatos' family came from the

The "Great School of the Nation"
towering over Phanari

island of Chios. A doctor of medicine from the University of Padua, he became prominent in the Seraglio, due to his extraordinary medical skills. Using his linguistic aptitude and knowledge of international affairs, he soon rose to become Chief Interpreter and later State Councillor, with plenipotentiary powers to draft and sign the Treaty of Karlowitz with Austria in 1699.

Tournefort speaks of the many talents of this founder of a dynasty of Moldavia ospodars. The two had discussions on medicine, botany and the Erasmus system for pronouncing ancient Greek. Tournefort ends his narration by observing that "nothing's guaranteed in the Ottoman Porte", noting how often the sultan's protégés met an untimely death.

Phanariotes are portrayed in Romanian historiography as corrupt greedy tyrants, heading a system where everything was for sale; in Greek literature they are portrayed as selfish and unwilling to put the national cause before their own vested interests in the Ottoman system, of which they were major beneficiaries.

Their stance vis-à-vis the Greek cause is intriguing. Much like the patriarchate, they represented the Ottoman status quo. Nevertheless, their readings and contacts abroad reminded them of an illustrious Greek ancestry. Greeks, amidst their political disasters, found inspiration in the widespread respect for classical Greece. A common faith that their destiny was to rise again developed as the French Revolution called the nations of Europe to rise and bring down the multi-ethnic, authoritarian empires.

Greek merchants in the diaspora propagated the new creed: Greeks should rise and establish a state modelled on the new political ideals. Phanariotes retorted with a utopia, anxious to keep their privileges intact. They held that the Turks, military strength aside, were uncultured and incapable of trade, government or art. They claimed that by virtue of their positions, culture and influence, they could effect a "takeover from within", eventually Hellenising the Ottomans. They combined Greek nationalism with the imperial tradition of Byzantium and Orthodoxy's ecumenical nature. This nationalism, centring on the primacy of Greek language and culture and its imposition on non Greeks, was typically Byzantine.

They had some grounds for believing in its success, having managed to tie the Ecumenical Patriarchate to the Greek cause. In the Ottoman confessional system, the patriarch headed all Orthodox people, be they Balkan Slavs or Orthodox Arabs. Those having nothing in common with the Greeks but religion were forced by the patriarchate to accept Greek bishops and services in Greek, something Balkan Slavs would soon rise against.

The Greek revolution was dominated not by the Phanariotes but by local warlords, diaspora intellectuals and the commercial bourgeoisie. This rising class had different interests and aspirations; its relations with the Phanariotes were hardly harmonious. Many interpreted the Greek struggle for independence as, inter alia, a fight between the traditional centres of Greek power, both resident in Phanari (patriarchate and Phanariotes), and the ascending bourgeoisie.

Members of the latter founded the Filike Etaireia (Society of Friends) in Odessa in 1814, with the chartered aim to free Greece. The new society, founded on freemason principles, would successfully lead to revolt. The new heralds did not, and could not, totally ignore the Phanariotes, well connected with Europe's royal houses and nobility, familiar with the Ottoman system and trained in politics and diplomacy. Many eventually joined the Etaireia, contributing their organisational skills and rallying in Europe for support.

The revolution erupted in February 1821 in Phanariote territory, the Principalities, which were a demilitarised zone (under a treaty between Turkey and Russia), where local rulers were Greek. Leadership was given to the Phanariote Prince Alexandros Ipsilantes, who had had an illustrious career in the Tsar's army. The revolt was crushed and Ipsilantes killed. Patriarch Gregory V, under Ottoman threats to massively slaughter his flock, excommunicated the revolutionaries. Nevertheless, by March the Peloponnese was aflame; the Aegean islands and the Asia Minor coast followed suit.

It was local chieftains who led the Greeks. After the death of Ipsilantes, the Phanariotes retired. This new leadership would later constitute the ruling class of the nascent Greek state. It was not only this loss of national leadership that dethroned the Phanariote class. Phanari paid a very heavy toll for the revolution, notwithstanding that the Phanariotes neither instigated nor controlled it.

Turks responded with massacres. In Constantinople, the main target of Turkish wrath was Phanari, its institutions and residents. Angry mobs killed indiscriminately, plundered the Phanariote mansions and set them ablaze. European ambassadors, clerics and merchants documented the destruction in detail. Greeks were put to the sword all over the city. The streets of Pera filled with Greeks begging for the relative safety of embassy precincts. The Galata quay was filled with refugees on a daily basis, as extended families rushed to leave the Ottoman realm, preferably for Odessa.

The culmination of reprisals was the hanging, on Easter Day 1821, of Patriarch Gregory V be-

Hall of Ceremonies of the Great School, detail

Mural from the Great School depicting Constantine the Great, Constantinople's founder

fore the main gate of the Patriarchate. The leader of the "Orthodox nation" was judged responsible for failing to contain the revolt. Even more than the massacres, this action sent shock waves abroad. Russia threatened military intervention and the massacres in the capital stopped. The same patriarch who had vilified the revolution would, because of his death, be registered as a martyr and hero by the Greek state. The Patriarchate's main gate remains closed to this day, as a protest against the hanging.

Phanari lay in ashes. Many Phanariotes fled to Russia, France and Egypt, constituting the most refined stratum of the Greek diaspora. Few opted for Greece, looking down at the new classes ruling the fortunes of the small state. Most of those who remained in Constantinople settled in Pera, whose embassies, heavy foreign presence and absence of Muslims created some illusion of safety. Pera became the new force, and its markedly secular and westernising élite took over from the Phanari theocracy the leadership of Constantinopolitan Hellenism.

If Phanari retained a distinctive atmosphere, it was due to the presence of the Patriarchate and its schools. Yet it steadily degraded into the petty bourgeois district of the 1900s described by a Constantinopolitan called Spatharis as a neighbourhood where housewives competed with each other in cooking, housekeeping and needlework, and spent their free time gossiping.

Women from the Black Sea region on the doorstep of an old Greek house

Spatharis mentions an entire army of elderly Greek bachelors, forced to postpone their weddings until they had found a husband for each of their (many) sisters. They never did…

• • •

The most impressive access to Phanari (Fener in Turkish) is by hopping on one of the Golden Horn ferries, departing from Karaköy or Eminönü. The trip offers marvellous views over the channel and the familiar landmarks of the Old City skyline. It also gives the opportunity to appreciate the horn-shaped natural harbour that travellers described for millennia as a perfect port. Constantinople evolved around this narrow waterway, which divides its European part in two. Until the Great War, visitors were impressed by the forest of masts by the channel's shores, a sight long gone from the city panorama.

The boat ride is also a sociological experience. The Golden Horn boats carry Muslim zealots settled in Çarşamba – the hill above Phanari – home from their jobs in Üsküdar, the other bastion of conservatism on Istanbul's Asian shore. Aboard, one encounters women completely enveloped in black cloth, sometimes with their faces totally covered, and men sporting Taliban-like attire and beards, which are banned by law in Turkey (the law doesn't seem to be enforced). Once I came across a polygamous family, a man with his three wives and flock of children. Polygamy is of course outlawed, and such sights make Turkey's urban westernisers shiver.

As the boat approaches Phanari, its most famous landmark, the imposing domed red figure of the Great School, rises like an immense chateau over the hill. Among Istanbul's most impressive silhouettes, it is visible from miles away and would have been a city symbol as much as the Galata Tower or Bosphorus Bridge, were it not for the anti-Greek hysteria prevalent for decades.

Only the wooden boat terminal survives unscathed on the waterfront. The coastal zone was completely deformed during "rehabilitation" in the 1980s. Mayor Dalan had many of the stone mansions of the Phanariotes lining the coast demolished to create a "seaside park". The result was predictably disappointing. The demolitions opened the way for a noisy coastal highway, congested with traffic. The existing main road of Phanari also became a highway. No local bothers to stroll in what is the dominion of the homeless, who either set up tents or sleep under the trees. Here and there the few mansions that escaped stand isolated. The once introvert quarter, secluded, haunted with memories, lost much of its mysticism when it was opened up to the sea and traffic.

To the north lies the old Jewish quarter of Balat, to the south Cibali, formerly an industrial quarter. The industrialisation that started in the late nineteenth century turned the channel into a smelly swamp by the 1900s. On January 6, 2003, the Ecumenical Patriarchate held the traditional Epiphany celebration of the "blessing of the water" in the Golden Horn, after decades of failing to get permission from the authorities. The ceremony, repeated every year since, involves throwing a cross into the water; several men brave the cold and dive to catch it. The image of young Greeks diving was triumphantly broadcast on Turkish channels, proof of the municipality's declaration that the Horn is now clean enough to swim in. But the filth still floats here and there, making me think that the brave Greeks diving for the cross don't simply defy the cold.

The surviving Phanariote mansions along the coastal road have their first floor buried in the ground – the result of earth accumulation over the centuries. Modest in appearance, they were built of stone and brick in two or three storeys, radiating a medieval air. Their upper floors usually project, resting on rows of voluted corbels; the tallest mansions are like a climax of projecting surfaces. For reasons of safety and privacy they had few openings on the ground floor, which was reserved for the servants. Windows were far more numerous on the upper floors. The narrow windows, covered with thick metal grills, are topped by pointed blind arches in the brickwork; under the roof runs a stone cornice.

It was in such modest mansions, whose fortress-like aspect reminded Theophile Gautier of medieval inns, that the Phanariotes resided: "Princes without principalities… treated by their servants like kings, consoling themselves for their demise with enactments of respect." In fact, a typical family of ospodars would reside in a three-storey mansion, whose narrow façade concealed an elongated building. Interiors concealed luxuries unimaginable. Gautier emphasises the contrast between plain exterior and lushly ornate interior, a common theme in Byzantine architecture. "In the East luxury is timid and shies from the eyes," he comments. He describes Phanari as "a sort of West End", contrasting its stone harmony to the wooden mass of other neighbourhoods.

Turkish and foreign writers misleadingly refer to these homes as Byzantine. The constructions themselves date from the seventeenth or eighteenth centuries; it is the style that follows the late Byzantine line, which dominated local civil architecture long after the Conquest. It was applied by the Ottomans in many of their hans, libraries and communal buildings. After the dis-

Kurdish family ascending the Phanari streets towards the Great School

astrous earthquake of 1509, stone was abondoned for wood. Only in Phanari and Galata did stone building continue.

Photographs from the turn of the twentieth century show the streets of lower Phanari lined with such mansions – a marvellous and peculiar sight extinguished by unfortunate urban planning. Today, a few survive along the coast, particularly near the Bulgarian church, while a few stand in the Phanari and Balat hills. Together with the two standing palaces they are our sole link to the Byzantines' secular architecture.

The Ecumenical Patriarchate of Constantinople, New Rome, stands within a walled en-

These girls are all siblings, their family moved to Phanari from Anatolia

clave, where it ended up after a century of wandering around. Given its huge spiritual resonance all over the Orthodox world, the absolute lack of magnificence in the premises strikes visitors. A large konak and a few stone buildings – modest to a fault – is all there is to it. The Patriarchal Church of St George is predictably in better condition than most others in town. It houses two mosaic fragments from Theotokos Pammakaristos (now Fethiye Camii), where the Patriarchate had resided from 1455 to 1587, one depicting the Virgin and the other St John the Baptist. These are the most precious relics of the Patriarchate, whose treasury is a great disappointment. Apart from some medieval manuscripts, not much is stored there, another demonstration of how destruction and plunder obliterated the city.

Much more magnificent is the massive silhouette of the "Great Patriarchal School of the Nation", familiar even to those who have never set foot in Phanari. Many Turks and tourists mistake it for the Patriarchate. The presence in Istanbul of an immense neo-Gothic redbrick building may perplex, but it is in tune with the architectural legacy of late Ottoman Greeks. The masterpiece of Pericles Demades demonstrates the wealth of that cosmopolitan community, the importance it attached to education and its openness to a wide variety of stylistic and aesthetic influences.

The current building dates from 1881, and the bricks used in its construction were carried over from France. The institution itself is much older, founded immediately after the Fall, in 1454, as a continuation of the Pandedakterion, the Byzantine university. Its operation under the auspices of the Patriarchate formed part of the privileges accorded by Mehmet to Gennadius. The school's first name was Patriarchal Academy; later names include Panhellenic Academy, Museum (the Greek word alludes to the nine Muses), Temple of the Muses, and Greek Museum of the Queen of Cities. All names convey that it was the most important Greek educational institution in the Ottoman capital. It remained so without serious competition until the foundation of the illustrious Greek schools of Pera.

The Great School was where dragomans and ospodars got their first education, before proceeding to universities in Italy or France. Education initially placed heavy emphasis on theology, philosophy and the classics. Yet as a new commercial bourgeoisie arose in the Greek community, it took more active control of education. The Great School was streamlined on secular lines, focusing on science and the classics. Its new building came to symbolise its new orientation.

There are currently 55 students in the immense premises, many among them Arabic-speakers from Antakya. The demise of the school, once the most prestigious academy in the Levant, echoes that of the local Greek community. Although exempt from the 1923 population exchange between Greece and Turkey, it was confronted with decades of intimidation and even pogroms. Its members fled, but the buildings remain as a testament to better days.

You enter through a gate at street level and climb a steep staircase leading to a court with glorious views of the Golden Horn and the Pera shore opposite. Similar views may be enjoyed from all windows on the school's northern façade. An unassuming main hall leads to the exquisite chamber of ceremonies on the first floor, whose ceiling and walls are painted with frescoes representing figures of Greek history. Pericles and Alexander the Great are depicted beside Constantine and the Apostle Paul, fusing what the community accepted as its two points of collective reference: classical Greece and Orthodox Christianity. Motifs of meanders, palmettes and other decorative figures taken directly from classical Athenian pottery decorate the frieze.

Next to the school rises Istanbul's only Byzantine church that remains in Greek hands, tiny Panaghia ton Mongolon (Virgin of the Mongols), also known as Mouhliotissa (medieval Greek for "Mogul Woman"). Its bizarre campanile with the vaguely gothic line is a later addition. Mouhliotissa's simplicity hides the fascinating story of Maria Palaeologina, a princess married to the Mogul Khan. Princesses were a major export of the Byzantine state, married off to 'barbarians" with whom the empire wanted to form marriage alliances. Maria lived besides the Mogul Khan for 15 years. After his death, she returned to Constantinople and founded a monastery (c1285), where she spent the remainder of her days. She dedicated its church to the Virgin protector of the Mongols.

Phanari's most bizarre monument is the Gothic silhouette by the shore at the district's northern end: Sveti Stefan, commonly known as "the Bulgarian Church". Its history is intertwined with that of the foundation of a "national" Bulgarian church, independent from the Ecumenical Patriarchate. The latter imposed Greek as the language of ritual and education on all of the empire's Orthodox subjects. Not only Greeks were influenced by the new ideas. The Bulgarians claimed, not unreasonably, that they were politically oppressed by the Ottomans and religiously and culturally oppressed by the Greeks. During the period they call "National Revival", they campaigned for the establishment of an independent church and a separate "millet" (confessional nation). Bulgarians wanted ed-

Byzantine relic from one of Constantinople's churches, kept at the Ecumenical Patriarchate

ucation and liturgy in Bulgarian and their Greek bishops to be replaced by Bulgarians.

In 1850 Bulgarian nationalists established the "Metoh" in a stone building on the Phanari shore, right under the nose of the Patriarchate and the Phanariotes, and rallied for their cause. An irate Patriarchate, already angered at the establishment of an autocephalous church in Greece, perceived their claims as a further threat to its ecumenical status. It campaigned against the recognition of an autonomous Bulgarian church. Yet a Bulgarian Exarchate was recognised by a Ferman (sultan's decree) in 1870. It has been alleged that the Porte allowed

Coat of arms of a Phanariote family over the gate of their mansion

for its creation in order to turn the Greeks against the Bulgarians in Macedonia, a territory that both nationalities coveted and that the Ottoman state was anxious to maintain. It is also alleged that the Porte wanted to pre-empt a Russian intervention in Bulgaria. Russians, under the new ascending current of pan-Slavism, espoused the cause of their "Slavic blood kin".

Recognition of the Exarchate, which soon became the prime vehicle for Bulgarian nationalism, prevented neither Bulgarian revolt (in 1876) nor Russian involvement. Russians stormed Bulgaria, ousted the Turks and helped establish an independent kingdom. Despite Bulgarian independence, the Exarchate's See remained in the Metoh, still standing opposite Sveti Stefan, and later moved to the quarter of Şişli, where it remains. Today, the Istanbul Exarchate only serves the needs of Istanbul's Bulgarians.

Sveti Stefan, inaugurated in 1898, is famous for being built entirely from corroborated iron – one of the world's few surviving prefabricated cast iron churches and the only Orthodox of that kind. The tender for its construction was won by the Armenian architect Hovsep Aznavour, who proposed the iron structure. The 500-tonne metal plaques were ordered from Rudolf Wagner and Sons in Vienna and were shipped to Istanbul via the Danube and Black Sea. The church was assembled on the spot within a week. The interior is also completely made of metal. The iconostasis was ordered in Moscow, where the icons, with the sweet forms and colours of the Russian style, were painted. The six bells were cast in Yaroslavl in Russia. The placid interior radiates warmth and beauty.

When Sveti Stefan was erected, there were about 30,000 Bulgarians in Constantinople. The community followed the general decline of non-Muslim communities under the Republic. It now numbers about 600 members, some of whom define themselves as "Macedonian Slavs". These remained faithful to the Exarchate and were expelled from Greek Macedonia after the Balkan Wars. Some now attend the Bulgarian church, others the Greek one. Most Bulgarians generally describe themselves as "Rum" (Roman), an umbrella term for the Orthodox.

A Patriarchate was founded in Bulgaria after Phanari recognised the autocephalous Bulgarian Church in 1950. Sveti Stefan is not only the most conspicuous reminder of the Bulgarian presence in town, but also an important monument of the Bulgarian struggle for independence, a struggle that started as a call for religious emancipation. At the same time, its architecture reminds of the innovative tendencies prevalent among the city's Christian communities at the time of its building.

Apart from the towering mass of the Great School, another symbol of Phanari is its famous row houses: constructions of medium height and three floors with very narrow façades, bay windows on the second floor, arched entryways and floors and ceilings of wooden beams. They are traditionally painted in deep reds, greens and ochre. Their eclectic decoration – heads of Hermes or Athena sculpted over the windows and columns decorating the main doors – betrays a society looking to classical Greece for inspiration.

Besides this influence of Greek antiquity, the

houses reflect various other influences. The row house as an architectural type was imported from Europe, but adopted elements of the vernacular, such as the square bay windows. The difference from the vernacular is the repetition of the façades and the basic layout; houses in a row differ only in decorative details. These constructions lack the size and the refined splendour of Pera apartment buildings. Nevertheless, they are elegant and profoundly human. Row houses addressed the needs and lifestyle of a rising petty bourgeoisie consisting of merchants, tradesmen, artisans and teachers; each housed one family. Similar houses are found in most formerly non-Muslim neighbourhoods, but the Phanari ones survive in large clusters, conserving the traditional Constantinopolitan cityscape.

Phanari preserved its Greek character until the 1960s. The Greek exodus was a result of a systematic policy of harassment, which included pogroms and evictions. The dilapidation of the houses seems to echo the desperation of their Greek owners, forced out against their will. It is a heartbreaking sight. A Turkish architect wrote that the houses "are crying, appealing to our souls".

Phanari is important as a case study of Istanbul's metamorphosis. The contrast between the built and the living worlds illustrates the dramatic alteration in demography and urban identity. Schools, churches and architecture betray a middle-class Greek past. Yet the current population is out of touch with this material world. Unable to develop some sense of attachment to the surroundings, the newcomers maintain a feeling of alienation.

The arrival of the peasantry was triggered by the dire economic conditions of the country. The immigration pattern is common to all Istanbul neighbourhoods abandoned by their previous inhabitants. First, one or two "pioneers" from a village established themselves in a particular district, usually occupying an abandoned home or paying a nominal rent. After settling and making ends meet, they called their families over. One family after another followed their tracks, until almost the entire village was transplanted to the neighbourhood. Most newcomers had never seen a city before and they grouped together in order to feel safe. This reproduced the segregation by local origins found in Mehmet II's time.

Phanari and Balat became magnets for migrants flocking in from the 1960s onwards, as they contained hundreds of abandoned houses. The first arrivals came from Kastamonu; others followed from Rize and Sivas, all in the Black Sea region. Gypsies arrived from Thrace, while recent years saw a massive influx of Kurds. Squatting in the abandoned buildings saved

21

newcomers from having to build shabby constructions in one of the shanties springing up on the periphery. Yet they had no means to repair the houses, which soon started to decay. Several families squeeze in homes intended for one.

As Turks overcame the nationalism of the past and started to take pride in Istanbul's cosmopolitan heritage, Phanari and Balat were hailed as an "open-air museum". A "Fener-Balat Rehabilitation Project" was launched, the first in town, based on a UNESCO feasibility report and financed by the EU and the Fatih Municipality. It follows the modern school, which rejects gentrification for tourist purposes but focuses on conserving entire environments and social units. Emphasis is put on social rehabilitation, while restoration involves the removal of later additions, so that buildings revert to their original form. The programme covers those houses whose owners accept the restoration.

Not many did initially, fearing they would be evicted and the houses sold to rich foreigners. Nurcan Atalan, the programme's press officer, explained that the uneducated settlers are influenced both by Turkish nationalism and by political Islam. "And also," she says, "by the claims of the extreme right that the Greeks are planning to return, reclaim their property and found a Greek Vatican around the Patriarchate." She says it took time to convince them to join the programme; many never did.

Programmes on family planning were launched, aiming at socio-economic regeneration. Most settlers give birth to many children. Men are often unemployed. Teenage daughters are normally not sent to high school, but made to wear the Islamic veil and stay at home. Most teenage boys are forced out of school to join the workforce. The programme aims to change all this and raise educational standards. Many local men work on the construction sites, ensuring that the local community is actively involved in the restorations. Local women are encouraged to take up handicrafts and participate in workshops.

Restoration work began in 2003 and is in its final stages at the time of writing. The change is immediately apparent in the districts' façades. Yet one cannot say the streets are clean, and the dereliction of the homes whose owners declined cooperation still catches the eye. It will be a long time before Phanari reverts to anything like its middle-class past – if it ever does.

Children of Anatolians playing football in a backstreet near the Great School

Awakening schoolbook memories: a walk by the Land Walls

Vegetable patches can be seen in front of this segment of the walls, near Silivrikapı, where the moat once was

"I wonder whether the grandeur of human achievement, the majesty of strength, the glory of antiquity, the pomp of memories, the melancholy of ruins and beauty of nature has ever been commingled to this degree... a spectacle simultaneously awakening wonder, respect and terror, worthy of Homer," wrote Edmondo d'Amicis about Byzantine Constantinople's largest relic, the land walls. Byron remarked that, although he had seen the ruins of Athens, Ephesus and Delphi, and had toured much of Turkey and Asia, he had never seen a sight that yielded an impression as strong as the prospect from the Seven Towers to the Golden Horn.

No matter how many times I have wandered along the land walls, I still experience that same feeling of awe that overcame me the first time I saw them. On every journey to and from the airport, my sight is fixed on them, towering by the coastal highway, stretching as far as the eye can see.

Built in 413 under Theodosius II, they stretch for about seven kilometres between the Marmara and Golden Horn, separating the historic peninsula of Constantinople from the Thracian plains. Combined with the sea walls, they formed one of the most extensive and sophisticated defensive works ever built. Only pierced twice, in 1204 by the army of the Fourth Crusade and in 1453, they defended Constantinople for a millennium.

The Theodosian walls consist of an inner (12 metres high, 5 metes wide) and outer (8.5 metres high, 2 metres wide) wall, jointly carrying 96 towers, some round and some cylindrical, at 55 metre distances from each other. Between every two towers of the outer wall stands one of the inner. A moat, 10 metres deep and 20 wide – flooded in times of siege with water from the Marmara and Golden Horn – ran in front of the walls, and ten gates, five public and five military, pierced them. Seven gates survive, serving traffic to and from Istanbul. With the erection of the Theodosian Walls, the surface of the walled city almost doubled, and included seven hills – as many as Rome. In an empire drenched in symbolism, this carried great significance.

The periphery is dotted with Byzantine relics. There are many poor districts and the area has seen dramatic changes over the past 30 years. Far from the city centre, the walls don't feature on many visitors' itineraries. During my first visit as a tourist in 2001, I took the suggestion of Edmondo d'Amicis to walk along their entire length and "follow the course of my own meditations". To reach them, I hopped on the banlieue train from Sirkeci. The rail road runs parallel to the shore. Its construction in the 1870s destroyed many Byzantine and Ottoman monuments, while part of the land walls and long segments of the sea walls were demolished. The ride offers a panorama of the sea walls and the domes and belfries of the once Christian quarters of Kumkapı and Samatya. For this reason I preferred the train for most subsequent visits.

Arriving in the deserted Yedi Kule station I walked to the shore. I soon reached the Marble Tower, a defence against sea attack, on the point where the land walls met the sea walls on the Marmara. It stood on the water with a scenic harbour in front of it, until the construction of the coastal avenue cut it off from the water. Its lower half is covered by white marble, hence the name; the upper part is laid out with parallel lines of white stone and red brick, and incorporated marble plaques bear the initials of the Palaeologi and the Cantacuzeni dynasties. On

Sulukule Kapısı (Gate of Lykos or Pempton) leads to the Gypsy district of Sulukule

its base, someone has sprayed "METALLICA" in huge red letters.

Right opposite begin the kilometres of ruined walls. Built of limestone, they radiate a golden colour in the sunshine. I shivered at the view. Scenes of Byzantine military triumphs crossed my mind: the emperor returning victorious from a campaign in Persia or the Balkans. And scenes of disaster: the turbaned mobs of the Conqueror laying a civilisation to waste, fires, desecrations, carnage.

I walked to Yedi Kule, or Eptapyrgion, the "Seven Tower" fortress. Two immense pillars of white marble project behind a lower front wall, marking the place of Constantinople's most famous gate, the Golden Gate. Built as a triumphal arch by Emperor Theodosius on the Via Egnatia, 1,500 metres away from the fortifications of the time, it was incorporated in the new fortifications of his grandson Theodosius II as the Golden Gate (its doors were gilded) and became Constantinople's ceremonial gate. After the Fall, it formed part of the Eptapyrgion fortress and was built in. The low wall in front is dotted with an ante-gate, framed by two impressive marble columns and lintel.

In the early years, Byzantine emperors were crowned in Hebdomon (Makrohori) in the presence of the imperial army, then took the Via Egnatia and arrived at the Golden Gate, where they were greeted by Constantinople's clergy and nobles. The cortege then proceeded to the Great Palace by the Hippodrome. The coronation ritual at Hebdomon, which was deeply rooted in the imperial tradition of Rome, was abandoned by 474; after that emperors were crowned in Haghia Sophia, and triumphal processions passed through the Golden Gate only after military victories.

One such is described by Robert de Claris, chronicler of the Fourth Crusade: "On this gate were found two bronze elephants so big, a miracle to watch. It was never opened, except when the Emperor returned victorious from battle. The clergy proceeded to greet him, the Gate opened and a golden carriage was carried outside... On its centre lay a throne, which seemed to be all gold. The Emperor, wearing his crown, sat on it and, crossing the gate on its carriage, proceeded to his Palace in acclamations and jubilation."

The last triumphal entry was that of Michael Palaeologos, who entered on a white horse on August 15, 1261, after his general, Strategopoulos, had liberated Constantinople from the Latin rule. The long procession was headed by the icon of the Virgin Hodegetria, Constantinople's palladium. Michael was crowned emperor in Haghia Sophia.

A Muslim cemetery lies between the Golden Gate and the road. The gate can only be entered from Yedi Kule fortress. It was once topped with statues of Hercules, of Prometheus and other legendary figures, described by amazed travellers as late as the eighteenth century. Plaques with carved eagles and crosses still exist. The Byzantine points of reference were imperial Roman tradition, the Orthodox faith and classical Greek heritage; an eclectic art mingled all three.

The Mikra Hrysi Pyli (Little Golden Gate) was opened close to the Golden Gate and intended for public use. Renamed Yedi Kule Kapısı by the Ottomans, it leads to the Samatya district. On the inner side, the Byzantine eagle is still visible on the tympanum over the door. Depicted on all gates and towers on the engravings of the early travellers, the Byzantine emblem was usually removed by the Turks. So were the names of the emperors. Many marble frames on the brickwork stand empty, the plaques having been removed.

Samatya is the Ypsoma Theion (Holy Height) of the Byzantines (Psomathia to the Ottoman Greeks). In this district was born Loxandra, maternal grandmother of writer Maria Iordanidou and heroine of Iordanidou's novel *Loxandra*, a depiction of lower middle class Greek Orthodox life in late Ottoman Constantinople. Samatya was also the birthplace of the father of Greek poet Constantine Cavafy. It's a shabby quarter of collapsing old homes, abandoned by their Greek and Armenian owners. As all other districts along the walls, Samatya – once a mixed Greek-Armenian quarter – has always been poor.

Flaubert, writing in 1850, contrasted its liveliness with the lethargy of Muslim boroughs. "The neighbourhood had an altogether different aspect... Girls with graceful hairstyles appeared in the windows, which had no grills. Young ladies sat on the doorsteps, watching the movement on the street. We could admire their delicate, pure traits without making them flee. In front of the cafés, men with the white skirts of the Greeks drank raki... It was a kind of Greek colony and the merry tones of that race had replaced gloominess." This juxtaposition of Greek merriness with the solemn serenity of Turks is a stereotypical image in many travelogues on the Ottoman city.

Many of Samatya's Greeks originated from Turkish-speaking Greek villages of central Anatolia. They had forgotten their mother tongue, but had kept their Greek consciousness intact. They bore Greek names, often the pagan ones of classical antiquity, and their art drew inspiration from Classical Greece as much as from Byzantium. In the decaying Samatya houses, Ionic capitals, marble pediments and cornices abound. Here and there, a wooden konak survives and a few Greek inscriptions may still be spotted. Greeks and Armenians were eventually replaced by poor Anatolians. The saying "Samatya turned Malatya", an Istanbul pun, doesn't imply that Samatya's new dwellers came from that city. It simply alludes to "Istanbul's takeover" by the Anatolians.

A minaret marks the ruins of the church of the Studion monastery, surrounded by stone walls with red brickwork. Here stood Byzantium's most revered monastery, dedicated to Saint John the Baptist and founded by Studius, a Roman patrician and ex-consul in the reign of

Leo the Wise. The basilica was completed in 463. The monastery's estates extended to the Marmara and included a private anchorage. According to the Book of Ceremonies, a tenth-century work of Constantine Porphyrogennetus, emperors would anchor here while visiting for the anniversary of St John's execution on August 29.

A stronghold of the Iconodules (those who venerated icons), the monastery was shut during the reign of iconoclast Leo V and its (later canonised) abbot, Theodore Studite, was exiled. Reopened by Michael II, it was to become, under Theodore, a repository of culture. Many of its monks became famous poets and composers of hymns, many more distinguished themselves in the study and copy of ancient texts and the illustration of manuscripts. They were termed "sleepless", as they took turns to sleep and sang hymns all day and night. The monastery's typikon (rule) was one of the strictest in the Orthodox world, and was adopted by many monasteries in the Orthodox and Catholic worlds.

Studion managed to preserve the Graeco-Roman heritage even in the darkness of Iconoclasm and it survived the Empire by 50 years. Its influence on politics was great; even coups were staged in its grounds. Here Emperor Michael V Calafates took refuge in 1042, fleeing a rebellion, until he was detected, dragged outside, blinded and exiled. Two dethroned emperors, Isaac Comnenos and Michael Doukas, finished their days as monks here.

The monastery was looted during the sack of Constantinople by the Crusaders and its relics were taken to Alsace and Flanders, where they can still be found scattered in village churches. A few years before the Fall, a Studite monk wrote: "No barbarian can see my face, no woman can hear my voice. For a thousand years, no useless man has entered Studion, none of the female sex trodden its court. I dwell in a cell that's like a palace; a garden, an olive grove and a vineyard surround me… On the one hand is the Great City with its markets, on the other the Mother of Churches and the World Empire."

Converted into a mosque in the sixteenth century and renamed Imrahor Camii, the basilica was decimated first in the disastrous 1894 earthquake and then in a fire in 1920. Although ruined, St John is the most ancient church of Constantinople to survive. It is significant for its proto-Christian style, incorporating Graeco-Roman elements. Unfortunately, it's always closed.

My entry was to be an adventurous one. A group of children spotted me desperately trying to climb in. They ran off and reappeared with a man who said that if I were willing to pay him some money, he'd help me. He left and reappeared with a ladder. We jumped into a walled courtyard, once an atrium preceding the church.

Before the central bay of the narthex stand four marble columns with awesome Corinthian capitals; two marble doorframes survive between them. The nave is flanked by two aisles; six columns survive in the north aisle. The Russian traveller Steven of Novgorod described the church as "very large and high, covered with a slanted roof. Its icons are highly decorated with gold and shine like the sun. The floor is quite amazing, as if set with pearls; no painter could paint that way."

Traces of the opus sectile, the mosaic of inlaid coloured stone that so impressed Steven, survive on the battered floor, on which some chickens were walking about nonchalantly. The opus depicts geometric patterns as well as miniatures of animals and birds.

Besides the Studion I spotted a campanile in red ochre and a dome covered with laden scales. Approaching, I found a spacious yard, all trees and flowers, in front of a mustard-coloured basilica. A woman appeared from the house at one end of the yard, carrying laundry to hang. She noticed me and approached. She was from Antioch and didn't speak a word of Greek.

The oldest references to the church, dedicated to Constantine and Helen, date from 1563; it was probably erected after the Studion

One of those "plain fortified churches" that Greeks had to be content with before the 1856 reforms: Samatya

became a mosque. On its west façade are incorporated four marble plaques, two of which date from the early Christian era. One depicts Emperor Constantine and his mother Helen holding the cross, the second shows cherubim, the third a cross, whilst the fourth, and most peculiar, is a solar clock. The inscription above the inner door to the nave mentions 1805 as the church's inauguration date.

The interior is basic: the church burnt to the ground in the anti-Greek pogrom of 1955, and the photograph of a desperate Patriarch Athenagoras among its smoking ruins featured in the international press of the time. The church is the parish of the Karamanlı (Turkish speaking) Greeks of Cappadocia and inner Anatolia who

One of the last Greeks of Samatya with the church of Constantine and Helen in the background

PREMIER

Tombstone written in the Karamanlı script
(Turkish written with Greek alphabet)

settled in Samatya. Adjacent is the Fotiadeios, the parish elementary school. Alexander and Nicholas Fotiades who founded it were maternal uncles of the Greek poet Cavafy.

I entered the Eptapyrgion (Yedi Kule) fortress, built right after the Ottoman conquest. Two of its towers belong to the Theodosian walls, two are the pillars of the Golden Gate and three were constructed by the Conqueror and connected to the rest by a stretch of inner walls; the fortress has the shape of a pentagon. An addition to existing defences, it was guarded by Janissaries.

Initially, the Eptapyrgion housed the Ottoman crown treasury. Like its namesake in Thessaloniki, it was later converted into a prison. Many of its inmates were foreign envoys to the Sultan. Sultan Orhan II was also imprisoned here before his execution by rebellious Janissaries. In 1701, Pitton de Tournefort was denied access to "a sort of Bastille where the eminent are imprisoned". Foreign visits were banned after the escape of an imprisoned French knight, a prohibition that survived into the nineteenth century.

The fortress is now a rarely visited museum, where the attractions are seeing the Golden Gate and climbing the towers for great views over the land walls and the Marmara. Deprived of its ornaments, the Golden Gate is a sad sight. The walls seem to stretch endlessly, separating the less affluent districts of the walled city from the supermarkets, skyscrapers, factories, forests and parking lots of its outskirts.

• • •

That September morning was neither hot nor humid, facilitating my long walk and the evocation of my schoolboy readings on the rise and fall of empires. The Turks respected the walls, recognising their defensive value, but their upkeep was neglected. Tournefort mentions in the late seventeenth century that the walls were "pretty good", whilst Lord Byron was amazed to find them "perfectly defensible". All travellers mention the Greek inscriptions and coats of arms adorning them and they describe a picturesque vicinity beyond them, with shady cemeteries, fields, forests and vineyards.

A series of earthquakes, sieges and the cannon assaults during the 1453 siege ruined large sections of the walls. Ironically, their greatest destruction took place in peacetime, with the construction of the railway in the 1870s. An even greater disaster was the restoration plan of the late 1980s devised by the municipality and funded by UNESCO. "Rebuilding" rather than restoration appropriately describes the intervention.

Visiting Greek writer Kostas Stamatopoulos wrote in the 1980s: "Thousands work in the immense construction sight… They advance fastly… Everything is uniform, of white stone and shiny red brick… Everything's brand new." The bulk of restoration was carried out between Eptapyrgion and the Belgrade Gate, where brand-new towers sprang up, like part of the décor of a Las Vegas nightclub. Many archaeologists denounced the "disappearance" of surviving Greek inscriptions and emblems.

Nevertheless, the walls remain a vivid contact with the Byzantine glory they sheltered for centuries. The tranquil atmosphere of their surroundings, where once silence and vegetation reigned, has been irrevocably damaged as huge concrete constructions, highway overpasses and traffic replaced forests and fields.

The moat has also disappeared, filled with the debris of road construction. Where the moat once ran stretch narrow fields, tiny greenhouses and playgrounds. Corn, lettuce, melons and rocket are cultivated here: it is said that the best salads in town grow out of the walls. Here and there are areas covered with graves; under the shade of some trees is a tent hosting the peasants who cultivate the fields. This is a traditional area of gypsy settlement and I saw gypsies strolling around just as d'Amicis did 150 years ago.

The Gate of Pege (meaning "source") or Selebria, now Silivrikapı, suffered nightmarish restoration. It was here that general Alexios Strategopoulos made his surprise assault and liberated the city from the Latins in 1261. The gate's name comes from the famous Zoodohos Pege (aka Balıklı) monastery in the forest opposite. According to the legend, Justinian – who suffered from kidney problems – ran into a group of women visiting a source in the woods opposite the walls. They informed him that the water had healing power. He drank and was healed, then decided to erect a church from surplus material destined for Haghia Sophia. A successor built a palace and the place became a resort, described as idyllic by Procopius in *de Edificia*.

The Justinian temple was destroyed by quakes, and the church – turned monastery – was rebuilt more than once. According to a well-known legend, as Turks entered Constantinople in 1453, a monk was frying goldfish in a pan. When mourners fleeing the massacres broke the news, he did not believe them. "Only if those fish turn back to life and swim will I believe our city has fallen," he said. The half-fried fish, the legend goes, jumped into the fountain and began to swim. The monastery was thereafter known as "the fish monastery" (balık is Turkish for fish).

The present church dates from 1833. Its courtyard is covered in marble tombstones originating from disappeared Greek cemeteries. Many are decorated with carvings of scales, scissors and other objects alluding to the profession of the deceased. Some bear inscriptions in the Karamanlı script, used by that isolated Greek community in central Anatolia: Turkish written with Greek letters. In a crypt under the church is the holy water with the descendants of the "resurrected" goldfish. The backyard houses the tombs of a number of ecumenical patriarchs of Constantinople.

The monastery was severely vandalised in the anti-Greek riots of 1955: the basilica's interior was ravaged, the monks' cells burnt and the patriarchs' tombs smashed, bones scattered around. An elderly monk was burnt alive. "From the vaulted ceilings, heavily wrought brass lamps had been torn and still lay scattered on the floor. The iconostasis, with saints depicted in the pre-Raphaelite manner of Russian Romanticism, was sorely battered," wrote Turkish-Jewish writer Edouard Roditi, visiting after the pogrom. As in other Greek shrines, the damage was restored, but the trauma is indelible.

Exhausted, I arrived an hour later at the Gate of Adrianople (Edinekapı), built on the highest of the seven hills. From this gate the Conqueror entered the city, as a huge marble plaque on its inner side commemorates. Later, sultans used it after being girded by the sword of the Conqueror in the nearby mosque of Eyüp.

I immediately noticed the iron campanile of the Greek church of St George further down. Church and school stand around a small courtyard covered with a pergola. The school is austere, its windows in redbrick frames. Corinthian capitals top brick pillars in the corners. A merry crowd had just finished their meal and were sipping Turkish coffee under the pergola. They greeted me amiably.

"After such a pilgrimage you should light a candle and make a wish," a white-haired, bearded man wearing a t-shirt and a pair of black trousers said. He was the priest. One of the women was his wife; the others were Arab Christians from Antioch, who guarded parish churches. The priest's wife said their children were in Greece. "They left, but we wouldn't. We come and go." She offered me chocolates.

The church is a basilica with a vaulted roof. Its exterior is of fortress-like simplicity; the interior of painted wood boasts an imposing wooden iconostasis with silver-coated and painted icons. I crossed myself wishing that one day I would settle in this marvellous city. Two years later, my wish would come true.

A young boy led me to another church nearby, the Virgin of the Heavens at Salmatomruk, hidden behind a massive wall like most Greek shrines built before the 1850s. The guardian, Vassilis, was apprehensive. He kept my camera to make sure I wouldn't shoot the interior, of light blue and white wood and interesting icons. Madame Marianthi, his wife, was more forthcoming. "Of course we're afraid," she told me. "So many churches have recently been broken into, icons stolen. It's difficult to live here. Look around. They're all covered in black, like ravens."

Vassilis relaxed a bit. "Look, these boroughs were always poor. But this... fervour is something new. We were raised in Samatya, but had to leave after the events... You know, in 1955..."

Marianthi jumped in. "I'll never forget that night. We feared for our lives. We couldn't stay in Samatya any more. Our own Turkish neighbours led the rioters to our homes, schools and churches! Is it possible to talk to them again? They looted everything we had... some of them beat us." The couple were interrupting each other, breathless with excitement.

"On the one side of our street in Samatya only Greeks and Armenians lived; on the other were Turks. They were poor and ignorant, but I don't recall even one veiled woman," Marianthi said. "Islamists are now throwing stones at the church and at our windows. But we aren't afraid. We shall never leave. Never. This is our city much more than it's theirs." They made me promise I'd leave the area before dark.

Abandoned Samatya houses, now collapsing

Imperial district turned slum: Blachernae

In Istanbul it is hard to escape a recurring sense of loss: no civilisation fought harder than the Byzantine to preserve the past for future generations, yet so much... in its own art and architecture has vanished.

John Ash

Narrow, muddy streets, shabby buildings, smoky coffee shops filled with unshaven males, women in black chadors and men in felt caps and baggy trousers set the background of Ayvansaray. Absolutely nothing reminds you that this corner was once an imperial district, the object of the world's envy, an excess of wealth and magnificence.

The neighbourhood, situated in the north-west corner of the walled peninsula and stretching from the shore of Golden Horn to the seventh hill, was the Byzantine region of Blachernae, an area of gardens, royal pavilions and monasteries. The Comneni decided to move their permanent residence here in the

The crescent replaced the cross atop the elegant Virgin Pammakaristos after its conversion to a mosque

eleventh century, abandoning the Great Palace, whose upkeep was judged too costly. Among the shabby constructions of today abound ruins of a resplendent past.

Right before the ugly third bridge on the channel, the walls of the Golden Horn meet the land walls. From below the bridge one may enjoy an impressive view of the land walls descending. The strongest segment of the fortifications in sight are thought to have been the ramparts of the Blachernae Palace. Unfortunately, they have been "restored" to resemble a Legoland castle. The monumental spectacle is marred by the incessant moaning of traffic from the bridge and the peripheral road running all along the walls to the Marmara.

Ascending the Blachernae hill and making way through shanties, one reaches a fenced off enclosure. Its walls and towers – modest and undistinguished – and a series of dungeons and substructures are identified as the last standing vestiges of the palace. They actually belong to a reinforcement of the walls, protecting its environs; the view from the other side, by the peripheral road running along the walls, clearly shows this segment is higher and stronger than others.

A royal pavilion existed in what was hilly countryside with panoramic views over the channel, far from the city, already from the sixth

Christ Enthroned, mosaic in the apse of the funerary chapel of the Pammakaristos

century. During the early and mid-Byzantine years, Emperors resided in the Great Palace, the vast compound between the Marmara and the Hippodrome. By the eleventh century that complex was in disrepair and its upkeep was extremely costly. The Comneni decided to settle permanently in Blachernae, greatly extending and embellishing the imperial palace on the hill.

The surrounding shabbiness makes it impos-

St Gregory the Illuminator, the Evangelist of Armenia, mosaic in the parecclesion of the Pammakaristos

sible to understand why the dynasty abandoned the glorious views of the Marmara for this area. But at the time of the Comneni, orchards and scenic country separated Blachernae from the city. The absence of any buildings nearby secured the palace residents a bird's-eye view of the Golden Horn, the city, Pera and the Marmara. Blachernae was away from the crowded markets, the Latin colonies and the

St Euthemius, mosaic in the parecclesion of the Pammakaristos

Hippodrome and its turbulence.

Byzantine Emperors never forgot the Nika revolt of 532, when both Haghia Sophia and part of the Great Palace burnt in the conflagrations. The Blachernae was a kind of Versailles of its time, an imperial refuge sheltered against the prospect of a revolt by its remoteness and by heavy guarding. Detached from the city and its populace, royalty led a life of opulence.

The most famous descriptions came from foreign visitors under the Comneni. Although brief, they convey stupor at the sumptuous interior and courtly ceremonies. The earliest is that of Odo de Deuil, a Catholic monk who arrived in 1147 in Constantinople as ambassador to King Louis VII of France. While Odo was amazed at Constantinople's riches and splendour, stating that it is "the glory of the Greeks", he was at the same time shocked at its sheer size, the squalor of some of its quarters and the high crime rate. "Exactly as it surpasses other cities in riches, it surpasses them in evil as well."

Blachernae was the sight that most impressed Odo; he devotes more lines to describe it than he does to any other. "What they call the Palace of Blachernae, although not high, is impressive because of its elegance and extraordinary construction. On three sides, it offers its residents the triple pleasure of gazing alternately on the sea, the country, and the city. Its exterior is of almost incomparable beauty and its interior surpasses anything I could say. It is decorated throughout with gold and various colours and the floor is paved with cleverly arranged marble. So much that I couldn't tell whether it is the subtlety of the art or the preciousness of the materials that gives it the greater beauty or value."

Benjamin of Tudela devotes much praise to the riches of Constantinople and the imperial palace of Manuel Comnenus (1143-1180) in particular: "This King Emanuel built a great palace upon the seacoast, in addition to those his forefathers built, and named it Blachernae. He plated its columns with gold and silver, and engraved thereon scenes from past battles and of his own combats. He also set up a throne of gold and precious stones; a golden crown was suspended over it by a gold chain, so that he might sit under it. It was inlaid with jewels of priceless value, and at night time no lights were required, for every one could see by the light the stones gave out."

Both writers mention Blachernae being by the sea, which isn't correct. The palace was close to, but not by, the water (unlike Bucoleon). The "gold and various colours" that Odo mentions were probably mosaics, whereas the marble floor is clearly an opus sectile. The "engravings" on gold and silver mentioned by Benjamin are more enigmatic. A few years after their description, in 1204, Blachernae, like the rest of the city, was pillaged by the Crusaders and the riches it contained were gone forever. As is the case with most edifices of the unfortunate Byzantine capital, no trace survives from the palatial complex. Only the strengthening of the city walls marks the point where it stood.

In the bleak days after 1261, when the Greeks liberated a ruthlessly plundered Constantinople, life centred on its north-west corner around the palace. In the engravings of visitors to the late Byzantine city, such as that of Christoforo Buondelmonti, houses appear only in this vicinity. The rest of the walled city appears as an endless plain intercepted by the huge forms of churches and pillars.

Further uphill stands one of the city's most interesting and least visited monuments, known in Turkish as Tekfur Sarayı (Palace of the Prince). It is identified with the palace commissioned by Constantine Porphyrogennetus. Built in the late thirteenth century, the building is shown in the lithographs and miniatures drawn by travellers to fourteenth- and fifteenth-century Constantinople. Although many believe this palace belonged to the Blachernae complex, the great distance between the Porphyrogennetus Palace and what is identified as the latter's ruins do not make this very credible.

The palace is of primary importance to art history, as one of the very few pieces of Byzantine civil architecture standing. Its walls survive intact; only the ceiling and floors have disappeared. The façades are decorated with the typical geometrical lace of white stone and red brick, which becomes quite intricate over the rows of arched windows. On an outer wall, frames of white marble betray the location of a series of rectangular windows, later built in. The Palace, until recently closed off, is now being restored.

During my first visit I found a hole in the surrounding wall and was able to jump into the small court. The main façade is the best preserved of any Byzantine palace. I entered the ground floor, noting scattered bases of columns, possibly identical to the ones surviving on the façade. I managed to climb on the side-wall reaching the third floor. The view, both of the ruins around me and over the city below, is one of the best in town. The sovereign who commissioned the palace made a good choice of setting: before me lay the source of the Golden Horn on one hand, the channel and the hills of the city on the other. Adjacent to the walls, the palace was like a fort, from where the sovereign could contemplate his realm.

The building fell to several inappropriate uses during Ottoman times. At one point it housed exotic species such as giraffes and elephants. Later it was secretly used as a brothel. Finally, in the early eighteenth century, the Grand Vizier Ibrahim Pasha inaugurated a workshop for the production of decorative tiles in the vicinity. His effort was intended to liven up the industry, previously centred on the city of Iznik (Nicaea). As a result, a new type of decorative tile appeared, named the Tekfur Sarayı tile. The workshop's precise location – whether

Elementary school children, opposite the Pammakaristos

it was situated in the palace or in an adjacent building – is unknown.

The building's most interesting feature is the covered balcony on its eastern façade. Characteristic of the civil architecture both of the Byzantine Greeks and the Genoese, the covered balcony later became a symbol of the Ottoman house, sometimes taking the form of a projection of the entire floor. Known as *cumba* in Turkish, covered balconies (or bay windows, as they are often called) are found in the old towns of Asia Minor, Greece and the Balkans. They are yet another inheritance of the Byzantine style.

A short distance downhill, on a small cob-

The legality of veiling pre-teen girls is debated in Turkey

bled square shaded by huge trees and surrounded by konaks, hides Istanbul's most resplendent treasure, the complex of The Saviour in Chora, today called Kariye Museum. Kariye is a Turkish corruption of the Greek word *chora,* meaning "country". The church was part of a monastery dedicated to Christ the Saviour. First established in the fifth century, it was situated amidst the fields that stretched between the western boroughs of Constantinople and the Theodosian walls. Many believe that the monastery was named Chora because of its situation among the fields, "in the country". Others argue that the word bears a mystic meaning and point to its inscription on the church's mosaics.

The monument's exterior, despite its exquisite harmony, leaves no hint of the splendour it conceals. Chora is the highest expression of Byzantine art. The quality and beauty of the mosaics and murals make it one of the masterpieces of the world's cultural heritage. At the same time, it is the Byzantine capital's best-preserved monument and the one that best conveys the effect of mystifying, otherworldly splendour. A visit to the church is a revelation to anyone unfamiliar with Byzantine decorative art, and the only chance to get a good grasp of it in Istanbul.

The main church is dedicated to Christ the Saviour, whilst the burial parecclesion (chapel) is dedicated to Anastasis (the Resurrection). The parecclesion and the outer narthex combine to form an L-shaped corridor surrounding the main church. The dome of the main church is surrounded by two domes of the inner narthex and one of the parecclesion. The four modest-sized domes give the exterior plasticity and elegance.

The core of the extant building dates from 1077-1081. Maria Ducaena, mother-in-law of Alexius I Comnenus, built the current church as an inscribed cross or quincunx, a style in vogue at the time. Early in the twelfth century, the church suffered partial collapse, perhaps due to an earthquake, and was rebuilt by Isaac Comnenus, Alexius's third son. But Chora took its present form two centuries later, in the time of powerful statesman Theodore Metochites, who endowed it with its fine mosaics and frescoes between 1315 and 1321. It is thanks to Metochites that the church can be acclaimed as one of the masterpieces of all time.

Metochites was one of the most important intellectuals in Byzantine history, a man of great learning and abilities. His name is associated with the new movement that sprang up under the Palaeologi, which promoted the study of the classics as well as intellectual pursuits. Metochites himself was an all-rounder. He was versed in history, wrote poems and volumes on philosophy and astronomy. He lived in a period of political decay and external danger: the Empire, which never overcame the sack of Constantinople by the Crusaders, was now attacked on all fronts by the Turks, the Catalans and the Genoese, and split by internal feuds.

Against such a background, a group of intellectuals spurred a renaissance of the arts and letters, known as the Palaeologan Revival. The Chora was the life work of Metochites, who withdrew and died there as a monk, and is buried in the funerary chapel. Chora survives as the most tangible expression of the Byzantine Renaissance.

Metochites represented a whole school flourishing in an era when political and military disasters and internal anarchy had driven Byzantine Greeks to profound soul searching. There was discontent at the decay and corruption that swept the imperial machine, exhausted after a millennium of confrontations on all sides. Many intellectuals found solace in the aesthetic and spiritual glory of the ancient world, and rejected the ascetic tendency of the Orthodox faith, developed by the hermits in the deserts of lower Egypt and Syria. These thinkers were as much concerned with this world and its pleasures and virtues, as they were with the coming one. As the empire shrank and lost its multiethnic, universal character, intellectuals started rediscovering their ethnic Greek identity. They began to redefine themselves as Greeks, alongside being Orthodox Christians spiritually and Romans (citizens of Romanía, the Roman Empire) politically. Interestingly, foreigners had always called the Byzantines "Greek" – it was only the Turks who took up the word "Roman".

The ideas of the school Metochites is said to have founded can be clearly identified in Chora's art. One can immediately discern important differences between the murals and mosaics here and those in the other Byzantine churches in town. Colours in Chora are resplendent and remind one of the Italian masters. A bright black, which seems to radiate the light of darkness, has no equivalent elsewhere in the city. Neither has the extensive use of white in the background of the mosaics and the friezes, or in the clothes. The forms also come as a surprise, going way beyond the stylised Byzantine ascetic line to adopt the naturalism and vivacity of Hellenistic and Renaissance art. Attention is paid to perspective, while Byzantine iconography is famously two-dimensional. The meanders and palmettes liberally used in friezes are directly taken from classical Greek art.

The lively colours and naturalism of forms is enough for many experts to term the art of Chora humanist. Even more astonishing and unexpected are the themes of the mosaics. In one, the baby Virgin is displayed struggling with her first steps, watched attentively and affectionately by Anna and a nanny. In another, Joachim and Anna embrace tenderly, after the latter announces her pregnancy to Mary. One can almost hear the weeping of the mothers in the Massacre of the Innocents, clutched together in collective mourning. Sensitivity and deep skill in the use of image and symbols permeates these mosaics, qualities reaffirmed in the murals of the burial chapel.

On a technical level, what surprises is the use of white, not black or grey, for the folds of cloths. This makes the cloth appear like a cloud of coloured light, a veil of air. The trick was later used by the Cretan painter El Greco, who managed to fuse his Byzantine iconographic background with the dream world of the Renaissance. Clearly the Chora demonstrates what course Byzantine art was proceeding towards, and what could have been produced had history taken a different route.

The decoration of Chora reflects the aesthetic preferences of Metochites and the refined aristocratic circles of the imperial capital from where he descended. Compared to them, the much acclaimed Byzantine mosaics all over the Balkans seem rustic and coarse.

The Chora monastery was an important centre of learning, and Metochites had founded the richest library that had existed in Constan-

The magic of mosaics and coloured marble in the Chora

tinople after the Latin sack of 1204. The church was converted into a mosque in 1510, but fortunately for the world its mosaics and frescoes were not excised but whitewashed over. Its art was uncovered in the late nineteenth century and it became the first Byzantine church in town to become a tourist attraction, visited by,

Mural of the Resurrection, parecclesion of the Chora

among others, Kaiser Wilhelm during his state visit to Constantinople. After loving restoration by the Byzantine Institute of America, it was made into a museum in 1948.

The area from Chora to the Pammakaristos, another Byzantine treasure, now called Fethiye Camii, comprises two of the districts called Little Tehran – Draman and Çarşamba – where Islamist zealots live. Women here are covered under thick black chadors, men sport felt skull-caps, baggy trousers and the peculiar Islamic beards with trimmed moustaches on the upper lip. The inhabitants live a miserable existence in stupefied fervour and ignorance. Polygamy, although illegal, is thriving here, families have far more children than they can support and many girls are shut in their homes, barred from attending school, where they would have to unveil. The area is a no-go zone for the secular élites. It hits the news whenever there are demonstrations in favour of abolishing the secular Republic and reinstituting a Caliphate, where the sharia would be the law of the state, or when the antiquated mores of the inhabitants make good substance for satire in the press.

Amidst all this ignorance and ugliness hides the Pammakaristos, the second most important church of the Palaeologi dynasty to have survived in the city. It is believed to have been built under Andronicus II Palaeologus (1282-1328), most probably on an earlier structure. The church housed the Ecumenical Patriarchate for more than a century (1456 to 1587) until it was converted into a mosque by Murad III (1574-1592). Most unfortunately, nothing of the original decoration survives in the main body of the church. Yet the sublime art of the mosaics of the funerary chapel (parecclesion) attached to the church are an indication of how much was lost – victim of vandalism or (most likely here) earthquakes.

The mosaics of the parecclesion are identical to the ones in Chora in style, technique and classicist references. The dome is supported by four columns of coloured marble and acanthus capitals, and decorated with a mosaic of the Pantocrator surrounded by prophets, all drawn in stunning realism. A magnificent composition of the Enthroned Jesus, flanked by the Virgin and John the Baptist, decorates the apse; the shades of green on the latter's dress are so vivid, that they can only be compared with a work of the Italian Masters. They bring to mind the orgy of colour in the jungle-like vegetation of the Bosphorus hills, which may well have been the artist's inspiration. The upper sections of the walls, the arches and intrados are adorned with mosaics of saints, including a stunning one of St Gregory the Illuminator, who evangelised the Armenians. Some of the figures give the illusion that they are about to move or speak. I always lose sense of time in the parecclesion, amazed by the effect of colour and form.

What a different world outside! Once I entered the premises of the Pammakaristos together with a photographer friend, Cathy Cunliffe, to shoot some pictures for a travel article. We were carefully studying the intricate decorative elements on the façade, when a young boy approached me. "Hello," he said repeatedly, eager to draw attention. I did eventually turn to him and was asked: "Are you one of us, or are you an infidel?" I said that I was not a Muslim, if that is

The eastern façade of the Palace of Constantine Forphyrogennetus (Tekfursarayı), with the covered balcony

what he asked, taken aback by the word infidel (*gâvur* in Turkish). "I just wondered where you were from," he insisted. "Why, exactly?" I asked. "To determine whether you are good or bad." I laughed: "Which means?" "Which means if you are from Iraq, that is good, if from America, it is bad." I told him I was from neither place. He was baffled. I *was* an *infidel*, but still fluent in Turkish and from neither Iraq nor America. The boy stared at us with awe as we were shooting the photographs. We were a curiosity.

I remember another instance in the vicinity. I had entered a tiny convenience store to buy a bottle of water. The store was run by two young Taliban-looking brothers. "Where are you from?" they asked. They proceeded to ask me what religion I was, even though my having said I was Greek should have informed them that I was evidently non Muslim. "Christian," I said. "You must now change to Islam," they said smilingly. "Pardon?" I said. "Now that you came to live in Turkey you must change to Islam," the elder repeated slowly, thinking that despite my Turkish I hadn't understood. "How about this week? We know a good teacher," the other said. "How about next week?" I said and walked out.

"It sounds like another country," my Turkish friends said when I recounted the event.

To be fair, I must acknowledge that no matter how strange their looks and lifestyle may seem to outsiders, especially to my secular Turkish friends, the locals in areas such as these are normally neither violent nor rude, and would very rarely tell off a foreigner, or even a Turk, for challenging their rules. Once I had visited the Pammakaristos with my friend Solita, and after the visit we became really hungry. It was during Ramadan, when Muslims are supposed to fast during daylight hours. We were starving. We passed the traditional coffee houses, where men of all ages chatted and watched television without smoking or sipping their habitual tea. It was funny in a sense – tea and coffee houses without tea and coffee – or even water. We found a bakery where delicious hot pies were being prepared and bought to be eaten after dusk. We devoured two in front of the poor baker, who couldn't even have a sip of water, and we chatted casually in Greek as the locals passed and looked on, without exhibiting any sign of shock.

Immersed in conversation with Solita, I hadn't noticed the girl approach. Her hair was uncovered and she was carrying a huge bowl with something I couldn't see in it. She asked, smiling shyly, "Brother, will you taste some? I was wondering whether the salt was okay. You know, I can't..." I smiled and tasted something delicious – a sort of salad with raw minced meat. "This is great," I said approvingly. The girl thanked me politely and left satisfied, and then another came and another and another. Women, veiled and uncovered, young and old, asked us to taste their food, anxious to hear it was properly done. "Should I add more salt?" "Can you taste the cinnamon?" "Does it need more cooking?" was asked to us a dozen times. By the time we rose to leave, we were stuffed. What nobody asked us was whether we were Muslim, and thus disobeying Islam's rules.

It is something of a habit to place small children at the windows in Istanbul's poorer neighbourhoods

The old “New Town”: the Pera shore

Galata: the "stranger in town"

"Galata is mysticism.
It is poets and the evocation of freedom. It is banks, bankers, the Stock Exchange, the Ottoman experience of capitalism. Galata is bohemians. It's the port, refuge of sailors lost in the world... warehouses, hans, agencies, bon-marchés, commerce. Galata is its bridge, from where poets contemplate the sea.
It is European architecture... Circassian beauties, French adventurers. It is debauchery, menus of carnal desire on offer in damp rooms with the scent of hot moisture. Galata is the tower... it is liberation..."

Leaflet of the Galata Festival, 2002

Panorama of Galata from Eminönü,
on the opposite shore of the Golden Horn

Old Greek apartment buildings at the foot of the Galata Tower, Kuledibi

Upon its construction in the nineteenth century, the Galata Bridge joined not shores, but worlds. On the south, the Old City had, since the Conquest, been the epitome of the Orient, the setting for the fantasies of mystified Europeans. "A theocratic city of the past, full of mosques and palaces and barracks," wrote Bertrand Bareilles, a French teacher living in Constantinople, in 1918. On the north, the Italianate enclave of Galata and Pera, domain of foreigners, churches, lively nights, libertarianism, riotous carnivals and European ways, represented the West. This shore, sheltering all that was heathen and scandalous, enchanted Muslims, some of whom came here secretly to drink and indulge in forbidden pleasures.

From Byzantine times Galata was "the stranger in town", a city within the city. Under the Ottomans, it became the European enclave of an oriental metropolis. Drawing foreign merchants and adventurers from all over Christendom, Galata was only nominally ruled by Constantinople – Byzantine or Ottoman.

Constantine founded a fortified port, Συκαί (Sykies, meaning "Fig Trees"), on the shore opposite Constantinople called Πέρα (Pera, meaning "far away"). When and why the name Γαλατάς (Galata) appeared is debatable. Some mention a Celt notable called Galatis, something hardly surprising for a world city like the Byzantine capital, where every race was represented. Others attribute the new name to milk (its plural is Γάλατα in Greek), holding that the milkmen supplying Constantinople dwelt here.

Galata's importance was initially defensive. Tiberius erected a castle on the shore, from which a thick chain stretched to the fortifications of the acropolis in Constantinople, rendering the Golden Horn impenetrable by attacking fleets. For centuries, nobody had succeeded in breaking through. Even Mehmet the Conqueror wouldn't attempt to, but ordered his soldiers to carry galleys overland from the Pera hills into the channel.

The rise of Italian trade brought Venice, Pisa, Genoa and Amalfi into constant war with the Byzantines and one another for domination. Manuel Comnenus was the first emperor to grant significant trade concessions to those merchant republics whose expatriates settled within Constantinople's walls. Referred to as "Latins" by the Greeks, they constituted at times a fifth of the population.

Greek-Latin relations were suspicious at best. After the 1054 schism between Orthodoxy and Rome, religious fanaticism was added to commercial rivalry. The Fourth Crusade gave Catholics a pretext to take advantage of a dynastic feud, seize Constantinople in 1204 and plunder it ruthlessly for weeks. The sack and 60-year rule that followed left an indelible trauma in Greek collective memory.

After Greeks liberated Constantinople in 1261 they banned Catholics from the walled city. To check the power of Venice, Emperor Michael Palaeologos granted Galata to its fiercest rival, Genoa. The Genoese organised the town on the model of Italian city-states. It was ruled by a committee of 24 seniors (the Podestà) which was only nominally a vessel of the emperor and reported to a notable sent every year from Genoa. The colony was called Magnifica Communità di Pera, and its communal authorities survived well into Ottoman times.

Until the settlement of the Pera hills, the Latins used the name Pera for their enclave, "Galatas" being in use by Greeks only. The port assumed the appearance of a medieval Italian town, a warren of narrow, winding streets lined with fortress-like buildings. It was frowned upon by Greeks as "the nest of libertines and the corrupted Latin clergy".

During the 1453 siege, the Podestà fled and the Genoese surrendered without fighting, thereby securing several privileges: Catholic churches were left unmolested and Galata's traders were exempt from many taxes. The sultan appointed a governor and Greeks flooded in, preferring life within a quasi-autonomous Christian enclave. They quickly became the majority.

Galata remained the base for Western commercial infiltration. Merchants flooded in from Europe, creating the community of "Levantines" – a mixture of European expatriates united under the Catholic faith, a community prominent in city life well into the twentieth century. Ambassadorial missions followed. In 1535, France became the first nation to open a proper embassy and gained extensive commercial privileges, the *capitulations*. Europe's other

asya
MAKİNE TİCARET ve SANAYİ A.Ş.
TEL:235 24 10-235 53 98
FAX:255 41 98
asya
MAKİNE TİCARET ve SANAYİ A.Ş.
OĞUZ MAKİNA
BUK

Buildings opposite Doğan Apartments. Abandon and decay reign

nations followed, aiming at similar privileges. Commerce in the Levant was in the hands of the Levantines and local Greeks, Armenians and Jews, many of whom acquired the citizenship of European states and worked as the local representatives of their companies.

Embassies and the affluent later moved out of congested Galata to the hills above, founding the exclusive borough of Pera. The coastal zone of Galata turned into a strictly port and financial area, a City of London of its time. The rich settled in Pera, whilst Galata's coastal zone was peopled by those of more modest means. Edmondo d'Amicis wrote: "Almost all roads are narrow and winding, each with its wine stores, patisseries, barbers, butchers, Greek and Armenian coffee houses, retailers, workshops and shacks. Everything is murky, damp, muddy and slimy, like the lower class neighbourhoods of London. Almost all of Constantinople's trade comes through here. The Stock Exchange, customs houses, branches of companies, warehouses are all here… Were it not for the turbans and fezzes one wouldn't think one was in the East."

Galata became the dying empire's window to modernisation. Its municipal council pulled down the medieval walls, built new streets, introduced horse-drawn tramways, gas lighting and an underground funicular. A number of famous European architects and artists transplanted the European styles of the time. Until the proclamation of the Republic, ending the Capitulations and barring foreigners from many professions, Galata remained what it had been since the Comneni: a bastion of cosmopolitanism, a European enclave in the Levant.

• • •

Bridging the Golden Horn and uniting the two parts of Constantinople's European shore had been many a city planner's dream since Byzantine times, when a wooden bridge existed midway down the channel. In Ottoman times, the necessity was stronger, as neighbourhoods spread on the channel's northern shore. Even

Perşembe Pazarı and its "Genoese Buildings", like a snapshot from medieval Galata

Leonardo da Vinci had come up with a bridge plan to join Galata and Constantinople. A first attempt produced a wooden bridge in 1845. But the first proper Galata bridge was a floating construction of the 1860s. Until then, boats did the Galata-Eminönü transit.

That first bridge rose to allow large ships to pass; more than 100,000 people crossed it every day. A new bridge was inaugurated in 1912, amazing people with its innovations. "It had a double tramway rail; we marvelled that it opened and closed and the rails would match, so that the tramway resumed operations immediately. It had wide sidewalks and tram pillars had two electric lamps each: the bridge was festively lit for the inauguration! All this at a time when Constantinople had no electricity and tramways were driven by horses and mules..." wrote Spatharis.

In service until 1992, this second bridge became part of city life and was loved and its praises sung by many locals. With the restaurants, cafés and panoramas over the Golden Horn and Asia, the bridge was not a mere crossing point, but a belvedere and part of the city folklore. From there departed the ferries to the Princes' Islands. The bridge burnt in 1992 and was sadly replaced by a concrete monster.

The new bridge, like its predecessor, is a colony of fishermen. Fishing rods project over both sides day and night, targeting the brave fish that venture into the dirty channel. The Fish Market, by the north-west end of the bridge, dates from medieval times. "There are sold the prettiest and best fish of the world," wrote Pitton de Tournefort.

Galata Bridge leads to Karaköy Square, the late Ottoman city's centre of banking, insurance and finance. The area is named after the Karaites, a Jewish sect that once dwelt here. Until the late 1950s Karaköy was a wide, crowded cobbled street, lined with shops and impressive buildings. Most, including Istanbul's only Art Nouveau mosque, were demolished to widen the square, now more like a junction of avenues. The Stock Exchange, in a Karaköy backstreet, was also demolished.

The square marks entry into the centre of Constantinopolitan capitalism, legendary Rue Voevoda, better known as Banks' Street. It was once the quarters of the voevoda (Ottoman governor), later the headquarters of most foreign and local banks and of the famous tobacco monopoly, the Régie. Local banks now occupy the impressive mansions. The grandest is that of the Ottoman Bank, an austere neoclassical edifice of the French expatriate Alexandre Vallaury. The bank was a joint Anglo-French venture, whose director was English or French, by rotation. The ultimate symbol of foreign capitalist penetration, the Ottoman Bank was Ottoman only in name.

The building is associated with tragedy: it was stormed, in August 1896, by Armenian revolutionaries of the Dashnak Party, a desperate attempt to draw world attention to massacres of Anatolia's Armenians, Abdul Hamid's response to their calls for administrative reform. The revolutionaries won worldwide sympathy, threatening to blow the building up if Europeans did not intervene. As negotiations were underway, organised groups of religious students massacred about 20,000 Armenians all over Constantinople.

The area around Banks' Street is one of my favourites: it houses most of the remains of Genoese Galata. At the corner of Kart Çınar and Galata Kulesi streets stand the remains of the Palazzo de la Commune, seat of the 24-member Podestà. That council of notables was reassembled after the Conquest and presided over Galata's churches and guilds until 1682.

The Palazzo, erected around 1315, was an attractive brick and stone edifice with elegant mullioned windows, in the typical austerity of the Genoese style. One can only admire it in old engravings. Its present state is disheartening: the façade on Banks' Street was incorporated into a nineteenth-century apartment block, while the stonework on the remaining ones is concealed under plastering. The mullioned windows were replaced by large modern ones and the doors by ugly glass entrances.

The most spectacular street in Galata, and one of Istanbul's most interesting, is Perşembe Pazarı leading from Banks' Street to the port. Named after a market held here every Thursday, it has some of the oldest buildings in town. Of stone and brick, they were built in a local style – grilled windows are crowned with blind arches and projections of the upper floors rest on rows of stone corbels.

These elegant structures are commonly termed 'Genoese houses'. However, their age and creators are uncertain. It is widely held that they were built – possibly by Levantines – in the aftermath of the Fall. Their style is eclectic and incorporates elements from Genoese, Byzantine and Ottoman civil architecture – a style particular to a city where all major ethnic groups made their contribution. The castle-like design of these "buildings of the Franks", lacking windows on the ground floor and with grills on the few others, betrays that they were erected "to suit an age of insecurity", as Bertrand Bareilles wrote.

Perşembe Pazarı is our only image of a European medieval port in the Orient, dedicated to commerce. The street may be architecturally enlightening, but it is also enchanting to walk

along, particularly at night. The forms, the shades, the dim light and the desolation bring to mind childhood fairytales of knights, princesses and heroism. In daylight it's hard to overlook the crowds and the profusion of ugly neon signs: the buildings host workshops and the street until recently had as many signs as an American highway.

Nearby stands the solemn figure of the old Genoese Cathedral of San Paolo e San Domenico, the early-fourteenth-century basilica of a Dominican monastery. It was converted into a mosque shortly after the conquest of Granada – a retribution for the end of Muslim rule in Andalusia – and the expulsion of Muslims from Spain. Its conversion sent a clear political message: the Ottoman state was prepared to champion the Muslim cause all over the Mediterranean.

The confiscated cathedral was handed to Iberian Arabs who settled around it – hence its name of Arap Camii (Arab mosque). The tower-like campanile became a minaret. Apart from the replacement of the cross with a crescent, the exterior hasn't changed much. Its architecture is starkly plain and completely devoid of the symmetry of Europe's Romanesque or Early Gothic churches. The building resembles a huge warehouse, an enormous stone box with a tower. Only its size impresses, intended to send a clear message of Genoese power to the Byzantine authorities opposite. The cathedral was, after all, the creation of a people fairly set on the pursuit of profit, a people practical and devoid of artistic aspirations. The Magnifica Communità never excelled in the arts or letters.

If the exterior remains as it was before conversion, the same isn't true for the interior. "The stained glass and gothic inscriptions on the doors are still there," noted Tournefort. No longer: the stonework has been whitewashed, Ottoman stained glass has replaced the original and a Muslim altar is lit by green neon.

• • •

Kemeraltı is Galata's busiest street, leading from Karaköy Square to the Bosphorus. On its southern side stretch Galata's once Greek and Armenian quarters, poor and squalid compared with those of Pera. Despite the presence of churches, synagogues and reputable schools, Kemeraltı was notorious for its brothels (church and brothel often coexisted on the same block). Those "houses", as well as the *cafés chantants*, had built Galata's fame among sailors from Odessa to Buenos Aires. The demolitions undertaken by the municipality in the late 1950s to broaden Kemeraltı made it lose – together with most of its brothels – its picturesque air.

The woman on the poster holds an Efes beer, the same kind being drunk by this old sailor. By the Galata embankment

My first ever visit to the area in 2001 was quite eventful. Entering Kemeraltı, I noticed a stone mass on the left. I took it to be a chunk of the Galata fortifications until I saw a small belfry with an iron cross. I then discovered a door on a narrow side street. I rang the bell and waited. Nothing. I rang again and again and was about to leave when I heard footsteps approaching. The head of an elderly woman appeared through the gate's grilled window. "Are you Armenian Catholic?" she inquired. "Absolutely. From Lebanon," I said, knowing that the community's headquarters were now based in that country. It worked. She told me the church was named Surp Hisus Pirgich – Jesus Christ the Saviour. She rushed off to fetch the keys.

The plain exterior conceals Istanbul's most splendid Armenian Catholic shrine, a large basilica with several chapels in the side aisles. The altar is surrounded by six Corinthian columns supporting a crown, which symbolises the firmament, and is decorated with an imposing oil painting of the Resurrection, in the style of the Italian Masters. An inner dome rises above it. On the wall behind, a fresco depicts a pagan theme one would hardly expect in a church: a half-naked woman in classical dress, possibly Aphrodite, resting on a pedestal. The organ, the stained glass, the oil paintings in the side altars – everything gives the impression that a corner of Italy was planted here.

The architecture and aesthetics are the product of a community firmly attached to the West. The Armenian Catholic church was essentially the child of the eighteenth-century Armenian monk Mekhitar from Sevasteia (Sivas). Mekhitar aimed at raising the cultural and spiritual level of his compatriots and believed that union with Rome would be the most effective way to do it. He founded the Mekhitarist order in 1700 in Constantinople, but the violent protests of the Armenians faithful to the Apostolic (Orthodox) Church led him to move his order to the island of San Lazaro in Venice. The Armenian Catholic community, famous for having given up its native language for French in everyday life, never became a major force among Ottoman Armenians, despite ardent proselytising. Its members were spared in the genocidal onslaught of 1915, and today the bulk of the community lives in Lebanon or else in the diaspora.

In Surp Hisus Pirgich, I recalled a passage from Maria Iordanidou's novel *Loxandra*. The writer describes how her mother attempted to have her interned in a Catholic school. "Dressed in her white and turquoise drapes, the Virgin stood at the back end of the court, her chest pierced, her bleeding heart showing!

Belle Époque apartment buildings by the Galata Tower

An organ was heard. Anna had never heard an organ before... The nuns led her to an inner court full of girls all dressed in black. The girls walked in a circle; in the centre, an elderly nun held a rosary and murmured... Anna discovered that most of the girls were not Armenian, but *Arméniennes Catholiques*, spoke only French and were called Marie-Thérèse or Marie-Louise... As they knit, a nun was murmuring, Je vous salue, Marie...."

Searching for the Greek parishes, I came across the shell of a synagogue on Alageyik Street. Built in 1895 and burnt in the 1950s, Or Hadash belonged to Constantinople's small Ashkenazi community. It's a sad sight now. Lógs stick out of its broken windows and trees grow in the hall. Above the sealed door are a relief of the Ten Commandments and a fading Hebrew inscription. Ivy has covered the main façade, and the small court in front of it is filled with piles of rubbish.

Some steps away a policeman guarded what I took to be a police station. There was a metal detector at the entrance to a small court, on one side of which stood a guardroom. I had a sudden inspiration: why not ask the police for directions to the churches? Some rather prohibitive-looking men were passing through the detector, the guard checking their IDs. I passed too and headed to the guardroom.

"A Greek church? You're looking for a church?" the officer said, disbelieving, bewildered, but polite. "I'll see what I can do." He dialled a number and had a short conversation. "In Karaköy there are Greek churches, Armenian churches, synagogues, even an English church," he said sounding confused.

A woman in her fifties appeared wearing red underwear with black lace under a red satin robe. Her hair was dyed blonde, her face painted like a carnival mask. "Honey, I'm off to buy cigarettes," she told the guard, then looked at me. "Hi sweetie, can I do something for you?" "The gentleman was only looking for a Greek church," the policeman said. "Are you Greek?" she said. "How nice! I don't even remember when I had my last Greek client. I remember a bit of Greek. Been in the market for quite some time... If you want, I'll walk you to the churches myself." How could I refuse? "I must wear something decent," she said. "I'm Christian too – Armenian."

She vanished then reappeared in a modest black dress and a black hat, looking perfectly normal with her hair concealed. She had even removed her makeup. "Did you really not know this is a 'house'?" she said. "How could I?" I replied. "As soon as I saw the guard, I took it for a police station." She laughed. "You know, this is the largest 'house' in Istanbul. It used to be run by the famous Madame Manukian, the nation's largest taxpayer for years. Such a lucrative business," she said nostalgically. "Why is there a policeman, a detector and a guard post?" I asked her. "For our safety. You see, Turks drink before coming, then fights break out. Also, there are those Islamic freaks who threaten to kill us. No sex before marriage for most of them here. Muslims preach so much on girls' purity, but even married men come. Do you know that prostitution is organised by the state all over the country? We are sacrificed so that others arrive 'pure' on the wedding bed..."

"Are there many Turkish girls working as prostitutes?" I asked. "Sure," she said, "especially country girls. They believe they're sheltered in Istanbul's anonymity. Once, a client recognised his sister among the girls. You should've seen the scene. Every day we have 'honour crimes' for much less than that. As for the foreigners..." The mere mention of the word upset her and she lit a cigarette. "Those bloody Natashas have ruined the market. Go to Lâleli, to Aksaray or anywhere in the Old Town. The market is tall and blond. What can we do? It's globalisation." She laughed. "And those transvestites. There's no woman prostitute left in Pera. If you don't have a willy you're out of business! Well, here we are!"

Before us stood a red ochre building with tiny comes. "This is St John," she told me. "It now belongs to the 'Turkish Orthodox Patriarchate.'" A bit further down was another red church with a beautiful campanile. "This is the Panaghia – their headquarters," she said. "Take care and don't say you're Greek. I must go now. I'm scared of these people. I suppose you know they've joined the fascist party." She crossed herself very discreetly, said, "Hope to see you again," and walked away.

•••

Panaghia Caffatiane, once Galata's prime church, was occupied by the infamous Papa Eftim – an apostate Greek priest and collaborator of Atatürk – in 1924. It is now the 'Patriarchal Church' of a patriarchate-family business, whose 20-odd members – Eftim's descendants – are all enlisted in the "Nationalist Action Party".

The "Turkish Orthodox Patriarchate" has occupied Galata's churches, called for the expulsion of the Ecumenical Patriarchate and tried to convince the public internationally that there are no Greeks but only "Turkish Christians" in Turkey. On the gate outside the Panaghia an inscription reads: "Independent Turkish Orthodox Patriarchate. Archbishopric of Istanbul". I felt as though I was entering the wolf's lair.

There was a row of funeral wreaths against the wall of the courtyard. A row of tombstones was incorporated in it, belonging to Constantinopolitan Greeks and dating from the last half of the nineteenth century. The church was closed, but there was someone in the parish office. I approached him. "It opens on Sundays," he said. I claimed I was a student of Turkish history from the States and was just curious about the community. He picked up the phone and had a brief conversation.

"Since you've come from far our leader is coming to show you around," he said. I feared he would ask for an ID, but he didn't. "What are all these wreaths for?" I asked. "Our Patriarch has passed away," he replied. I noticed the stone campanile, one of the prettiest in town.

Twenty minutes later a young man in a suit appeared. "So you've come from the States," he said in pretty decent English. I tried on a bit of an American accent. He stood on the side as I toured the basilica, dating from 1840. On its site stood a Byzantine chapel, and a church was founded shortly after the Turkish conquest.

Mehmet the Conqueror had a number of Christians forcibly moved to Constantinople from the Crimean town of Caffa (Theodosia), as part of his repopulation plan. The latter brought over the silver icon of the Virgin, now in the Panaghia's narthex. Built in the 1470s, Panaghia Caffatiane became Galata's largest Greek church, mentioned by all travellers. It was destroyed by fires and rebuilt several times, the last in 1840. Occupied by Papa Eftim in 1924, it escaped the 1955 vandalisms. It boasts an impressive iconostasis, which imitates an ancient temple, with an exquisite fresco of the Last Supper on the pediment. An Epitaph was abandoned in the middle of the nave. In the aisles, beautifully embroidered procession drapes rested against the wall. The place was palpably neglected and the plastering was peeling off the ceiling. The "Turkish Orthodox Patriarchate" lacks the means or the will to restore. In the absence of a parish, its main source of income is rents from leasing the seized properties, which include two other Greek churches in Galata. They will, no doubt, remain a no-go area for Greeks so long as they are in the hands of the Eftim clan. I thanked the man in the suit, who – I would later learn – was Eftim's grandson.

The area around the churches and along the shore still houses most of Istanbul's shipping offices. The docks are in the immediate vicinity, and Galata continues as the heart of Istanbul's commercial shipping. Here, in a huge brick warehouse, Istanbul's modern art museum was inaugurated in 2004.

Returning to Karaköy, I mounted the Yüksek Kaldırım towards the Tower. Starting from the

square, this is one of the city's most famous and steepest ascents – hence the Turkish name meaning "standing cobbles". Until the 1950s, Yüksek Kaldırım was the most famous set of steps in the Levant, known in Greek as *Ta Skalakia* (The Stairs). One hundred and eighteen cobbled steps connected Karaköy with Constantinople's grandest boulevard, Grande Rue de Péra.

In the 1950s the stairs were replaced with asphalt to make things easier for cars. Because the asphalt becomes slippery in wet weather the municipality recently resolved to pave the ascent with granite plaques. Old buildings line both sides. Most were Greek shops, ateliers and warehouses. They are now occupied by small businesses selling electric appliances on the lower part of the street, musical instruments further up.

Constantinopolitan Greek writers describe *Skalakia* with marked nostalgia. George Theotokas wrote in *Leonis*: "It was a fairytale place, maybe the most crowded of Constantinople's Christian quarters, at the same time the seat of the most splendid flea market the human mind could imagine – the meeting point of the commercial daemons of Turkey, Greece, Russia, Latin Europe, Israel, the Balkans and the Caucasus.

There was an intermittent flood of broken toys and musical instruments of all kinds, drawings and postcards of all corners of the earth, paper angels, Christmas toys, traditional dresses, carnival costumes and masks, old books with precious covers, big portraits of Napoleon or Victoria or the Sultans, stamp collections, photographs of nude women, pies and nougats in an unbelievable variety of kinds and tastes and shapes...

From both sides of the street, vendors advertised their stock, each in his own language, mixing all languages up in the end."

All this was well over by the end of the Allied occupation of Constantinople (1918-1923). Today, the occasional African immigrant can be spotted selling illegal CDs, but long gone are the days of the touting crowds.

I reached the roundabout by the Tower, where the now disappeared stairs gave way to the famous Grande Rue de Péra. Instead of heading to the Tower, I turned left, taking in Serdar-ı Ekrem Street, lined with impressive eclectic buildings and the ubiquitous covered balconies. It used to house some of the most important Levantine families of the late Ottoman city. Despite being so close to the lower zones with their countless brothels, this was the domain of affluent merchants of all nationalities and of Constantinople's rich Greek captains.

Impressive mansions cover all styles, from ornate eclecticism to highly stylised Art Nouveau. Ever since I first came here this border zone between Galata and Pera has been one of my favourite strolls, an arena to practise one of my favourite hobbies: "talking with the buildings". Those silhouettes, some crumbling and others painstakingly restored, have so much to tell of a refined multinational society of legendary wealth and elevated tastes.

Today, deprived of its non-Muslim communities, the area nevertheless remains highly diverse. Restored buildings, such as the massive Italianate Doğan apartments, are inhabited by bohemian expatriates and affluent Turks, many of whom are involved in the arts and literary scenes. Rents are skyrocketing; living in an apartment with a view over the Marmara, the Golden Horn and the Old City means spending a small fortune.

Yet gentrification is far from complete; the grand eclectic mansions have the most unlikely neighbours. Right opposite Doğan appartments, built as Appartements Helbig for the rich Belgian family of that name, stand grand buildings with broken windows and collapsing balconies. By the Crimean Memorial Church, built to commemorate the British dead of that war, stands the fabulous Art Nouveau Appartements Papacopoulos, a 1907 five-storey residence, whose ceilings are painted with scenes from Greek mythology. Once, I visited one of its flats while a team of restorers was repairing the ceiling frescoes and replacing the panes in the immense oval window looking onto Haghia Sophia. The glamorous aspect of the refurbished flat contrasted sharply with the aspect of the six children of a destitute family living in the same building.

The cylindrical Galata Tower, dominating the borough, is a Genoese construction of 1349. It remains one of Istanbul's tallest silhouettes visible from miles away. The most prominent landmark on the northern shore of the Golden Horn, it rivals the Old City's huge mosques and was adopted as the symbol of the Beyoğlu (Pera and Galata) municipality.

Built as the tallest point of the Genoese fortifications, named "Tower of Christ" and topped by a huge cross, it lost its defensive importance after the Ottoman conquest. At the height of Ottoman power nobody could threaten the capital, and the Tower, just like Yedi Kule, was converted into a gaol for prisoners of war. For a short period it housed an observatory. According to an urban legend, Hezar Fen Ahmet Çelebi, the seventeenth-century mechanic, flew from the Tower to the opposite shore of Üsküdar, in what is claimed to have been the first flight in history.

The administration later took advantage of the Tower's panorama and used it as a fire

Typical apartment building, Kuledibi

Abandonment and desolation, Lower Galata

watchtower – like the purpose-built Serasker Tower in Beyazit. The guard would raise a red balloon whenever a fire was detected, setting the population and the authorities on alert with the cry "yangın var!" ("there's a fire!") The cry epitomised terror for the inhabitants of a city whose entire neighbourhoods were often consumed in the flames. The Tower served this purpose until its 1964 restoration, thereafter becoming Istanbul's most celebrated belvedere.

I had left the Tower last on that prolonged first Galata stroll, waiting to admire the sunset from atop. Before entering, I noticed the incorporated marble plaque, commemorating the day and time of conquest, which mentions that the Genoese Governor handed over Galata's keys without fighting. I headed straight to the observation deck. Despite my fear of heights, I remained there for more than an hour.

Never had I seen such beauty of colour and form unfold before me, nor have I since. The Golden Horn was visible in all its length. So was the Marmara and its islands, behind the peninsula of the Old City, and the lower part of the Bosphorus until the first bridge. Even the dirty waters of the channel reflected a seducing azure from the distance.

The city unfolded beneath me: rows of buildings amphitheatrically set on hills surrounded by a garland of waters. The Old City's dense tissue of red roofs was pierced here and there by domes, minarets, vegetation and the familiar

Typical late-nineteenth-century houses near the Crimean Memorial Church

forms of its monuments. From the Asian hills in the background, minarets and roofs radiated a golden light. A multitude of ferries doing the Europe-Asia commute left paths of steam and wrinkles on an otherwise still surface.

The sky slowly turned fiery, the clouds a fantasy of violet, orange, gold and pink, waters purple-grey, the silhouettes of hills and buildings blackened. The cries of the seagulls flying all around the Tower added much to the dreamlike quality of the view. I was frozen by the beauty of it and agreed to leave only when the guard asked, "Well, are we spending the night together?"

Where buildings are the narrators: Pera, the Paris on the Bosphorus

"Pera sidewalks are the daily stroll of a Europeanising crowd, international and bewildering, reminiscent at times of Paris, at times of Italy, Alexandria or Athens... When it comes to brasseries, beer-houses and wine bars, Pera has much more to offer than Athens. At times, you have the impression you are in Munich or in Belgium...."

G.S. Frangoudis, *Constantinople*, 1899

My first sight of Pera moved me deeply enough to change the course of my life. It was a glimpse of the famous Grande Rue, the now pedestrianised Istiklâl Caddesi, on a Friday night – my first ever night in Istanbul. I found myself here a few hours after the cruise ship on which I was working, saving money for a gap year, had anchored in Galata. Within minutes I resolved that this was

Bay windows and fire-escape ladders, a typical Pera townscape the place to be. Money saving and gap year plans dissolved before the façades of the Grande Rue, and for the next year and a half my prime concern would be preparing my move to Istanbul.

That evening is a sequence of images indelibly stored in my brain. I had walked from Galata to the Pera quarter of Tepebaşı, then arrived at the roundabout of Galatasaray, a few hundred metres from my present home. Was it some kind of festival? Streams of people strolled casually around. Young boys and girls dressed in fashions you would expect in Barcelona or Tel Aviv; elegant elderly couples walking hand in hand beside riotously made up transvestites and women with headscarves. Bookstores were still open at half past ten. Melancholy classical music poured into the street, complementing an atmosphere that did not fit into any of the categorisations in my mind. This wasn't Europe, it wasn't Latin America and it certainly wasn't the Middle East.

The architecture cast the spell, a spell still with me. The Grande Rue remains grand, a procession of ornate façades representing all the styles popular during the Belle Époque. On the hills above the point where the Bosphorus meets the Marmara and the Golden Horn spreads an enclave of neoclassicism, eclecticism and Art Nouveau, which – despite the flight of its original inhabitants – retains a character markedly different to the rest of the city. Most Pera buildings are decaying, but, strangely, their abandonment makes the place even more bizarre, even more enchanting.

Pera is the antithesis of tourist-poster Istanbul. It isn't minarets but belfries and church cupolas that rise over densely built quarters of apartment buildings with impressive entrées, niches with statues and delicate ironwork on their doors and balconies. In Pera, what is familiar to the westerner takes precedence over what is "exotic". Looking at the veiled women and moustachioed peasants who seem (and are) out of place here, one can only remember the nineteenth-century travellers, who commented that "were it not for the fezzes, one would forget Pera is in the Orient".

The architecture shouts it out: Pera was Ottoman Constantinople's Christian enclave. A minority quarter until the 1970s, it is remembered as the city's most developed area, the only one that provided facilities for an urban lifestyle – municipal gardens, theatres, luxury hotels, department stores, cinemas, commercial arcades, cafés, patisseries and restaurants of all kinds.

Pera is a recent settlement. The name, however, is old. The Byzantines called the entire northern shore of the Golden Horn "Pera" (meaning opposite or faraway), while the "Latin" settlers spoke of their "Magnifica Comunità di Pera", referring to Galata. Pera proper began as an extension of Galata. Its first settlers were wealthy merchants, expatriate and Greek, fleeing a town that "suffocated every sunset, when the Voevoda shut the gates". From the late fifteenth century, overpopulation and poor sanitation made Galata synonymous with epidemics. The confiscation of the Latins' cathedral and the settlement of Arabs created tensions with the Levantines. Desire for space and the wish to make the best of the panoramic views led the rich to the hills with the vineyards, known as *les vignobles de Péra*. Settling outside the fortifications was now safe: Ottoman power had been consolidated and no enemy could threaten the capital.

The neighbourhood's development was tied to the arrival of the European embassies. France took the lead, sending Knight Jean de La Fort in 1534 as its first permanent ambassador to the Porte and erecting a palace in Pera the following year. The treaty between Francis I and Suleiman the Magnificent included the famous 'capitulations', granting France extra-territorial jurisdiction to rule on the commercial disputes and personal status of her subjects in Ottoman lands. The capitulations fell within the Byzantine tradition of permitting foreign traders to live according to their own laws in personal and work matters.

The French soon established an ambassadorial chapel and a court, before which cases of extra-territorial jurisdiction were brought. The Venetian Republic established an embassy in 1560, England in 1596 and the Dutch much later in 1702. The other nations of Europe followed, striving for privileges equal to those of the French. Embassies – fortified compounds with gardens, palaces and chapels for the expatriates – were built close to one another on the slopes descending to the Bosphorus. Between them spread monasteries of Europe's main orders.

Pera was, like Genoese Galata, very much the child of commerce and European penetration in the Levant. The new district attracted Constantinople's wealthy Christians. Expatriates moved their residences from the squalid Galata back streets to the idyllic slopes of Pera, where they could enjoy the panorama of the "garland of waters" and be closer to their countries' embassies. Large numbers of local Greeks and Armenians came either to work as interpreters and administrative staff in the embassies or simply to live in their proximity.

Pera attracted Christians for the same reason Galata had done so earlier; it enjoyed a great degree of autonomy. Freedoms here were even more extensive and the absence of

Muslims made the authorities indifferent about life in the "town of the infidels". Pera was under the control of the embassies, and living in their shadow gave Christians confidence. Pera was their new shelter. Travellers were very impressed by its social mix, which featured Levantines, Greeks, Armenians and expatriates from all over Europe. Every known language was spoken in Pera. This, and the presence of language schools operated by the embassies, granted Pera the title of "Babel".

"[After the Galata Tower], an ascent of some 300 paces leads to the hill's summit, which is level, about 200 paces wide and 2000 paces long. A road filled with houses, gardens and vineyards crosses in the middle. This is the most pleasant part of the city. From here and the slopes below one may enjoy a panorama of the Golden Horn, the Propontis, Constantinople's seven hills," wrote Pierre Gilles in the 1550s, describing the street grandly named Grande Rue de Péra. The slopes leading to the Golden Horn were filled with Muslim cemeteries, whose cypresses and funerary stelae, crowned with turbans and inscribed with arabesques, enchanted travellers.

In 1700, Pitton de Tournefort could "now distinguish Pera from Galata. Pera is not simply the latter's suburb... The Palace of France is an attractive building, whose chapel is served by

Architectural detail above the main door of apartment buildings, Sakız Ağacı Street

the French Capuchins, at the same time teachers of the *Children of the Tongues*. Those young men the King raises in Constantinople so that they be trained by the monks in Turkish, Arabic and Greek and later serve as interpreters to the French consuls in the Levant's ports." The language school was inaugurated in 1665 by Colbert, Louis XIV's genius minister of finance, and was financed by French guilds. Its operation was seen as essential for safeguarding French interests in the Orient. The French embassy shaped the colony's cultural life and propagated French culture among the Christians, staging the plays of Racine and Molière and poetic soirées. Economic antagonism shortly took a political-cultural dimension.

Art Nouveau elegance, Harbiye

The sultans' indifference to Pera was best demonstrated during the French Revolution. Upon news of the fall of the Bastille, French and Levantine republicans occupied the Palais de France and ousted the royalist ambassador, Comte de Choisel Gouffier. They walked up and down the Grande Rue sporting tricolour badges and annoying the ambassadors of England and Austria. Badge bearers were not allowed in Pera theatres, and the Austrians asked the sultan's foreign minister to intervene. The latter replied that "those foreign merchants are our guests" – as far as he was concerned, they might as well go about with grapes on their heads!

"Lois, Justice, Force": the old French Ambassadorial Court

Until the beginning of the nineteenth century, the Grande Rue ended at today's Galatasaray roundabout. On the site of present Taksim Square spread the Grand Champs des Morts, a vastness of Christian and Muslim cemeteries. The main artery leading from Taksim Square to Cihangir is still called Sıraselviler (row of cypresses), although grand eclectic apartment buildings replaced the trees. Pera's second artery was an ancient caravan road, crossing the Grande Rue at the point of present Kumbaracı and Asmalı Mescit streets. This crossroads, midway between the Galata fortifications and Galatasaray, was at the heart of the

Levantine coat of arms, Galatasaray

new district and gave central Pera its Greek name – Stavrodrómi (crossroads). The name is by far the most appropriate for a district that began as the crossroads of races, languages, lifestyles and ideas, and remains so even after the loss of its multi-ethnic character.

The Grande Rue was associated from the outset with pomp and pose. Perotes boasted of their "Little Paris by the Bosphorus", without a doubt Constantinople's busiest and most elegant quarter, "a frontline post of Europe under the regime of the Turk". Yet the problems inherent in Ottoman rule plagued this bastion of Europeanism. One was the complete lack of urban planning: Pera was densely built, with few communal spaces. Double rows of bay windows almost covered the streets. "Two- and three-storey houses on both sides of the street almost touched one another," wrote Hans Christian Andersen during his 1841 visit. "One certainly doesn't need an umbrella here in rainy weather." All writers dismissed Pera streets as narrow and dark, full of dust in the summer and mud in the winter.

Street lighting was another problem. Before the advent of gas, Pera and Galata streets were poorly lit. At night, Costantinople's Muslim boroughs were deserted and silent, Turks shutting themselves inside after their night prayers. Yet in Galata and Pera, a second cycle of life began after dusk. Perotes ventured out to eat alfresco and drink in the taverns, attend theatre plays and other spectacles. The police required all pedestrians to carry a lantern. Those failing to comply were immediately arrested. The Turkish assumption was that anyone venturing outside after dark must be of dubious character. Pera streets in those days must have been quite a spectacle with all the lanterns moving about in the dark.

One can't help noticing the fire-escape ladders. Spiral in form and brightly painted, they line the back alleys to remind one of a long history of disasters: fires obliterated Pera with great voracity and at regular intervals, spreading fast because of dense building, wooden houses and deficiencies in the water system. The most disastrous, in 1870, consumed a third of Pera within a matter of hours, leaving more than 100 dead. It changed the borough's aspect for ever. Wooden buildings were forbidden from then on and rebuilding turned Pera into a district of multi-storey Parisian-style *appartements,* built in the European vogues of the time. The eclecticism of the 1880s and 1890s was replaced by Art Nouveau at the turn of the twentieth century. Yet in these buildings elements of the vernacular – the bay window being the most conspicuous – were incorporated to create an architectural hybrid, neither European nor Ottoman. The Pera *appartements* are the architectural expression of Levantine cosmopolitanism.

Rebuilding took place at a time when the empire was desperately attempting to catch up with the world. The administrative reforms of 1839 and 1856 gave non-Muslims a nominal equality before the law and enabled Christians to erect impressive cathedrals, schools and other communal buildings. The absence of Muslims and their religious prohibitions permitted the sultans to experiment with European innovations in Pera, such as the telegraph and the telephone, before allowing them elsewhere, making it experimental terrain for urban reform.

While Muslims in the Old City lived in the darkness, under an obscurantist clergy, light spread over Pera. In 1856 the foreign-owned Compagnie de Gaz de Dolma Bahché illuminated two kilometres of Pera heartland, along the Rue des Petits Champs (present Meşrutiyet Caddesi) and the Grande Rue all the way to Taksim Square, where a huge municipal garden took the place of the cemeteries. Again in 1856, in a remarkable move, the imperial residence moved from Topkapı Palace to Dolmabahçe, in close proximity to the embassies.

It was after insistent pressure from the latter that Constantinople acquired proper municipal authorities, divided in 1857 into 14 municipal districts, on the model of the French *arrondissements.* Galata and Pera formed what was proclaimed a "Model District". In 1869 it became the first area to be served by the horse-drawn tramways of the Societé de Tramways de Constantinople. One is amused by the writers' descriptions: runners holding long wooden sticks and blowing trumpets ran in front of the tram shouting "vardaaa!" (make way!), trying to disperse the streams of pedestrians and stray dogs from the tram's direction.

In 1873, a short underground funicular, still operative and known as Tünel, joined Pera's namesake roundabout with Galata's Karaköy Square, where the Stock Exchange stood. Galata's bankers and insurers could thus reach their

Pera homes without having to mount the hill – steep, crowded and full of brothels. Initially, the mullahs had forbidden Muslims to get on the Tünel, claiming that travelling "in the depths of the earth" contravened religious law!

Galata and Pera were not only positioned opposite the walled peninsula, but developed in complete opposition to it. While the latter lived in a slow pace unchanged for centuries, with eunuchs and harems and a Muslim theocracy, the former lived with telephones, telegraphs, cafés, beer houses, department stores and multi-lingual bookstores. The first "moving images" were projected in the Sponeck beer house in 1897, and Pera quickly become Constantinople's cinema land.

"Pera is the West End of the European colony, where one can find the joys and comforts of life," Edmondo d'Amicis wrote. Belle Époque dolce vita made it the place to be. The new *appartements* "of Parisian elegance" harboured a social phenomenon: for the first time, people from different ethnic and religious communities lived in the same building. Families from the upper social strata of all non-Muslim groups frequented the same clubs, salons, theatres and restaurants, putting an end to the Ottoman tradition whereby different "millets" lived side by side without intermingling. The traditional model of the Ottoman city, where different enclaves were set up for different ethnic groups, was also challenged in Pera. Civic life was secularised, and a "proudly cosmopolitan" class emerged.

"Cosmopolitan" summarises the Pera experience. The Grande Rue and all other main arteries of the sixth municipal district were lined with signs in Greek, French, Armenian, Ottoman, Russian and Ladino. Bertrand Bareilles describes an archetypal Pera scene: "Two Levantines sit in a beer house called True Macedonia, owned by a Greek from Karpenissi, which nevertheless serves Pilsen imported from Munich. They start their meal with three olives and a glass of raki, and continue with Russian caviar and English-style steak." Maria Iordanidou recalls the municipal garden at Taksim: "We would go there in the evenings with my mother and grandmother to eat German bread, Hungarian salami, Swiss gruyere and grilled mackerel, and drink Bavarian beer." Pera Greeks who moved to Athens remember the French movies, Italian operettas, and balls where all the European tunes were played and different nationalities mingled. This cosmopolitan experience defined Pera Greeks to such an extent that it made them feel superior to their compatriots, even those residing in other neighbourhoods of the city.

If the buildings of Pera could talk, they would narrate the series of tragedies that eradicated that cosmopolitan society. The buildings of the Grande Rue witnessed all the dramas of contemporary history. The street was filled with blood during the Armenian massacre of 1895, ordered by Abdul Hamid. Maria Iordanidou vividly describes in *Loxandra* how Constantinople's Kurdish butchers were recruited for the massacre and used their cleavers to slaughter Armenian civilians, and how the city's stray dogs licked up the victims' blood.

It was in Pera that the Young Turks staged demonstrations to celebrate the establishment of the constitutional monarchy in 1908, in which the minorities participated enthusiastically. They paraded down the Grande Rue and the Rue des Petits Champs to celebrate, believing that it was a regime of liberty and equality, not one that had spelt out the plans for their destruction in detail.

Pera was the epicentre of the frenzy during the five years of Constantinople's allied occupation, following Ottoman defeat in the Great War. Those "armistice years" (1918-23) were years of joie de vivre for Ottoman Christians, who had suffered greatly during the war (Armenians outside the capital were subject to massacres and death marches in 1915, and so were the Greeks in the Black Sea region and all over Asia Minor). The Grande Rue was filled with the flags of the victors, a tide of refugees from sovietising Russia and allied soldiers. Locals marvelled at new inventions and new ways. Maria Iordanidou describes the frenzy of those years in *San Ta Trella Poulia* (Like Birds Gone Mad):

"In July 1914, when Anna left for Russia, she had bid farewell to the dignified Constantinople of the nineteenth century. The Constantinople of horse carriages, weight carriers and its Greek quarters, where the ghost of grandmothers still haunted the kitchens… In August 1920, Anna returns to jump from the Middle Ages to the twentieth century. Karaköy Square is filled with Anglo-French troops, Greek soldiers, Russian refugees, Jewish, Levantine and Greek nouveaux-riches. Gone are the weight carriers and carriages. Cars! French camions beep deafeningly in Galata's narrow streets.

"*Nous avons gagné la guerre*: Madelon de la Victoire is sung in bars and grill-rooms that pop up everywhere. Beer barrels block the entry to Recep's pastry shop. The *General Gubernator* of Astrakhan is selling piroshki on the Galata bridge. Hurdy-gurdies adorned with Greek flags play *The Boys of National Defence did away with the [Greek] King*. Photographs of Venizelos adorn all the cafés. And everybody sings *Tipperary*.

"In front of the *Hôtel de Londres* Greek soldiers are dancing *kalamatianos* in the middle

Demonstrating for peace on İstiklâl Caddesi, formerly the Grande Rue de Péra

KİRALIK
DERPA ATAKKABI
İNDİRİM
simit sarayı
iddaa
ÖZSÜT

of the street, and the Grande Rue is closed to traffic because Scots in leopard skins parade, playing gaidas and drums. *Hôtel Tocatlian* is like a corpse surrounded by worms: entrepreneurs, foreign spies, drug dealers, pimps and prostitutes of all kinds. Shameless glamour, frenetic partying, a carnival. The Whore of Babylon dressed in purple and red and gold is touring the streets of Pera and Galata.

"*Ochi chorniye!,* I want to live! resounds from the cafés-chantants. Bring champagne! Russian aristocrats are the singers, selling their last diamonds to pay for the champagne. Levantines wore ferajes and play Turkish ladies, because local colour is sought after and Turkish women have gone into hiding."

Greek defeat in the Asia Minor campaign (1919-1922) and the Exchange of Populations that followed it sealed the fate of Anatolia's Greeks and Greece's Turks. But it also made almost half of Constantinople's 300,000 Greeks leave in a matter of months, fearing that a massacre like the one in Smyrna would take place. Pera nevertheless retained a Greek majority and a linguistic and ethnic diversity, remaining "a polyglot city". An extortionate "property tax" levied on non-Muslims in 1942 failed to make Greeks leave their Pera homeland.

The most shameful memory after the Armenian massacres was the government-organised attack on the Greeks of the night of September 6, 1955. Organised groups of looters attacked Greek shops, houses and shrines all over Istanbul in an event that, in its organisation and execution, closely resembled Berlin's Kristallnacht. In a few hours, 4,348 shops, 99 restaurants and 11 hotels (90 percent of all Greek businesses), 26 schools, three cemeteries and 45 churches were vandalised; another 35 Greek shrines were set ablaze. A considerable number of Armenian and Jewish properties were also looted.

In Greece, this event is remembered as the worst eruption of anti-Greek hatred in modern times. Its aim was to intimidate Greeks into abandoning claims on Cyprus, but more so to force Constantinopolitan Greeks out. It turned into a spasm of social hatred and a violent assault on all minorities, seen as "infidel", "foreign" and "rich". The Grande Rue was covered with the shattered glass from shop windows, piles of expensive imported textiles, smashed refrigerators, thousands of shoes. Martial law was proclaimed, and tanks paraded along the main streets. The next day, groups looted the Pera shops, whose stores had been shattered during the violence, for spoils in an orgy of destruction and theft. The 50th anniversary of September 6, 1955 was remembered with commemorations in 2005 and named "Istanbul's night of shame".

It is a very positive development that people now freely talk of the mistreatment of minorities in the past.

The "September Events" forced tides of Greeks abroad. Years of hysterical nationalism followed. In 1964, the Turkish government expelled all Constantinopolitans who were Greek passport holders, as tensions in Cyprus reached a peak. The expelled, and their relatives who left with them, amounted to more than 20,000 people. Emptied of its residents, Pera was left miserable and derelict. Peasants from inner Anatolia and the Black Sea coast, flooding the city to find work, replaced the Perotes. The coarse, unrefined appearance and manners of the newcomers and, even more so, their Islamic fervour and the clothes that went with it, sat badly with the refined world of Pera. The newcomers squatted in the apartment buildings; seeing them as temporary residences, they did not bother with the slightest repair. Prostitution reigned.

"The Grande Rue at night became an altogether different street, the hangout of an altogether different crowd," remembers Adelaide Mercenier, a Levantine who grew up in the Pera of the late 1960s and early 1970s. Having worked for years as the press attache of the Greek embassy in Ankara she now lives in Greece. "After dusk families retreated; even when visiting friends or relatives, everybody took care to return home before dark. At night the streets were illuminated by the neon lights of seedy bars. There were street fights, knifings and drunkards, and we children could not venture out."

Poverty and sleaziness enveloped Pera like a shroud of dirt. Urban Turks, resident in Teşvikiye and Nişantaşı who had once walked the streets of cosmopolitan Pera, were struck with horror when visiting. Pera became the prime object of their nostalgia for the good old days. But it was too late. State policies had borne fruit – the borough was ethnically cleansed. The widespread gentrification of recent years has attempted to restore some of the lost splendour. But a place is its people more than anything, and although the buildings are here, the Perotes are absent. The past cannot be revived. But it is often evoked by nostalgia, the nostalgia of a society that is beginning to feel pride in the multicultural legacy of its city.

• • •

Bertrand Bareilles wrote that Pera was "in many respects a Greek city". According to French traveller Jean Thevenot, visiting in 1656, "noble Greeks" were the majority in Pera already at that time. Besides, most Levantines also spoke

Greek as a native language. Descending from families established in Constantinople for centuries, they shared their professional and personal life with the Greek Orthodox. Many single Catholic merchants arriving from Europe married local Greeks. Their descendants also intermarried with Greeks, and a peculiar community, Catholic and Greek-speaking, was born. Many female names found on tombstones in Galata's cathedral of San Pietro and San Paolo are unmistakably Greek – Xanthippi, Despoina, Penelope. Such families helped make Galata and Pera Greek-speaking towns.

So long as the star of Phanari shone bright, Greek notables preferred to live there. It was only after its destruction in 1821 that Pera became the heart of Hellenism, not only in Constantinople or the Ottoman Empire, but worldwide. By the end of the nineteenth century, Pera's more than 80,000 Greeks, the *Stavdrodromi Greek Community*, was the most distinguished in the Greek world.

Bareilles attributes the fluency of "Frankish" Perotes to the Greek maids working in Pera households. "These nannies and maids come from the [Aegean] islands of Tenos and Andros. They prefer to work under the Europeans, where they can stick to their habits, their dialect and gestures. [Thanks to them], all of Pera's French children are fluent in Greek." Most elderly Jews raised in the district speak Greek very comfortably, while many Bulgarians and Levantines use it as a first language at home – a reflection of Greek dominance over Pera life.

It was on seeing Pera that I appreciated the sophistication and aesthetics of the old Greek middle class. Before, I had always listened with disbelief to stories of the elderly, featuring a refined and cosmopolitan urban Greek bourgeoisie. Greece has excellent medieval and traditional architecture in island and village communities, but no large urban centre to be acclaimed as the creation of such a class. Driven by a vulgar impulse to maximise profit and ignorant of the need to conserve, Greeks turned their big cities into concrete monstrosities. Refinement and aesthetics remain in memory only. Pera became for me the living proof that Greek urbanism had existed, and had indeed been capable of grandeur and taste. Despite the Greek exodus, the demolitions by the municipality and the overall neglect, Istanbul is much more enlightening on contemporary Greek urban architecture than any city in Greece. Large parts of Pera's tissue seem to have changed little, if at all, over the last hundred years.

The façades and the arched passageways bring to mind those black and white archive photographs depicting men in frocks and

women with feathered hats and corseted dresses parading up and down streets lined with patisseries and movie halls, or posing collectively before sumptuous churches or in the interiors of dance halls. The best places for an insight into that world of frothy long dresses, good manners and much pretension are the Pera Greek schools. Two of them still function with a small number of students: the Zografeion and Zappeion Lycées.

During my first visit to the Zografeion I felt as if I was being guided around a luxury hotel. The neoclassical building, once a boys' school, is tucked away on Turnacıbaşı Sokağı, a few metres from the Grande Rue (Istiklâl) and the Greek consulate. I was expecting to find the building in a state of decay, with broken windows, dripping roofs and rusty furniture. Not an unreasonable expectation, as Turkish state policy ever since the late 1950s has prohibited even the slightest repairs in the schools. Many closed because of lack of students, and are slowly collapsing all over the city. Others were demolished. But nothing seems to have marred Zografeion, built by architect Pericles Fotiades in 1892 with money donated by Christakis Zografos, the wealthy Greek banker. Zografeion was inaugurated to rival Phanari's Great School.

The first surprise came when I saw the sparkling marble floors, the polished wooden doors and the overall cleanliness and luxury of the interior. The next came as I noticed that the children running around during the break were speaking to one another in Turkish, and spoke Greek only when replying to one of the teachers. There were, of course, very few children considering the size of the buildings, even though Zografeion is one of the most populous of the handful of surviving Greek schools. Pupils, as in all Turkish schools, still wear a school uniform, abolished in Greece in 1982.

Behind the glamorous appearance – befitting a school built to serve the most distinguished Greek community of its time – hide signs of the community's slow death, the number of students in the classrooms being the most evident. Under the Sultan, Constantinople's Greek schools operated in absolute freedom and were completely self-governing. All classes were taught in Greek and their content chosen by the school's administration. Latin, French, Italian, German and English were taught, along with (Ottoman) Turkish, although Constantinopolitan Greeks did not speak Turkish unless they were lawyers, worked for the bureaucracy, were involved in commerce or came from the interior of Anatolia. This appears strange today, given that Turkish has become the first language of the few Greeks left – a triumph of the nationalist policies of a century.

Typical Pera apartment buildings
on my street, Galatasaray

Moves for the imposition of mandatory Turkish instruction in Greek schools were made after the Young Turk Revolution in 1908, but were met with unrelenting Greek hostility: at a time when nationalist sentiments ran high, anything Turkish was considered anathema. Ottoman Greeks pretended to ignore or preferred to forget that they were subjects of the Sultan. The Great War gave Young Turks the much-wanted pretext to strike. The Ottoman language was imposed in all curricula. Much of the fierce Greek opposition was due to the difficult Arabic script in use at the time.

"Among the other adventures the Great War brought was the instruction of Turkish... Unbelievable as it may seem, Turkish was not taught in Constantinople's Greek schools. Why would it be in any case? Constantinople was an international city. One could communicate in any language, and most of all in Greek! So why ever learn Turkish, which was written in the Arabic script from right to left?" wondered Eleni Halkoussi, the Constantinople Greek actress who studied in the Zappeion, the most exclusive school for girls in the Greek world. She narrates how "the girls" greatly exploited the timid kindness of the Turkish men sent to remedy their ignorance of Turkish. "We felt very vindicated when Mustafa Kemal substituted the Latin script for the Arabic hieroglyphics, of which we had learnt nothing more than the first letter, ELIF, a perpendicular line..."

Today Greek schools operate in a problematic environment. Instruction is bilingual: natural sciences are taught in Greek, and all social sciences in Turkish and by Turkish teachers. The schools are subject to the ministry of education, which appoints a Turkish deputy director to ensure that students are indoctrinated with the official position of the state in subjects like history and "national security" (a class taught here). Only the history of Turkey is taught, Greek history and culture being ignored. Human rights lawyer Fethiye Çetin complains that "Turkish teachers teaching history in Greek and Armenian schools attempt to make students hate their own identity." Until recently the Turkish deputies reported to a special Committee on Minorities, supervised by the secret service. Monitoring every activity of the Greek teachers, they operated as spies for the government. The Greek letters above the doors of Greek schools were excised by special order of the ministry of education in the aftermath of the September Events...

To be fair, the taming of virulent nationalism in recent years means most Turkish deputies are now decent people. The Committee on Minorities was abolished in 2005, and some deputies are even a great help to the school, as the current director of Zografeion, Yannis Demircioğlu, stressed. The main problems the schools face today stem from the depletion of the very community. There are too few Greek children, and in many schools the majority of students are Greek Orthodox Arab speakers from the Hatay region. The common medium of communication between students of different linguistic backgrounds is Turkish. Many students speak only a very basic Greek, and at times it is distorted to the point of being incomprehensible. The schools, once renowned for their strictness, are now too lenient, trying to help students faced with often impossible problems. Excessive leniency means that the schools, once famed all over the Greek world, are no longer competitive. Most affluent Greeks opt to send their children to private French schools.

Stelios Mumbayacioğlu, a retired teacher and one of Pera's last Greeks, has a memory from his elementary school years in Phanari's Great School: "I was naughty in class and the teacher smacked me quite hard. I remember that my only concern was to erase the rash from my cheek before returning home: if my parents learnt of my punishment, there would be a second round. I walked to the Phanari quay and washed my face with freezing water – it was a winter day – until the rash was gone." But quality was the other thing they were known for. I had once complemented Demetres Mandacioğlu, an elderly Greek from Prinkipo, on his rich vocabulary and received the proud reply: "But I graduated from the Great School!" in the same way a Briton would refer to Oxford or Cambridge.

Zappeion, the old high school for girls, is a huge *Style Empire* building beside Haghia Triada, Pera's largest Greek church; both buildings are visible from Taksim Square. Zappeion is huge blackened and desperate for restoration. It was once a boarding school for the daughters of the cream of the Greek world: its students came from as far away as Odessa, Alexandria and Marseilles. It is now a mixed high school with a few students and it also houses the city's sole Greek kindergarten. The statue of Zappas, the Greek tycoon who financed the building and operation of the school, no longer decorates the main staircase; it was damaged during the lootings of September 1955 and is kept in the school's library. A bust of Atatürk, flanked by two huge torches, replaced it.

And yet the statues of the Muses and the frescoes with scenes from Greek mythology are still there in the theatre and the ceremonial chamber. They remind of the words of the Ecumerical Patriarch Bartholomeos during his speech at the first ever conference of Istanbul Greeks held in their homeland in the summer

YAZICI
KUMAŞ
245 03 81 - 245 37 49
EFES
Pilsen
ÇAYKENT
TEKEL BÜFE

of 2006: "Even if the people are gone, stones remain and shout they were here, their voices like a threnody coming out of graves."

• • •

It was the desire to be steeped in this melancholy mass of memories that made me wish for a flat in Pera. Its legacy, moreover, perfectly suited my determination not to (and inability to) identify with any single cultural and ethnic background. It is funny how things happen at times. In one of my first ever walks in the city as a tourist, I ended up in Cihangir. The region was not indicated in my guide: modern tourists pay less attention to the Pera districts, focusing on the "exoticism" of the Old City. As was the case with their travelling ancestors, Pera seems to either bewilder or annoy them, spoiling the oriental vision they are after. I got lost in the maze of Cihangir's alleys, its brightly painted houses and Belle Époque *appartements* and its outdoor cafés. I loved it; it was tasteful and civilised and charming, at once familiar and strange. Here is where I would like to live some day, I proclaimed, and I remember exactly at which crossroads I made that wish. Almost two years later I moved into a house a few metres away.

I spent the first two months socialising and looking for some sort of employment. And trying to learn Turkish. My favourite hangouts were the alleys of Tünel, where I befriended a group of anarchists. They were jobless, extremely willing to talk about politics, religion, family, you name it, and quite fascinated at the case of a Greek moving to Turkey. For more than two months I must have been something of a cult figure, sitting on the stools of the area's tea houses and cafés and conversing with enthusiastic and oddly dressed youngsters. The "conversation" involved my being lectured, eagerly taking notes and opening and closing my dictionary. "I see. So you say you had a child by artificial insemination because you were against the institution of marriage? Interesting. No, sorry, will you say that again? No, *alienation* is not in my dictionary. Why don't you try to… sketch it?" Bless them; I was competent before I knew it.

I remember the days and nights in Cihangir very vividly. I shared the first floor and basement of a Greek house of the 1930s with Sophia, a Greek musician who had come to study Ottoman court music. I have a profound aversion to Ottoman court music (and most folkloric tunes of the Balkans and Middle East for that matter), an aversion that Sophia's early morning or midnight studying did not help appease. Yet I developed a strong affection for Sophia, which continued and deepened after our (disastrous, *she* insists) cohabitation. Nei-

Backstreet in a rundown neighbourhood near the Armenian Catholic Cathedral

ther of us spoke any Turkish in the beginning. Everything was new, either exciting or overwhelming. Our landlady was a solitary soul, rather depressed. A convert from Islam to Christianity, we both found her newfound zeal irrelevant and at times embarrassing.

Despite its markedly "European" appearance Cihangir retains a very vivid and particular local colour. My most vivid memories have to do with the freezing winter mornings and the street sellers. On those grey mornings everything was paralysed under snow and I had no courage to venture out of bed. A determined Sophia would nevertheless storm my bedroom, having resolved we should go out for the week's shopping. Threats and violence wouldn't produce the desired effect; on the contrary, Sophia would soon make her way under my thick blankets, initially complaining, soon fast asleep.

Then the procession would start. We had memorised the order: first would come the seller of simit (bread rings eaten as a snack), then the seller of pies "Cheese pies, meat pies, potato pies!" and lastly the man selling potatoes and onions ("patateeeees, soğaaaaaaaan!") "Let's wake!" Sophia would mumble. "In a while," I would say. "Wait for Aygaz." Aygaz, the liquid gas company, has hundreds of small vans going about the city to distribute silver-coloured tubes with the precious fuel, which most households use for their stoves. "Taram, taram, taram, taram, taramtaram, tamtam, Aygaz!" the taped music went down the street. "Alex! Out we go!"

But my favourite Cihangir voice appeared late in the evenings. It was the seller of Boza, a white drink from fermented millet. This street seller was the only one with a good voice; he was good enough to become a singer, Sophia said. He would go about crying: "Booooozaaaa! Vefa Bozaaaaa," and we would run to the window magnetised, surrendering to the power of his voice. Neither of us liked Boza, but we would occasionally go out and tip him for his voice. He carried a metal scale on his back from which hung two metal pots with the drink; he used tin measures and poured the drink into glass bottles. Scale, pots, bottles and caps would jingle as he walked every evening, weekdays and holidays, rain or snow, along Cihangir's streets.

We had to leave Cihangir after about a year because of the many problems in the house; our churchgoing landlady had neither the money nor the energy for its upkeep. I ended up in Şişli, two metro stops north of Taksim Square. I didn't like its concrete mass, so reminiscent of downtown Athens and so distant from its past as the area of villas for Ottoman pashas and rich Christians. But the noisy moving clouds, Istanbul's seagulls, had followed me from Cihangir to my new home, and I could hear their cries day and night. The most charming aspect of Şişli were the old Jewish ladies I spotted every now and again, chatting melodiously in Judeo-Spanish in the middle of the street. After a few months I moved back to what I felt was my natural territory – Pera.

There was again something supernatural about my new move. While still resident in Cihangir, I was walking down the slope from Galatasaray, and my attention was drawn by a row of elegant old Greek houses with bay windows. "If only I could find an apartment in one of those," I wished. Weeks after my decision to search for a flat in Pera, a friend informed me of a vacancy in one of the buildings I had spotted. Within a month, I was in my present home, a flat in a hundred-year-old Greek *appartement*. My bay window looks out on Haghia Sophia and catches a glimpse of the sea, reminding me of what drew the first settlers to Pera.

The front façade of my flat with the bay window looks on Yeni Çarşı, the steep street that descends from Galatasaray to the Bosphorus. The upper zones of Yeni Çarşı are gentrified territory, inhabited by journalists, writers and bohemians. My back windows look on the *French Street*, a rather coy rehabilitation project which turned a back alley of Galatasaray into a would-like-to-be Montmartre. At night, the repertoire of its cafés ensures I am put to sleep by tacky songs of the 1960s and 70s. But the lower slopes of Yeni Çarşi are home to completely different sounds and crowds: two villages of Arabs from the zone of Siirt in south-east Turkey have resettled in the area almost in their entirety. Arabic is spoken on the streets, women go about envelopped in black chadors and some men sport Taliban-like baggy trousers and beards. Gypsies celebrate their famous weddings in an open space a few metres from my house, with drums and bagpipes and dances.

Once, the buildings and streets of Pera served as the place of interaction for people of different races, who nevertheless belonged to the same class. Today, even though they have lost their multi-national character, they house people of very different backgrounds. If the diversity of races and creeds is almost extinguished, a great diversity of lifestyles and social backgrounds persists in the Pera of the twenty-first century. Turks use *kozmopolit* as an adjective for places. Unlike its Greek-derived original, *kozmopolit* does not necessarily denote the co-existence of different ethno-religious groups in the same area, but the mingling of lifestyles and the tolerant atmosphere this creates. I think that most Turks, at least in Istanbul, would cite today's Pera as an example of the usage of the word.

Tarlabaşı and Tatavla: from "Little Greece" to ghetto

Typical scene in Tarlabaşı: old Greek homes, Anatolian dwellers

It's like an open wound in the very heart of Istanbul, only a couple of yards from Taksim Square. The alleys of Tarlabaşı, with their rundown buildings and reputation for crime, are an altogether different world. The moment you cross busy Tarlabaşı Bulvarı you leave the buzz of the Grande Rue and its side streets way behind. The architecture is still Pera eclecticism. But there are no cafés, no bookshops, no passages and no crowds of wanderers. No outsider ventures here after dark.

Even the name Tarlabaşı makes "White Turks" – the nation's secular, westernised middle classes – shiver. Istanbulites remember the existence of the "alleys of dereliction" whenever a building collapses, burying its tenants alive or when shootings between rival drug gangs result in deaths. The rest of the time the city pretends to ignore Tarlabaşı, much more famous for its transvestite brothels, cocaine dealers and young delinquents than it is for its decaying mansions and churches.

Tall transvestites parade next to gypsy women with flowery headscarves, in streets filled with debris from demolitions. Laundry hangs above the streets to dry, like tattered festival flags. Brightly painted houses of Belle Époque elegance are a sad sight with their broken windowpanes, collapsing roofs and dismembered balconies projecting above the streets. The streets themselves are crowded with groups of dirty children shrieking and playing chase while the occasional flock of sheep wanders by. This is Istanbul's most central and most notorious ghetto.

It wasn't always like this. Looking at the architecture gives you a hint of the neighbourhood's middle-class past. Tarlabaşı was Pera's largest borough. It spread on the slopes between Stavrodromi (central Pera) and the Tatavla gorge as the narrow zone around the Grande Rue became congested with upmarket stores and the mansions of the wealthy. Greeks who couldn't afford the *appartements* of Stavrodromi imitated the Pera lifestyle a bit further downhill, forming an almost exclusively Greek borough.

Architecturally and socially, Tarlabaşı – settled in the 1850s – was the transition between the aristocratic cosmopolitanism of Stavrodromi and the parochial modesty of Tatavla on the opposite hill. It was divided into two zones, still distinguished by the architecture. Its upper slopes, close to the Grande Rue, were a modest continuation of the exclusive boroughs of Galatasaray, Petits Champs and Taksim. The architecture is that of central Pera, albeit less ornate. The hundreds of grand Art Nouveau apartments of Upper Tarlabaşı are fading testimonies of affluence and elegance. Plaques with the names of Greek architects survive on their walls. Their gloomy decay made Greek writer Kostas Stamatopoulos call Tarlabaşı "a vast necropolis of the 1900s". Doctors, owners of small businesses, actors, writers and artists lived in the area. Its steep alleys are those "narrow Pera streets" mentioned by Maria Iordanidou, whose family moved here around the same time.

Architecture in Lower Tarlabaşı, bordering the gorge that once separated Pera from working-class Tatavla, is more modest. Two- and three-storey homes once housed less affluent Pera Greeks: tailors, schoolteachers, barbers, artisans. Despite their modesty, homes in this area follow an elegant line, with attention to decorative details. They are profoundly human and dignified and create a harmonious cityscape.

Tarlabaşı was less cosmopolitan than other

Gypsy women in Lower Tarlabaşı

54

34 HNZ 96

Pera districts, with a small Armenian community and some European expatriates beside an overwhelming Greek majority. It was only after a mass influx of Russian refugees from the October Revolution that the area became multiethnic. Degradation started as Greeks left in tides to be replaced by Anatolian peasants. Yet the Greek presence was strong all through the 1970s. "Here the faint heart of Constantinopolitan Hellenism continued to beat until the early 1980s," wrote Greek lawyer and regular Istanbul visitor Thrasyboulos Papastratis, who has been visiting Istanbul since the 1980s. Not one Greek family remains.

The final blow was dealt by the piercing of Tarlabaşı Bulvarı in 1986, a plan carried out under mayor Bedrettin Dalan, who also demolished the Phanariote mansions. Those Tarlabaşı demolitions dominated debates on city planning during the 1980s. The aim was to divert the traffic of the pedestrianised Grande Rue. Yet mayor Dalan was a member of ex prime minister Turgut Özal's Motherland Party and a known subscriber to the ideology of "Turkish-Islamic Synthesis", a nationalist creed invented by the 1980 junta and further developed by Özal. Dalan was on a mission to "cleanse" the city of its non-Muslim heritage, many academics claim, pointing to the fact that the bulldozers sent to demolish "those houses of Greeks and

Syr ac women praying, Constantine and Helen Church, Tarlabaşı

Armenians" were adorned with Turkish flags.

Dalan proceeded with his plan with the blessing of nationalists, who pointed out that those buildings did not deserve protection, since they had been built by "foreigners" and "were not a product of Turkish culture". Some of the most elegant *appartements* vanished and the busy new boulevard severed Tarlabaşı from the Pera heartland. As the Grande Rue became the centre of Pera nostalgia, Tarlabaşı was left to destitute immigrants.

Ignore pleas not to venture in and feel safe to indulge in a long tour in daylight. True, the neighbourhood is home to the penniless, the unemployed and the criminal. Nevertheless, nobody would treat a foreigner disrespectfully. The only nuisance will be the children, begging you to take photographs of them. Your foreign looks and/or camera will protect you. What makes Tarlabaşı a face of Istanbul not to be missed is the combination of its explosive social cocktail with the architecture of those now gone.

Kallyoncu Kulluğu Street is the heart of Tarlabaşı. According to former resident Bertrand Bareilles, it was once the centre of the famous Carnival of the Pera Greeks. The carnival filled the Grande Rue and proceeded to Tarlabaşı. There, dressed like their classical ancestors, or sporting false noses and beards, revellers danced the night away. Writing in 1918, Bareilles comments that during the carnival, the Grande Rue from Taksim to Asmali Mescit was all serpentines and confetti and fireworks, and looked "like the Boulevard des Italiens during Mardi Gras".

Kallyoncu Kulluğu is lined with impressive Greek buildings adorned with meanders, statues and pediments bearing busts of Hermes or Athena. Crosses drawn by the soot of burning Easter candles are still visible above the main doors. Some of the buildings are empty; through the broken windows of others one can see goats in what was once a sitting room with its plaster reliefs on the ceiling and peeling tapestry on the walls. In others, firewood is piled in a bay window from where a "*kokona*" (elderly Greek lady) would once watch the street.

Washing machines and ironing boards are grouped in the grand marble entrances, for communal use by several households. More than 20 people are often cramped in a flat, sometimes together with their livestock. Most are refugees from the East, who flooded Istanbul after their villages were burnt down and emptied by the armed forces in the 20-year war with Kurdish separatists.

Tarlabaşı is crowded. Its three main groups, gypsies, Kurds and transvestites, are all "marginals". They form the social category of "Black Turks", as opposed to the "White Turks" of the urban élites. Childbirth rates are high and the streets here are filled with swarms of ragged children. Turkish professor of English literature Murat Belge described in an article entitled *Two Nations in the same Country* how such children greet him with "hellos" and "goodbyes" in English, unable to imagine that he and they belong to the same society. Every time I visit these quarters myself, I feel that my Turkish friends come from an altogether different country. The difference first apparent is the one of material conditions, but there is much more in the schism between "white" and "black" Turks.

Gypsies are the oldest group, already having inhabited Dolapdere (on the foot of the Tatavla hill) by the seventeenth century. Gypsy women can be distinguished by their headscarves adorned with coins or embroidery. Famous for their merry tunes and dances, gypsies face as much discrimination as they do in Europe, having a reputation for lawlessness and petty theft.

Kurds are the most populous group in the area. The harsh, guttural tones of Kurdish dominate, as do the gloomy tones of Arabesk, a type of music mimicking – as the name suggests – Arab melodies. Kurdish gangs fight each other for local control and Tarlabaşı Kurds often make headlines over the frequency of 'honour crimes'.

Originating from the barren wilderness of the country's south east, where traditional communities are feudally organised and governed by inherited codes of honour, Kurds are a tough lot. Violently uprooted, they have to face daily the bitter realities of socio-economic exclusion, which often leads to crime. Young men, freed from the rigid social control of their closed rural communities, are often ready to do anything in the anonymity of the city for some quick money.

Most Tarlabaşı Kurds are street vendors and waiters, shoe polishers, gigolos, rent boys in gay bars or security staff in the strip clubs of Pera backstreets. Many are unemployed and spend their time in street fights and arguments. Revealing the reality of their lives are the scars many young men proudly exhibit, "medals" inherited in some fight. The prime expression of Kurdish identity are the street fires lit during the Newroz, the Persian New Year celebrated by the Kurds, when children and youths jump over the flames. Kurdish songs with a marked anti-state message are also sung at this time.

The transvestite and transsexual prostitutes – extremely tall, fond of silicone, very painted and cheeky – give the most character to the ghetto. Despite their abnormal height they insist on wearing high heels. Their omnipresence at night in downtown Istanbul is surprising to visitors, who don't usually expect to see such sights in a Muslim country. Most work in the streets, but Tarlabaşı is the headquarters of the trade. Transsexual brothels proliferate around the Armenian Catholic monastery and in Büyük Bayram Sokağı, on the Pera side of Tarlabaşı Boulevard.

According to the novels *Loxandra* and *Leonis*, Tarlabaşı, particularly the area of Abanoz Sokağı, has always been a seedy area. Nevertheless, in the 1900s it catered to an upmarket crowd, in contrast with the brothels of Kemeraltı and Kuledibi. Theotokas writes in *Leonis*: "It was a narrow cobbled street, like hundreds of others in Constantinople, but busier. Doors were open, grilles shut in the ground floors. Some benign old ladies sat peacefully outside. Women stood in doors and windows, lightly dressed, with ribbons in their hair, lips and eyes

brightly painted. They even smoked, shamelessly, in the open. But nothing much more... Men entered the houses in silence and order, and haggled with the ladies on the street."

The tranquil, almost dignified, image of prostitution in the 1900s has nothing to do with the sleazy, violent backstreets today. Pimps, transsexual prostitutes and extortionists constitute the Pera underworld, and its brothels and unsavoury bars, patronised by Anatolians, have a violent air absent from Theotokas' narration.

The African refugees of Tarlabaşı have been called "pariahs among the pariahs". Easily spotted because of their colour, they are an easy target of harassment both by minority groups and the police. Kurdish and gypsy children throw stones and dead rats into their apartments, and the police have a reputation for brutality when dealing with them. They usually sell illegal CDs on the streets or work in construction. Most of them came here duped by slave traders, who promised them they would arrive at "an EU country"; most want to move towards Italy or France. If Africans find permanent work they have do it for a fraction of the money given to locals. Rumours of their involvement in drug trading worsen public attitudes towards them.

Tarlabaşı is a major outpost of the drugs trade. Sometimes while walking its backstreets I have noticed men in dark suits talking in parked

Neighbourly talk, Tarlabaşı style

cars. Once I even heard shots – they say it is the crug dealers who mainly cause shootings in Tarlaɔaşı. Many teenagers are involved in drug trafficking and many spend their evenings sniffing glue or turpentine from plastic bags. Those *tinerciler* (turpentine guys) pose the greatest danger to the outside visitor, since they are usual y unaware of their actions and thus highly dangerous. To be fair, though, they are few and far between in daylight.

I discovered Tarlabaşı by chance. Walking down the namesake boulevard, I was thunderstruck: a shepherd was walking his 40-odd sheep down the hill. I followed him and noticed the patches of lambs' wool hanging on doors and window shutters. Women were sitting on chairs, weaving. Others had spread their carpets out on the street and were using water pipes to wash them. Clothes, carpets, tablecloths and curtains hung above the street to dry. The newcomers have imported their village life to the city: red peppers hang on the windows and pasta is spread on the terraces and yards to dry in the sun.

In every second corner a blackened shell remains from a collapsed building, and you can see goats and hens being raised in what was once the ground floor, beside broken bathtubs and heaps of firewood. From time to time another building collapses. Sometimes, several families who have taken refuge in it are buried under the rubble. Open spaces, like scars, remain after the rubble is collected. They are used as parking lots, camping grounds for the Ramadan tents and for the massive animal slaughtering for the feast of Kurban Bayramı.

The bizarre silhouette of well-kept Haghios Konstantinos, the Greek church, contrasts with the surrounding decay. "I only show up to look after the church, then flee before dark," Madame Eleni, the caretaker, confessed to me. "It used to be a decent neighbourhood, but now it's the third world." She showed me around the church, a daring eclectic construction of 1861 whose exterior incorporates Byzantine and Gothic elements. Its interior pays tribute to ancient Greek glory, a favourite reference for the community in a period of national revival. The marble iconostasis imitates the façade of a Greek temple. Haghios Konstantinos has been rented to Assyrian Christians, fugitives from the turmoil in the country's south-east region.

Somewhere in the district's lower zones, among beautiful decaying houses, a sentence sprayed on a wall caught my attention: "I will f… the mother of anyone dropping their garbage here." Ottoman fountains were scattered around. I returned to the upper zone. The magnificent Armenian Catholic Seminary now hosts the Istanbul Art Centre, where Sinem, my student of Spanish, would later take flamenco classes. One of the few grand buildings to have undergone restoration, it is occupied by dance, theatre and painting groups. Yet its surroundings are full of transvestite "houses".

Further towards Taksim, on Karakorum Sokağı, stands a very western-looking church,

VESTEL

All the way from the Iraqi frontier to Tarlabaşı

which is in fact the cathedral of a very eastern community: the Archbishopric of the Assyrian Orthodox. The Assyrians, or Syriacs, as they are also known, claim to have established the first Christian church in the world. They conduct their services in Aramaic, the language of Christ. Dispersed between Iraq, Syria and Turkey, their heartland in Anatolia is in the Tur Abdin region around Mardin. Their cathedral was built with stones carried from that area. Many Assyrians fled to Istanbul or abroad, suffering both at the hands of the government forces and of the PKK, a Kurdish separatist organisation. Their Sunday service, held in Haghios Konstantinos, is

"One for two million [old] liras" the sign reads

an interesting experience: women enter the church with their heads covered in lace and the sexes are seated separately. The faithful raise their hands to pray, in the same way as Muslims – a gesture which, as I learnt in Cairo, derives from the Ancient Egyptian rite.

The only time my presence in Tarlabaşı created some friction was when I was photographing a row of Greek houses for this book. I spent some time trying to capture their architectural details on camera, watched attentively by a crowd of women and children. An elderly woman approached and asked me why I was shooting pictures. "There are two types of people who come here to photograph," she said. "Those who admire the buildings and say that they are of historical importance, and those who claim that they are derelict and have to be demolished. To which group do you belong?" "By all means to the first," I answered, assuring the women that I wasn't photographing the derelict buildings for some public authority to include them in its demolition list.

An announcement by the authorities that more than 5000 buildings in the city wouldn't withstand an earthquake of 7 on the Richter Scale has worried Tarlabaşı residents. "We don't want our homes to be put down, and we don't want to be relocated," the woman said. I said that I believed a restoration project will be launched for Tarlabaşı, like the ones underway in Phanari and Balat. "Haven't you heard of that programme?" I said. Not surprisingly she hadn't. "If they restore the buildings they will evict us and sell them to rich foreigners," she said. "For the state, we simply don't exist."

• • •

Tatavla was founded in the sixteenth century, a Greek village on a hill isolated behind a gorge. Its settlers were sailors and workers in the Ottoman navy; abducted from the Greek islands, they were brought to work in the imperial arsenal in Kasımpaşa. A population with different customs, originating from all over the Aegean, the newcomers settled around the church of Haghios Demetrios, which they founded in 1535.

European travellers knew the village as San Dimitri and as such it appears in engravings. Tatavla was the only hamlet – together with Kydonies (Ayvalik) in Asia Minor – where settlement of non-Greeks was prohibited by order of the sultan in 1793. The prohibition, in which local Greeks took pride, remained in force until the Republic's proclamation.

The settlers were joined by hundreds from all over the Greek world, eager to live in a Greek haven and freed from cohabitation with Muslims. Tatavla grew and prospered, evolving from a workers' neighbourhood to a mixed community. Many wealthy Greeks arrived, especially after the looting of Phanari in 1821 and the massacres in Chios in 1822 during the Greek War of Independence.

Yet life remained parochial. Tatavla's fame was based on its folklore of carnival and lent. Some of the traditions, conserving a pagan, bucolic character, scandalised contemporary morals. Tatavla conserved both its parochial character and Greek majority up to the 1970s. Today, bereft of its Greeks, it has become a concrete mass, stripped of all memories of the one-time village of timber houses.

The name Tatavla always caused confusion to Greek writers. How do you spell it? Even worse, how do you decline it? It's a Greek-Turkish hybrid (Ta Tavla, meaning "The Stables"), dating from the time when the sultan used the area as pasturelands. The original settlers retreated to the hill of San Dimitri, separated from the rest of Constantinople by the forested gorge, when their parish church in Kasımpaşa was converted into a mosque.

From the outset, the isolated Greek hamlet acquired a reputation for "libertarian" ways. "A district of dirty wooden houses and narrow streets on a hill, passage for seamen and shipbuilders, sheltering the basest elements; locals indulge in the worst entertainment and debauchery. The moral scum of ancient Ionia and Phrygia survives in the figures of the dancers in Tatavla taverns and wineshops," wrote the German traveller Hammer in 1822.

In a similar vein, Constantinople resident Skarlatos Vizantios complained of the wine houses of Neapoli (the present Dolapdere) where "effeminate dancers still perform in some establishments, but no longer sit by the doors, dressed and talking in a manner renouncing their sex". Transvestite dancers, a local attraction, had become a thing of the past in Vizantios's time (the 1870s), but transvestites in general made a spectacular comeback a century later.

Vizantios describes Tatavla as "a beautiful and clean district of elegant wooden homes scenically covering the hill and steep narrow streets". According to Andreas Syngros, writing in the 1890s, it was the difficult topography which isolated Tatavla. Life on the hill remained "archaic". The presence of a stream in the gorge, which often flooded in winter, as well as the legendary steep ascent, made access "an odyssey" in rainy weather. This is the origin of the famous Constantinopolitan song "Pull, Driver Pull, Let's Head to Tatavla!", expressing the determination necessary for the ascent.

Outsiders didn't often venture up the hill, except for the celebrated Lent festivities. The local community was organised around its two main parish churches, Haghios Georgios and Haghios Athanasios, and resembled a Greek village. A big square at the site of the current bus terminal hosted the beer gardens Acropolis and Ararat, where local Greeks would kill time.

There were no *appartements* in Tatavla, but two-storey houses, and no tenants; every family owned a house. There were no shops apart from small convenience stores; street vendors sold the necessities. "Customs and ideas were completely different to those in Stavrodromi," wrote Syngros. "Anybody wishing to introduce Pera customs was doomed to fail."

Constantinopolitan writers mention the pe-

TENNIS

culiar Tatavla lent festivities. "Clean Monday", marking the end of carnival and the beginning of lent in Greek tradition, was celebrated with great joy. Greeks from all over the city gathered to eat beans and other foods appropriate for fasting, to sing and dance in the open air. Bertrand Bareilles complained of the cacophony of hurdy gurdies, mixing music from a variety of cultures.

The festivities, named Baklahorani, were held in front of the cemetery of Haghios Eleftherios and the churches. Maria Iordanidou called them "a pagan commemoration". The most puzzling event was a procession on horseback of prostitutes from other parts of the town, popularly called "the procession of the Amazons".

The spectacle was well documented by Greek writer Leandros Mihas: "The prostitutes mounted on horses and paraded to the location of the festivities. They were dressed uniformly in velvet jackets and short velvet trousers, silk stockings and high heels. They wore sailor hats and held a whip in their hand. Their faces were covered with velvet masks." This parade, its origins lost in the pagan Greek past, added to the excitement surrounding Baklahorani and became a legendary topic of conversation in the boys' schools and athletic clubs of the Greek community. Its procession in front of the churches was a sight to see, and the Patriarchate never interfered to condemn it.

A young mussel seller

Until World War I, local Greeks carried Greek flags and wore patriotic costumes during festivities, danced traditional dances and sang their national anthem and patriotic songs. All Greek national holidays were celebrated with fervour. Yet the community was decimated by several blows it received from the Young Turk Revolution in 1908, including the law on Turkification of names (1924), which banned streets and squares from having Greek names. A fire in 1929 destroyed much of Tatavla, leading to its renaming as "Kurtuluş" (Salvation).

Today nothing remains of the gorge between Tarlabaşı and Tatavla, described by French writer Gerard de Nerval in the 1830s as green and foggy, reminiscent of the Alps with its vegetation and wooden houses, but the turns of Dolapdere Avenue betray the stream's course.

On the foot of the Tatavla hill stands an interesting silhouette – the Evangelistria church. Although Greek, it has many Armenian elements: pointed windows, pyramid domes on the twin bell towers, interesting reliefs on the stone exterior. A work of 1894, judging from the date on the pebble mosaic of its courtyard, the church took 18 years to complete. Its interior with the marble iconostasis is much more Hellenic. Evangelistria is a good example of how the Constantinopolitan community assimilated different influences from its long past and multi-ethnic environment to produce a local eclecticism unknown in Greece.

Evangelistria is on the edge of the once dodgy borough of Neapolis, still with a bad reputation. Most residents are gypsies. The slopes are dotted with concrete; the tiled roofs mitigate the asphyxiating effect of cement. There is a profusion of satellite plates and drying laundry. Walking in the streets involves making your way through crowds of children and heaps of garbage; the dirty water that housewives throw from the upper floors of houses is a constant hazard.

"One reaches Tatavla by a street lined with beautiful wooden houses, slightly reminiscent of the Chinese style in their ornaments," wrote the french poet Gerard de Nerval about Akartsa, the legendary ascent to the main square of Haghios Demetrios uphill. He referred to the intricate carved finishes of the wooden roofs and balconies in local architecture. No specimen of it survives on Akağalar Caddesi, as Akartsa was renamed, now an array of concrete boxes. What survives is the inclination; so steep is the ascent that you arrive out of breath at the square. The latter, in front of the outer wall of Haghios Demetrios, is more like an open space where dozens of buses are parked, topped by two ugly electricity pylons, which unfortunately replaced the cypresses as the hill's landmark.

The church, dating from 1535, was restored several times. Its present form, from 1726, is a simple basilica without much to merit a visit. Its guards are a family of Arab Christians from Antioch. They offered me tea and said they had relatives in Thessaloniki. Their eldest son, who used the Greek name Yiorgos, offered to show me around. A student in the Great Patriarchal School in Phanari, his Greek was basic. Arabic at home, Greek at school, Turkish in the street: his linguistic reality.

A few houses away stands the former Central Boys' School, founded in 1886. Renamed Kurtuluş Mixed School, it strives to continue in operation with four teachers and two students. The building with the owl on its pediment, set behind a small garden right opposite the school, is the famous Tatavla Athletic Club. It gave Greece two Olympic champions in 1906: upon winning their medals they declared they wanted the Greek flag raised and the Greek anthem played, even though they were Ottoman subjects. The demand being granted, a diplomatic crisis ensued. The building was ravaged in the anti-Greek pogrom of 1955, like all Tatavla schools and churches. Today it no longer serves the community, operating as a common sports club.

Grand Haghios Eleftherios (1855), Tatavla's second parish church, once stood dominating the green of the surrounding plains, but is now lost amidst the concrete. It was the first domed church to be built in Constantinople after the Fall: the Tanzimat reforms, which instituted a nominal equality between Muslim and non-Muslim subjects, repealed the law that decreed only mosques could be domed. Looted in 1955, the church is in a derelict state, tiles peeling off its roof. In the nearby Greek cemetery, the Gothic lines of the chapel surprised me as much as the Turkish inscriptions on the most recent tombs, proof that Turkish has become the first language of Istanbul Greeks.

Few old timber houses survive on the hill. Yet quite a number of elegant Belle Époque homes line the streets leading to Pangaltı and its Catholic cemeteries. In some, elderly Greek women dressed in black sit in the bay windows and watch the street – a habit their foremothers had indulged in for centuries. A Greek *kokona*, vigilant at her bay window, is a stereotypical image of Constantinople's Greek quarters, and observing the comings and goings on the street was a *kokona's* favourite pastime.

The old ladies who look out of the windows now are lonelier than their predecessors: their families, if any, have fled to Greece, the States, Australia or some other corner of the world. They rarely have the opportunity to speak their mother tongue – usually only after Sunday mass. They sit and stare at the street with an empty look. Their chances of glimpsing some familiar figure passing by are minimal. The last of the Madames, Istanbul's non-Muslim ladies, they are an image of a past era.

Istanbul's Jews: the "Minority of the State"?

A stone left on a tombstone to mark a visit, Jewish cemetery, Kuzguncuk

For a variety of reasons, any examination of the perplexing history of Turkey's Jews has, since the creation of the Turkish Republic, taken on markedly political overtones. That community's history, and especially the invitation of Spain's expelled Sephardim to settle in the Ottoman realm, has been used by the Turkish state as an argument to prove that the Ottoman Empire was tolerant and respectful to minorities, and to refute the bitter counter-accusations of Greeks and Armenians. Turkish organisations have used the "salvation" of Spain's Jews as a platform to win the sympathy of Jewish lobbies in the United States, where the Turkish Jewish diaspora has embarked in zealous lobbying on Turkey's behalf. Living under such a politicised background, the community itself has been left in the shade.

To make things even harder for those trying

to get a grasp of Istanbul Jewish culture, the community – unlike the homogeneous Greek and Armenian ones – is a linguistic and confessional medley and the guardian of a language and customs taken straight out of medieval Spain. Its history is one of the most perplexing in the Jewish diaspora. Yet what will also puzzle the outsider is that, unlike in the case of other minorities, the official voices of the community have a policy of portraying the Jewish experience in Turkey as completely trouble-free. Many prominent community members also regularly manifest their Turkishness.

Because of my interest in Judaism and my knowledge of Judeo-Spanish and Hebrew, I feel close to this 23,000-strong community. And I feel disappointed and sad to watch it being frequently verbally attacked both by Turks and by the other minorities, who accuse the Jewish community of having sold itself to the state.

Jews have been part of the local mosaic ever since Constantinople's foundation as New Rome. They first inhabited Khalkoprateia, the copper market, until Theodosius had them evicted from the walled city. They then settled in Stenon (present Hasköy), on the northern shore of the Golden Horn. The ghetto was described by Geoffroy de Villehardouin, leader of the Fourth Crusade, as "a rich and populous suburb".

Contrary to the claims of Turkish (and Turkish-Jewish) historians that Jews had a rough deal in Byzantium, anti-Semitic feelings never reached the level found in western Europe. Ecumenical councils condemned attempts to convert Jews, advocating that they were entitled to live as their customs demanded. Elias, the Nestorian bishop of the town of Nissibi in Upper Mesopotamia, wrote that Byzantines "tolerate Jews in their realm, permitting public cult and the building of synagogues. In Romanía [the Byzantine Empire] Jews openly say 'I'm a Jew', defend their faith and pray without having to account for it." The bishop lamented such treatment was not accorded to non-Orthodox Christians, branded heretics and persecuted.

Byzantine tolerance drew Jews from all over Europe. Ashkenazim from Hungary, Germany, southern Russia and Provence settled in Thessaloniki. Benjamin of Tudela, the Spanish-Jewish traveller, mentions Jewish communities in all major towns of Greece, the Aegean coast of Asia Minor and Cyprus. In his narration Byzantine Jews appear to live in peace and prosperity; the only significant tensions he saw were in Constantinople.

Benjamin reached the capital in the reign of Manuel Comnenus (1143-1180) and reported: "No Jew lives in the city; they've been sent beyond the Channel. They can only visit on business. There are 2000 rabbanites and 500

Karaites; a wall divides the two. Many are silk manufacturers, many traders. Quite a few are very affluent. But apart from Shlomo Ha-Mitsri, the Emperor's doctor, no Jew is allowed to ride. Because of the latter's influence, Jews enjoy many privileges. General oppression is worsened by the habit of tanners to throw their dirty water on the Jews' doorsteps. Oppression falls equally on good and bad Jews, but despite it they are rich, benevolent and respectful. The place they live in is called Pera."

Karaites, an ancient Jewish sect that originates from Baghdad and only accepts the Torah, rejecting rabbinical teaching, set its religious centre in Constantinople (it was moved to eastern Europe after the Fall). The oldest Jewish communities in Greece and Turkey are still called Romaniots (inhabitants of Romanía, ie Byzantium). Ironically, they are the only people to retain that Christian empire's name. Until early in the twentieth century, Turkey's Romaniot Jews mostly retained Greek as their mother tongue.

After the Fall, Mehmet the Conqueror founded the Chief Rabbinate, representative of the empire's Jews. In 1454 the rabbi of Edirne (Adrianople) sent an open letter to European Jewry, inviting them to "a country where everybody lives in peace in the shade of a vine or fig tree". During the rule of Mehmet's successor, Bayazid, one of the largest movements in Jewish history took place. In 1492, Ferdinand and Isabella of Spain decided to expel from their realm all Jews who wouldn't convert. Europe's largest Jewish community was thrown into turmoil. Thousands converted, but most decided to emigrate, leaving place names to testify to their centuries-old presence and taking the Spanish language and culture with them.

The new Ottoman Empire desperately needed skilled labour that Turks – nomadic warriors – couldn't provide. On suggestion from Constantinople's rabbi, Elias Kapsalis, Beyazid invited Spain's Jews to settle in his realm. Later, the invitation was extended to Spain's fleeing Muslims. A symbolic meaning was hidden behind the invitation: succeeding Byzantium, the Ottoman Empire was willing to stretch out a helping hand to all those that Catholic Europe rejected.

Ottoman Jewry became the diaspora's largest and most affluent group. Spanish speaking communities sprang up from Tangiers to Sophia and Smyrna. In Thessaloniki, Jews were in the majority from the 1500s to the early 1900s, which gave the city its alternative name – Madre de Israel. An amazed Spanish visitor in 1916 described it as "a Barcelona of the Levant". The newcomers were called Sephardim, from S'farad, the Jewish name for Spain. Their holy texts were translated into an old Spanish language known as Ladino, whereas they spoke a

Silver artefacts from synagogues

language called Djudeo Espanyol. The waves of Sephardim were followed by thousands of Marranos, Portuguese Jews who initially pretended to convert, then fled to the Ottoman lands to practise their faith unmolested.

In Constantinople, newcomers settled in the central district of Eminönü, by the bazaars, the Golden Horn quarters of Balat and Hasköy and the Bosphorus villages of Ortaköy (Europe) and Kuzguncuk (Asia). Balat, often called "Yahudi Balat" (Jewish Balat) became Europe's largest Jewish settlement. Jews continued to arrive as persecution raged through Europe. The Jews carried with them valuable innovations such as the printing press, introduced to Constantinople by the Nahmias brothers in 1493.

Jews willingly settled in the Ottoman realm. They retained an unending gratitude to their Ottoman saviours and were loyal to the state. Many were cultured and innovative and successful at infiltrating the empire's bourgeoisie and state apparatus. Alongside commerce, banking and medicine, Jews excelled in translation (for European diplomats and state officials) and diplomacy.

One of the most prominent was Portuguese "Marrano" Dona Gràcia Mendes Nasi, aka "La Senyora". A banker of legendary wealth, she organised with her nephew, Joseph Nasi, later Duke of Naxos and the Cyclades, the rescue of Marranos from Portugal's inquisition. When she fled from Italy to Constantinople, leading a Marrano caravan, she was triumphantly welcomed by the Sephardic authorities and presented to the sultan. La Senyora arrived with all her capital, and financed the naval battle of Lepanto on behalf of the Ottomans. Her power worried the rabbis, who accused Marranos of being crypto-Christians.

The slander led to the first schism in Ottoman Jewry: the Senyora and her community left the Chief Rabbinate and put themselves under the protection of the Magnifica Communità di Pera. Their descendants today, although subject to the Chief Rabbinate, maintain an "Italian Synagogue", also known as Call de los Francos (Synagogue of the Franks), in Galata. Echoing that submission to Genoa, many acquired Italian citizenship in the 1950s.

The second, far deeper, split was provoked by the teachings of a Smyrna Jew called Sabbetai Tsvi. Tsvi developed a creed mixing messianic with cabbalistic thought. Proclaiming himself the messiah, he toured the Ottoman Empire, calling Jews to assemble and resettle in the Land of Israel. Tsvi set the entire diaspora on fire, from Amsterdam to Baghdad. The Ottoman Rabbinate felt challenged and denounced him for subversion. Tsvi was arrested, brought before the sultan and given the option either to convert to Islam or die.

He opted for the former, bitterly disappointing world Jewry. Some 200 families followed his conversion and a new sect was born: the Sabbetaists or dönme (converts), who kept mystic Jewish rites under a Muslim veneer. Settling in Salonica, the community played an active role in the Young Turk Movement, the modernisation of the Ottoman Empire and the creation of the Republic. Considered Muslim, they left for Istanbul with the exchange of populations in 1923. Although they appear completely assimiliated, some at least retain their bizarre customs, making a secretive, almost underground, community.

The Sabbetaist crisis was temporary and the Ottoman Empire remained a promised land for Jews. Arrivals from Europe continued until 1910. A massive influx of Russian Jews fleeing the pogroms added to the tiny Ashkenazi community, while a reverse current of poor Ottoman Jews migrated, mainly to South America and France. Movements such as Hassidism, Reform and Zionism had no impact on Ottoman Jewry, conservative, linguistically fragmented and firmly attached to the state.

What did affect them was the Paris-based Alliance Israélite Universelle. Contrary to stereotypes of Jewish affluence, many Ottoman Jews lived in poverty. The Alliance set up schools, providing a secular-oriented education in French, orphanages and relief centres. Under Alliance influence, many bourgeois Jews substituted French for Djudeo-Espanyol.

No period better demonstrates Jewish loyalty to Turkey than that of Ottoman collapse. During the Greek Asia Minor campaign, Jews refused to participate in the Greek administration and on occasions openly challenged the Greek war effort. They were the only Ottoman minority that participated in the last elections for the Ottoman Parliament and didn't support the allied troops occupying Constantinople between 1918 and 1923.

Greek war actions in Asia Minor created friction. Jews campaigned on the Turkish side and provoked the wrath of the Greeks. The Greek army and local Greeks at times set Jewish shops and homes ablaze in Asia Minor towns, whilst some Jewish shops were looted. Jews lost homes and businesses in arson attacks on Asia Minor towns. Jews celebrated Turkish victory, which eliminated their primary commercial rivals – Greeks and Armenians. Former Chief Rabbi Haim Naoum was the only non-Muslim delegate in the Turkish representation to the Lausanne peace talks.

Unexpectedly, Jews became the prime target of the new Republic, founded on the nation-state ideal and by definition suspicious to minorities. After the Armenian genocide and the Greek exodus, commerce remained in Jewish hands and resentment therefore became focused on them. A century of continuous defeats and loss of territory made Turks develop a virulent nationalism, calling for religious, cultural and racial unity. Xenophobic voices started to claim that all "foreigners" (and non-Muslims were seen as such) hated Turkey and conspired against it.

The Turkish press began to accuse Jews of treason. The treason was not speaking Turkish, not intermarrying with Turks and leading a different lifestyle. Justice Minister Esat Bozkurt's words, "The real master of this land is the Turk; those who aren't pure Turks have only one right, the right to be slaves," epitomised the new order. The press accused Jews of ingratitude for speaking the tongue of their persecutors and of "living like foreigners". Conservative Muslims believed the Kemalist revolution and the secular Republic were nothing more than a Jewish plot against Islam. There was a rumour that Atatürk was a Sabbetaist. The press advocated expulsion of the Jews back to Spain or to Palestine.

Up against such hostility the community had to develop survival tactics. A Jew called Moise Cohen from the city of Serres in Greek Macedonia claimed that nationalism rested on language, not religion. He said Turkey's Jews should feel "Turks of the Jewish faith" and adopt Turkish as their mother tongue. He changed his name to Tekin Alp and pressed others to do likewise.

Torah scrolls in typical Sephardic style

Families abandoned surnames they had carried for centuries; first names were also Turkified. Turkish replaced French as the language of instruction. A "Citizen Speak Turkish" campaign was launched, forcing minorities to abandon their own languages. There was much pressure from the press on the Jewish community to renounce the special status that the Lausanne Treaty conferred on Turkey's non-Muslims. The community did so in 1927 and attacks subsided.

In 1934, a wave of riots decimated Jewish communities in Thrace, forcing Jews to flee to Istanbul or abroad. Turkish state policy regarding Jews was ambivalent to say the least. On one hand the government called in Jewish academics who had left, or been forced out of,

Nazi Germany to work in Turkish universities. On the other, it applied a ruinous property tax on all non-Muslims in 1942, aiming to end their prominence in business life. Those who failed to pay the exorbitant amounts were interned in forced labour camps, where some died.

In a world plagued by anti-Semitism, Jews' very right of existence in Turkey was questioned. Turkish Jews found refuge in serving the Turkish ideal. This, together with their past campaigning on the Ottoman side, earned them the animosity of the country's Christians, who were much more assertive in claiming their difference.

Turkish Jews in Israel and the United States maintain close ties with Turkey. The children of those persecuted for not speaking Turkish are now setting up Turkish language societies and culture centres. They actively campaign in Turkey's favour, and are portrayed in the press as the land's defenders against Greek and Armenian lobbies. In Turkey itself, Jews are the second largest and the financially most successful minority. They live a low-profile existence. Some have changed their names or use a Turkish name in public and a Jewish one in private. Many carry foreign passports (mainly Spanish or Italian) as well as Turkish ones. Three brutal attacks at Istanbul synagogues in 1986 and 2003 have made the community even more introvert and security conscious.

As is the case elsewhere, anti-Semitism is intertwined with popular perceptions of the state of Israel. Jews and Israelis are equated in the public's eyes and the traditional Muslim sympathy for the Palestinian cause creates resentment against the country's Jews. Yet what differentiates Turkish anti-Semitism is that it doesn't primarily target the Jews, but the dönme (Sabbetaist) community. The Sabbetaists or "Salonicans" are accused of pretending to be Muslim, whilst sticking to their ancestral Jewish creed. Due to their apocryphal faith, Sabbetaists are equated to freemasons and portrayed, especially in the Islamic press, as a secretive caste ruling the country much against the interests of "pure" Turks. The bigotry against Sabbetaists and the characteristics ascribed to them remind one of racist accusations against Jews elsewhere. Islamists have often launched a "witch-hunt", branding members of the secular ruling classes as dönme and hence "impure" Turks.

Despite Turkey's official intimacy with Israel, much challenged under the current Islamic government, anti-Semitism is widespread. Hitler's *Mein Kampf* was a bestseller in Turkey in 2005. Anti-Semitic proclamations in the press have deeply worried the community, which understandably has reacted by keeping an even lower profile.

Stained glass from Hasköy's Maalem Synagogue

The hidden face of the metropolis: Istanbul's Hebraica

Jews are the past of Balat, these lively children are its present

Istanbul's Jewish heritage is as rich and diverse as it is unexplored and forgotten. More than 25 synagogues, vast old cemeteries and dilapidating old quarters are scattered all over the city. Istanbul's Judaica are concentrated in the old ghettos of Balat and Hasköy, and the Bosphorus villages of Ortaköy and Kuzguncuk. Ever since the 1986 attack by Palestinian terrorists on Galata's Neve Shalom, the community's largest synagogue, any visit to Istanbul's Hebraica is done by permission of Turkey's Chief Rabbinate. This is a complication necessitated by security concerns, and should by no means dissuade the visitor as permissions are usually granted quickly and without much hassle.

The Chief Rabbinate is situated in a modest building in the Pera borough of Şişhane, near Tüne Square. Here was the beginning of Pera's Jewish land, with its heart at Kuledibi, at the foot of the Galata Tower. One can still spot Jewish dates and the coat of arms of Castile, a reminder of the Sephardim's roots, above the main doors of apartment buildings. An official from the Rabbinate's secretariat prepared my visit and I was able to see all major Jewish sites in three consecutive mornings.

I started my pilgrimage at Kuledibi, settled in the second half of the nineteenth century by Jews from Hasköy and Balat and Jewish refugees from Russia. Although some buildings are the superb legacy of an affluent middle class, Kuledibi was known as a poor neighbourhood rife with prostitution. Its most bewildering trait was the proximity of brothels and synagogues. To reach the gate of the Ashkenazi synagogue, you had to cross a row of brothels, elderly Jews remember.

Most Kuledibi brothels were Jewish run with Jewish prostitutes: families owning them had close ties with the other centre of Jewish prostitution at the time, Buenos Aires. More than 200 – mostly Ashkenazi – households survived on prostitution, which was exclusively in minority hands until the proclamation of the Republic. Jews dominated the Kuledibi area, Greeks and Armenians Abanoz Sokak in Pera and Galata's Kemeraltı. (Ottoman law prohibited Muslim women from prostituting themselves.)

The exodus of the poorest Jews to Israel in the 1950s ended Jewish prostitution. The borough today is a busy commercial quarter in daytime and silent at night. The large brothel at Alageyik Street is the sole reminder of past debauchery. Under gentrification, Kuledibi is becoming one of Istanbul's trendiest boroughs, a magnet for bohemians and yuppies alike.

By the Galata Tower, on Büyük Hendek Street, is Neve Shalom, Istanbul's largest synagogue. A dull 1950s building, it has been tragically associated with the community's greatest fear. Twenty two people died in an attack in 1986 carried out by the Palestinian terrorist organisation Abu Nidal. An abortive attack was made during the 500th anniversary celebrations of the Sephardim's arrival from Spain in 1992. In November 2003, a suicide bomber in a passing vehicle killed three worshippers and many Muslim passers by. This assault was planned and carried out by Turks, something that greatly upset the community.

Much more appealing architecturally is the Ashkenazi synagogue on Yüksek Kaldırım, near Karaköy Square. In Moorish style, the 1901 synagogue catered to Istanbul's small Ashkenazi community, mostly refugees of the pogroms in Tsarist Russia. The Star of David atop a long metal stick on the dome, visible from miles away, marks the position of the synagogue.

The guard, a friendly old man, was a descen-

The Italian Synagogue ("Call de los Francos") is situated near the Podestà building in Galata

dant of those pogrom refugees and could speak fluent Russian. As I couldn't, we managed with Hebrew and French. He complained that Greek Jews never visit (taking me for one). I explained there are few left, most having perished in the Shoah. I marvelled at the wooden interior and the dome, painted blue with golden stars. The guardian asked me to recite a Hebrew prayer with him. I managed that easily but gave myself away shortly after: as he pulled the curtain, inviting me to venerate the Torah scrolls, I kissed them (as I'd seen Istanbul Jews do) and automatically crossed myself! He looked thunderstruck and I felt very embarrassed!

Entrance to Jewish *apartment* with Christian and Jewish dates, Kuledibi

The Italian synagogue stands besides the Catholic monastery of San Pietro e Paolo and a portion of Galata's fortifications. The synagogue, replacing a much older one of the 1880s, is a couple of streets from the Palazzo de la Commune, where the ruling council of the Magnifica Communità di Pera convened. This is no coincidence: the Italian synagogue belongs to the Marranos, the community of La Senyora, which chose the protection of the Genoese over that of the Rabbinate. The synagogue only opens on Saturdays and festivals, or for special visits.

On its doorstep, a middle-aged blonde lady called Rashel was expecting me. To my amazement, she was wearing a kippa! This is the latest fashion in Turkish Jewry (this headgear is normally reserved for men). Rashel showed me around. The synagogue was in pristine condition, its interior less impressive than its gothic-style façade. My attention was drawn to the bright yellow caps below the chairs – essential earthquake protection for the faithful. Rashel said she spoke Turkish with her children at home, but she herself had been raised speaking Judeo-Spanish. "Assimilation is unavoidable," she said. "We're a small community. Television, the papers, everything is in Turkish. Most of my children's friends are Turkish." She lamented the death of Judeo-Spanish after half a millennium. "But we wouldn't want our children to be laughed at because of their weird Turkish accent, like we were at their age," she said. "We must keep a very low profile."

The pinkish building with a rose window and small dome on Karaköy Square is Zülfaris, built in 1671, Galata's central synagogue, now housing Istanbul's Jewish Museum. The wooden interior is the main attraction: the museum is essentially a political manifesto. It was inaugurated to commemorate the 500th anniversary of the arrival of the Sephardim – "The 500 Years Foundation" as it's called – and it aims "to show the world the bond of brotherhood between the Turkish and Jewish nations and the tolerance shown to Jews in Turkey since Ottoman times". More than just a domestic organisation, the foundation promotes Turkish interests abroad.

Typical row houses in Balat Aryentro

Jewish existence in Turkey is portrayed as full of happiness and free of persecution, in a "climate of unparalleled tolerance and acceptance". The Thrace pogroms of 1934 and the infamous property tax are unmentioned. Prominent writer Aziz Nesin protested against the "selective amnesia" of Turkish Jews, attributed by Turkish-Jewish writer Rifat Bali to a past of constant accusations of disloyalty. The community's press organ, Shalom, denies anti-Semitism exists in Turkey. Bali distinguishes between the "Jews of the state" and the "other Jews", not bound by the community policy.

From the Karaköy boat terminal I took the Golden Horn ferry to Balat, a district on the Old City shore of the Golden Horn. Once Constantinople's largest borough, it is named after the Greek word *palation* (palace). This area spread out right below the Blachernae Palace. Jews settled here from late Byzantine times and tombstones with Romaniot names have been unearthed. Some came from Balkan cities, fleeing the crusaders and the constant fighting between Greeks, Serbs, Bulgarians and Turks.

Balat's oldest surviving synagogues – Ahrida and Yanbol – were founded by Romaniots of Macedonia fleeing Ottoman conquest and ethnic strife. The street where Ahrida (Ohrid) synagogue stands is called Vodina Street, after the Slavic name of the Greek town of Edessa. The synagogues dedicated to Thessaloniki and Castoria are in ruins. These two synagogues were established by Romaniots carried over from those towns as part of the Conqueror's repopulation scheme. Then the Sephardic tide arrived. Balat once had 19 synagogues, each with a congregation of different origins and customs.

Migration to Israel and to more affluent districts left Balat with about 20 Jews. The old Jewish row houses, similar but slightly more modest than the Greek ones of Phanari, are decaying in the hands of poor Anatolians. Some synagogues have been closed for years. Only the shells stand of several others, whilst one or two have been converted to parking lots.

Balat had always been poor and shabby. Travellers' descriptions do much to undo the stereotype of Jewish plutocracy. The anti-Semitic Theofile Gautier wrote: "We reached a neighbourhood where walls looked leprous… the grey wood peeled off like dandruff… Skinny dogs slept in stinking black mud." Edmondo d'Amicis infiltrated Balat "which winds like some dirty snake along the shore of the Golden Horn" to judge whether Istanbul Jewesses were as beautiful as those of Morocco. He writes of a "smell of rotten wood, dirt, filthy children and "old men who look like resurrected lepers". The French teacher Bertrand Bareilles dismissed Balat and Hasköy as two of Constantinople's filthiest districts, where pools of still water "stink like a dead body".

Locals directed me to Ahrida synagogue. Seconds after I rang the bell, a blonde woman with bright blue eyes opened the gate. "Welcome honey, I love punctuality," she said in Spanish. Because of my Latin-sounding surname she had thought I was Sephardic. So this was Madame Corine, the guardian of Balat's synagogues. I'd been warned she could be "difficult". The first thing I noticed were the eyes, the second her voice, the voice of a commander ordering troops. The sheer volume and tone could make a criminal flee. I loved her to bits more than any synagogue she was Balat's treasure. "Well, want to be shown around or what?"

Istanbul's oldest synagogue is set in a walled and shady courtyard. The only thing that distinguishes its modest exterior – with its typical Ottoman pointed windows – from a hammam or bedesten (a type of Turkish covered market) is a canopy over the main door. Ahrida dates from Byzantine times. Destroyed by fire, it was rebuilt in 1694 in the tulip style of Ottoman baroque. The self-proclaimed Jewish messiah Sabbetai Tsvi tried to preach his theories here. When the rabbis complained, Tsvi fled to Salonica. The wooden interior boasts an internal hidden dome: at the time of construction it was prohibited for non-Muslims to add domes to their shrines.

Ahrida's most striking element is the bema, in the form of a ship. Some claim that it alludes to Noah's Ark; others that it symbolises the galleys that carried the exiled Sephardim from Spain to the Ottoman realm in 1492. Madame Corine said that men from other districts have to come to Ahrida so that the ten men minimum for a service to be held is met. There are no more than five Jewish men left in Balat.

Corine led me to her shop a few blocks away. She trades in iron parts, "one of only two women in Turkey", her Turkish husband Mustafa explained with pride. He is originally from Antep in southern Turkey, near the Syrian border. As much as Corine appears rather harsh and despotic, he is soft-spoken and mild. Corine explained: "My father died very young. I was older than my brother. I had to carry on with the business. It was tough. Mind you, we were brought up differently. I rarely ever ventured out of the house unaccompanied by my parents. Entering this market I joined another world. A world dominated by men. It's hard for a woman to command respect."

Their families didn't object to their marriage. Corine denied claims of Turkish anti-Semitism. "Unlike so many countries in Europe, no one vandalises our cemeteries," she said. But she denounced both the inactivity of the community in protecting certain shrines and the politics of the state, which often prefers to see minority monuments disappear. She spoke to me mostly in Ladino, with a lot of Greek thrown in. "The relations between the minorities were harmonious. It's from Greek friends that I know my little Greek."

Corine must have liked me, impressed that a young Christian who speaks Hebrew and Ladino was so interested in her community. She showed me something that visitors rarely have the chance to see: Yanbol synagogue, in the courtyard beside her shop, boasts a superb painted ceiling, depicting that city in Bulgaria from where parish members came in late Byzantine times.

Of the 17 other synagogues that once dotted Balat, only four stand: Ishtipol (of Jews from the Bulgarian city of Ishtip), Chana, once housing the rabbinical court, Selanico (of Salonican Romaniots) and Castoria (of Jews from that Greek city). The last three are ruined.

A number of churches are scattered around Balat: three Greek ones, Taksiarhes, the Virgin of Balino and St Demetrius of Xyloporta, and the Armenian Surp Hresdagabed opposite Yanbol synagogue. They testify to the presence of a Christian contingent, absent today like the Jews. The narrow streets are dotted with small shops. The rehabilitation of the Balat market is part of the famous "Fener Balat Rehabilitation Programme". Smoky coffee shops are frequented by Anatolian men of all ages, who kill time over tea, card games and backgammon. Corine walked me to the quay, from where I crossed by ferry to Hasköy.

Opposite Balat, on the northern shore of the channel, stretches Constantinople's oldest Jewish quarter. Starting off as Stenon, the area was renamed Pikridion, after a monastery founded there in the reign of Byzantine empress Irene the Athenian. Many more followed, the most famous becoming Haghia Paraskevi: a church dedicated to the saint still survives in Hasköy. Jews were settled here in the reign of Theodosius, who evicted them from the walled city. They were Romaniots, with a Karaite minority later added. The borough was renamed Hasköy in Ottoman times and received the Jews ousted from Eminönü in 1591, when the Yeni Camii was built on their quarter.

Greek historian Scarlatos Vizantios describes the district as "a crowded and filthy borough by the coast... exposed to the winds, the summer heat and the channel's fumes". Hasköy was inhabited "by Greeks and Armenians, largely artisans and tavern owners, but mostly by Jews". The Jewish contingent contained Romaniots, Sephardim and Karaites, and the shrine of the latter survives here. D'Amicis wrote of Hasköy: "Scarred dirty children play in the mud. Hunchbacked women in tatters sit working on the doorsteps.

The church of Surp Hresdagabed and the Armenian School remind that non-Jews also resided in Balat

The modern city peeps out behind the piled up tombstones of Hasköy's Jewish Cemetery

Mud and debris everywhere. As if we'd been travelling for a week, we started to miss Pera."

Present Hasköy is a concrete mess. A walled compound topped by barbed wire dominates a central square. The Hebrew inscription on a marble plaque above a gate proved I was in the right place. "They're waiting for you in the grocery store," an unknown man shouted and disappeared. Upon entering the store I saw a man holding a faxed copy of my passport. "You must be Mr Massavetas..." Jak, the guardian, doesn't live in Hasköy. Its last Jews opted for better neighbourhoods...

The shabbiness of the outer wall was succeeded by the serenity of a leafy courtyard. The external simplicity of the rarely visited Maalem synagogue shelters a sumptuous interior, recently restored in a most unfortunate manner. Garish colours and excessive use of polish have created "the apotheosis of kitsch", as an old Jew of the district complained. Maalem's bema has the form of a galley, like the one in Ahrida. The "hidden" internal dome is decorated with depictions of the Promised Land. "If you want the living memory of our community, go to the pension house," Jak said.

•••

The neoclassic façade of the former Alliance School for Boys contrasts sharply with the dreary surroundings. I knocked on the doorbell by the intimidating metal door. "Are you our Greek visitor?" a voice behind asked in Turkish. "Yes," I replied in Spanish, handing my passport. The door opened. "You're late. Everybody's waiting for you." The guard still spoke in Turkish. "I'm sorry, I got a bit lost." The director came towards the door and spoke in Hebrew. "The grandmothers are so impatient to meet you." "I hope communication won't be a problem," I said. "I speak Turkish, but my Ladino and Hebrew are far better." She smiled. "You won't need those."

I went up the staircase slightly bewildered. Around me, everything was spick and span, modern and in good taste. This didn't look like a charitable institution; it looked like a plush hotel. The staff walked up and down cheerfully in their immaculate white uniforms, some escorting one of the elderly to the garden.

"Don't tell me!" an old man exclaimed in Spanish. "You are our Greek visitor! I'm Albert. Come, let me show you my room." We took the elevator to the first floor. I followed him into a double room, neat and tidy. A small mezuza decorated the door. On the walls were pictures of a middle-aged couple, menoras and photographs of the Holy Land. "That's my wife," Albert continued in his characteristic medieval Spanish, pointing to an old black and white wedding photograph. "And these I have made," he said proudly, as I noticed some flowers made out of tiny coloured beads. "We keep ourselves busy with handicrafts. And these are from an excursion to Bodrum we made last year," he said, pointing to photographs of tanned and cheerful seniors in some seaside restaurant.

News does travel fast, even among the elderly. A grandmother walking with the support of a crutch appeared in Albert's door. "I think you're hiding our guest from us," she said. She then walked forwards and, to my amazement, said, in fluent, well-articulated Greek: "Welcome, my child. My name is Ester. I'm very happy to be able to speak Greek again. It's been some time. I've forgotten so much." I was dumbfounded. "But you speak like a Greek!" I said. "Certainly not like a Greek," she answered, "I speak like a Politissa (Constantinopolitan). I am Jewish, but my best friend was Greek. I grew up in Pera. Everybody in Pera was Greek then. Those who weren't spoke fluent Greek. Then they all left. Before they went, Pera was our little Paris," she said nostalgically in French. "You do speak French, of course? All well-brought up Greeks speak French. But come, I'll introduce you to everyone."

The corridor was now filled with elderly women talking eagerly in Judeo-Spanish. At our appearance, a chorus of "kaloselthes, kalosethelthes" ("welcome") furthered my astonishment. I had never expected that elderly Jews would be eager to freshen their Greek. "Athens!" a woman who introduced herself as Carmona said. "I would have so much liked to go there once. I have many friends there. After the Events (the anti-Greek pogrom in September 1955), many of our Greeks left. It was in '55, I think. The Greeks have gone now. But so has our youth, our relatives. That's life," she said, but remained surprisingly cheerful. "What can we do?" She told me she was raised in Galata, and her knowledge of Greek was natural, as there were only Greeks around. Most of her childhood friends were Greek. "They all remarked how the Greek I spoke was slightly different from the local vernacular."

One lady was Ashkenazi – the only one around. You could tell she had been a Grande Dame, a Pera socialite. "I am Caroline," she said in such a grand tone that everybody else burst into laughter. She spoke in a combination of Greek, French, Italian and German: "The Greeks had the best balls, I loved them. I loved their weddings, they threw rice and flowers on the couple. And Tatavla… the carnival… so many memories. They left and our lives became so boring, so parochial. I've been to Greece. Castoria, Kavala, Athens, the islands…"

"I am Vida," said another woman. "My great grandparents came from Castoria. I have been there. Half of my family remained in Greece, but some of them the Germans put in the oven," a typical manner here of referring to the Holocaust. Her hair was snow white and her eyes deep blue. She must have been a beauty once, I thought. "I came to Balat as a bride." she said. "Of course I speak Greek. It's a bit corrupted with French and Turkish, but Greek it is," she said proudly. "I miss Aspasia, my best friend. They lived on the floor above us. We had such a happy life! The Greeks do know how to have fun! Have you ever heard of the Tatavla carnival? I went there every year with

Typical street in Balat

Aspasia and her family. What a life! We dressed up, we drank, we sang, we made merry. Then that bloody Cyprus thing started and our friends were evicted... You must have so much fun in Athens. Do you play the laterna there often?" The laterna... how could I explain that this organ belongs to a life long gone and forgotten? Like the Tatavla carnival...

"What a life," Caroline mumbled. "Now the flowers have withered in our little paradise..." "What flowers?" I asked. "We, of course – the minority girls. The beauties of the Levant," Vida said thoughtfully: "We've lived interesting lives; we've seen so much and have so many stories to tell. But we're old; we'll soon die and our stories will die with us."

"We are the last Politissas, the last Estampolianas," Ester added. "Come, let me show you our garden."

As the elevator arrived, the women stood up in unison and sang for me in Greek: "Good bye, adieu forever. We talked over it, but it was but a dream, so we forgot all about it..." Constantinople's most famous song in the mouths of a Sephardic congregation. "Opa!" Ester cried out.

•••

Before heading to the Jewish cemetery I wanted to see a bit more of the old Jewish district. Here and there are scattered ruined synagogues – old rectangular brick buildings of medium height. Some are immediately identifiable from the barbed wire that encircles their walls. Often not more than a shell remains, used as a parking lot or warehouse. Other synagogues are sealed off, decaying silently away from the eyes of passers by. A gloomy sight and a gloomy thought.

Heading towards the coast, I noticed a Hebrew inscription above a door. A terrible noise came from the building's interior, and metal parts were scattered on the floor. A worker approached me. "This used to be a synagogue," he said. "Do you want to see the inside?" He called to a young man named Albert, obviously a Jew. "The synagogue is owned by my family, but we don't have the means to restore it." He led me inside. The noise was intolerable.

There was a wooden balustrade and a wooden ceiling with carvings representing geometric patterns and the Star of David. Here and there were holes in the wood. An internal dome was visible in the centre, amidst a chaos of stored materials. The building had undergone significant damage and was a heartbreaking sight.

Albert took me to the family business, in a modern building right opposite the synagogue. It was a small business dealing in iron parts, and the two young sons, Albert and Yosef Ozel, were actively involved. They were the last Jewish family with a business in the area, Albert said. They did not live in the district but in the modern suburb of Ulus, home to many Jews and Istanbul's Jewish school.

"Hasköy has gone to the dogs," Yosef said with contempt. The family had taken up a Turkish surname, and the brothers said they did not use the "Jewish" versions of their names in public. They preferred the Turkish names Alp and Yusuf instead. "Do you feel Turkish?" I asked. "No," they replied in unison. "In the army they called us *gâvur* (infidel) and so on. Neither do they accept us deep down, nor do we feel the same as them. We have another culture." "Your community says Istanbul's Jews *are* Turks – Turks of a different religion," I said. "They say this because they have to say it." Albert replied.

"So, when a Turk asks you, you wouldn't say you belong to a different *nation* – the Sephardic?"

"Are you out of your mind?" said Albert. Even local Greeks stress their Turkishness to stave off harassment." He spoke with the angry despair of someone who feels his situation is not understood.

I walked to Halıcıoğlu, on the next hill. "On every corner you encounter a new nation or creed... graves and mosques, churches and synagogues... beautiful Armenian ladies... you listen to Greek, Armenian and Judeo-Spanish..." wrote Edmondo d'Amicis about what is now a concrete mass bisected by the peripheral highway. Minority memories are entombed.

The huge Jewish cemetery spreads over a number of hills on both parts of the highway. It dates from 1582 and is still in use, comprising 22,000 tombs. Its inscriptions are a register of Istanbul Jewry – Romaniot, Karaite and Sephardic. It's an impressive sight, entire hills covered with what appear to be scattered stone boxes.

One segment is unfenced, full of weeds dancing in the air, but no trees. Cylindrical marble tombstones, like small sarcophagi, and rectangular tombs seem to have been sprinkled by some unknown hand. The oldest bear decorative reliefs representing tulips and other Ottoman symbols, and inscriptions in Hebrew and Ladino (medieval Spanish written in Hebrew letters). There's nothing resembling a path; struggling my way through, I often fell into holes. Here and there, tombstones were piled in heaps. The more recent inscriptions were in Turkish and in Turkish were the names of the deceased – the fruits of the Turkification campaign. People entered and strolled around; some gypsy families were actually picnicking on the graves.

The cemetery has always impressed: "It's a wide, open space, full of countless flat tombstones, the miserable image of a city destroyed in an earthquake, without a tree or flower… deserted and depressing as the site of a major disaster," wrote d'Amicis. Bertrand Bareilles found "tombstones with Hebrew inscriptions dipped in mud, not one properly erect".

Desolation reigns. Graves are covered by weeds, tombstones are broken, inscriptions illegible. In recent graves, piles of little stones, each denoting a visit, testify that relatives still come. What has changed dramatically from earlier travellers' times is the panorama: the slopes offer views of the Golden Horn's upper half. The familiar silhouettes of Phanari, Balat, the Byzantine walls and Tekfursaray lie opposite. But instead of cemeteries and parks, the city is now surrounded by slums, highways and flyovers. The source of the Golden Horn, once the idyllic picnic spot of the "Sweet Waters of Europe", is a wasteland of dirty water and slums. The constant noise of the automobiles from the highway kills any sound of nature.

Further uphill, a much better preserved section of the cemetery hides behind a tall wall. As if to answer writers' accusations, community authorities have planted a number of small cypresses. Some of the tombstones here are of stunning beauty and in excellent condition. I spent time deciphering the lines in Ladino and Judeo-Espanyol (written in a Latin phonetic script). This medieval Castilian tongue, with Jewish, Catalan, Greek and Turkish vocabulary, recalls the narrow, twisting lanes of the "Juderías", the Jewish quarters of Girona, Barcelona, Toledo, Salamanca, the fortress-like houses and synagogues, part of Spain's ethnic mix for centuries. On these hills, part of Spain survives, in exile for more than half a millennium… On the northern edge lies the less congested Karaite section. Here inscriptions are in Hebrew and Greek written with Hebrew letters.

I felt very moved deciphering the beautiful Hebrew script. Spanish first names (Angel, Gracia, Carmona, Vida, Dona, Carmen) for the Sephardim, whose surnames betray their roots: Toledano, Pisano, de Ávila, de Narbona, Romano. Romaniots often opted for Greek names (Polychronis, Stamatoula, Efrosinia, Maroula, Hannoula, Afendra), while many surnames of both Romaniots and Karaites could feature in any Greek phone directory (Axiotes, Galanos, Iacovides, Kandiotes, Kastorianos, Korkides, Livanos). The tombstones will perhaps become the last relics of millennia-old communities, wiped out by immigration and assimilation. To exorcise the feeling of desolation, I put some stones on the most decayed tombstones, marking my visit as Jewish custom dictates, and then rushed away as darkness began to fall.

Would-be conquerors turn refugees: Russians in Constantinople

Madame Alyeksandra, born a subject of the Tsar, is the guardian of Haghios Andreas, a rooftop church in Galata

Russians have had a long and intimate affair with Constantinople. Their futile attempts to conquer the Byzantine and later plans to claim the Ottoman capital for Christendom are well known. Much less known is the fact that there was a huge community of Russians in the last days of the Ottoman city. Many are surprised to find Russian tombstones in Istanbul's Greek cemeteries and Russian dishes such as chicken kiev and beef stroganoff on menus.

The affair goes back a very long way. The Rus, as they were then known, caused a sensation when they appeared in Constantinople in 860, a fair and noisy lot in narrow wooden boats. What brought them down the Bosphorus was the legend of Tsarigrad, the "City of Caesars". The rather amateurish naval attack was of course abortive. But the Russians had come out of their frozen steppes to make an appearance before the world. Constantinople had already exercised a grip on their imaginations, and would do so much more after their christening.

Orthodoxy was brought to Russia via a marriage alliance. Vladimir, Duke of Kiev (then Russia's largest city), formed an alliance with Emperor Basil II, marrying his younger sister, Anna Porphyrogennete, in 988. Greeks considered pagans as barbarians, and Basil set Vladimir's conversion to Orthodoxy as a precondition for the marriage. Vladimir accepted, more concerned about having to part with his concubines than with the pagan idols. He proclaimed his new faith a state religion, called over Greek missionaries and ordered that his subjects be baptised, if necessary by force. Vladimir and Anna were canonised by the Russian church.

Tradition portrays Orthodoxy's arrival as the result not of politics, but of Vladimir's soul searching. An inquisitive Vladimir sent envoys to investigate the monotheistic religions and propose one for the ruler and people of Russia, the story goes. After much wandering, the agents were so impressed attending a service in Haghia Sophia that they "didn't know whether they were in heaven or earth". They thus proposed Orthodoxy as Russia's religion…

Whatever the beginnings were, adoption of Orthodoxy tied Russians firmly to Byzantium. They copied its architecture, iconography, and liturgy and adopted the Cyrillic alphabet, an adaptation of the Greek for Slavic tongues. Constantinople became their alma mater, site of Russian pilgrimage and home to a Russian colony. The spell it cast on Russians is evident in the text of Russian visitor Anthony of Novgorod. When he visited in 1200, he left the most detailed list of Constantinople's monuments and relics of any foreigner lucky enough to admire it before 1204. Five more accounts of Russian pilgrims survive from Palaeologan times, mostly concerned with churches and holy relics.

When the Ottomans surrounded Constantinople, Russia, the "Great Orthodox Nation", had succumbed to the Mongols and wouldn't free itself until decades after the Fall. Loss of Constantinople deeply affected Russians, who became obsessed with the "restoration of the Cross on Haghia Sophia". But the Fall also meant that the political centre of the Orthodox world moved to Moscow, self-titled "Third Rome" and protector of all Orthodox people. A Moscow Patriarchate was established in 1589, yet Russians continued to flow to Constantinople as pilgrims and traders and the tsars continued to make donations to the Ecumenical Patriarchate.

Meanwhile, Greeks developed a myth that "the blond nation" would rescue them, reclaim-

The immense "han" topped by the Russian chapel of Haghios Andreas, Karaköy, Galata

ing their former capital for Christendom. The only Orthodox nation to have escaped Muslim rule was very much aware of these expectations. Russo-Turkish wars occurred every 20 to 30 years after Peter and Catherine the Great consolidated Russian power and turned their attention south. Taking the Crimea from the Ottomans, they focused on the Black Sea, the straits and the Aegean.

The tsars portrayed their campaign to control the commercial waterways as a war of Christian light against Muslim barbarism. Catherine the Great's "Greek Project" was a dream of the Russians recapturing Constantinople and restoring it as the centre of a reborn Byzantium. Catherine named her grandson Constantine, preparing him for the throne of the Palaeologi. Many Greeks joined the Russian army and diplomatic corps and planned a Greek uprising.

Russia remained cold when the Greek War of Independence erupted in 1821, fearsome that any development could upset the post-Napoleonic status quo. If foreign intervention did help Greek independence, it was the actions of England, France and Russia in the 1827 naval battle of Navarone – prompted as much by the will to check Russian expansion southwards as by humanitarian concerns.

This concern at Russian expansionism made England and France join forces with Turkey to attack Russia in the Crimean War in 1856, leaving us with the famous song words "and the Russians will not get Constantinople". They didn't, but they arrived once more at its very outskirts some years later.

In 1876 the Bulgarians declared independence and Turks responded by massacres. Russia marched to the aid of fellow Slavs, liberated Bulgaria and moved in on Constantinople. Russian cannons resounded in the city as they reached San Stefano, a remote suburb on the Marmara (present Yeşilköy). A terrified Abdul Hamid signed the treaty of San Stefano, which created a huge Bulgarian kingdom from the Danube to the Aegean. This was the last Russian advance on Constantinople. Russians erected a memorial outside San Stefano commemorating their victory and their 200,000 dead in Bulgaria.

The results of the treaty of San Stefano caused alarm in the great powers, who reversed them by the Treaty of Berlin that same year, creating a small Bulgarian kingdom, vassal of the sultan. Yet the monument in San Stefano stood, reminiscent of Russian desires for Constantinople. Unsurprisingly, the fiercely nationalistic Committee for Union and Progress ("Young Turks") that came to power in 1909 dynamited it. The action was filmed – the first Turkish film shooting ever.

pp 232-233: The abandoned rooftop church of Prophet Elijah seen through the windows of Haghios Andreas

Lycee Saint Benoît on Karakoy's Kemeraltı Street

When hundreds of thousands of Russians invaded after the Great War, they had no conquering intentions whatsoever, even though Russia and Turkey had once more fought in different camps. Russia withdrew from the war in 1917, after the October Revolution. Two years later, the collapse of the imperial "White Army" before the Bolshevik advance made millions of Russians embark for exile from Batum, Odessa and the Crimean ports. Constantinople was the first port of call. Constantinopolitans called the newcomers "White Russians", alluding to their allegiance to the Tsar. The first arrived in 1918 and they remained in great num-

Details of murals in the church of Haghios Andreas

for the beautiful and liberated modern woman. Harashos also introduced short skirts and short hairstyles. Russian aristocrats had been used to buying their clothes in Paris, and their wardrobes rejuvenated Constantinople's fashion scene. Russian noblemen brought in the "monocle" fashion, ever since associated with distinction.

Instances of Turkish men neglecting their wives for a "harasho" mistress became commonplace in the early 1920s, prompting much commentary in the satirical press and action from cheated wives. Many filed for divorce, which is interesting given the Muslim theocracy of the time. A committee of Turkish women demanded the expulsion of Russian women on account of their "immorality". Ironically, similar events have taken place 80 years later, after the influx of a new tide of economic migrants from the former USSR.

From 1920 to 1940, Russian joined Constantinople's linguistic melange. Those who stayed soon dominated the entertainment sector, setting up restaurants, bars and bistros. They became music, painting and language teachers, singers, musicians and dancers, photographers, receptionists, tailors and manufacturers of all sorts of quality products, athletes, flower sellers and interpreters. They introduced ballet to Turkey, furthered the teaching and appreciation of classical music, and cultivated impressionist painting and photography. Among the immigrants were members of the Smirnoff family, who brought vodka to the city.

After the Republic's foundation, many White Russians acquired Turkish citizenship.

Mass in the Russian rooftop church of Haghios Panteleimon

Today, only a handful remain of that extraordinary community, which for a decade numbered around 12 percent of the city's population. Many were driven away by the nationalism of the 1930s and 1940s, or simply looked for opportunities elsewhere. White Russians are now another chapter in Pera's romantic past.

One relic of those times is Rejans, the restaurant founded in 1934 by three White Russian dancers beside the Greek church of Panaghia in Pera. Unfortunately the borscht, the duck and the homemade vodka that the restaurant was once famous for have declined in quality and do not justify the high prices.

Neither of the Constantinopolitan Russians I have met – the term emphasises their roots in the city, distinguishing them from the economic immigrants of the 1990s – descend from the White Russian tide. Yet they are "white" enough: their ancestors arrived even before the revolution.

André Tekel goes by a French first name and a Turkish surname, but is Russian "to the bone". I met him by chance at Saint Benoît school, housed in the vast premises of a Benedictine monastery on Galata's Kemeraltı. Its monastic façade conceals unimagined luxury. The private French-language college, although a few metres from Karaköy's infamous brothels, is one of the most prestigious places in town.

Monsieur André caught me admiring the building from the street and invited me inside. He works in the school's administration. It was only after he showed me around that he asked me where I was from. We had spoken in French and I was amazed when he switched to fluent Greek.

André, like all members of old Pera's non-Muslim bourgeoisie, is fluent in Greek, French and Turkish. And, of course, in Russian. "My family arrived in the eighteenth century, under unclear circumstances. This was the first group of Russian settlers in modern times, much before the White Russians you know of. Very few descendants of those two groups survive to this day. I am one of them."

Monsieur André did not mention the economic immigrants of the 1990s. Maybe their bad reputation, especially due to prostitution, makes the 'native' Russians prefer to ignore them. I later met some White Russian elders who wrote the newcomers off as 'soviet bred'. "My family has been in town for more than three hundred years. I may have a Turkish surname, but my name is Christian; we keep our identity, our traditions. Before, I had many Greek friends, but they were forced to leave... I even went to a Greek school for five years," he said.

He is a Perote born and raised, and proud of it. He still lives in the quarter, unwilling to move to the more fashionable periphery. "If you could only glimpse old Pera... a real European enclave. Everybody spoke Greek and French, frequented theatres, cinemas, balls. We had comfort, but culture and refinement too." His wife is also Russian; their only daughter is studying music abroad.

"You must absolutely visit the Russian monasteries," he told me. I was startled. "There are three rooftop monasteries down in Galata, atop old hans. There's always a monk there." He smiled. "Galata was, and is, a mosaic – how long its colours will endure is another question."

An inscription in Russian and Turkish on the wall of an immense *appartement* gives directions to the chapel of St Panteleimon. A veiled woman sat barefoot on her doorstep, peeling potatoes in a big bowl. She directed me to the terrace. There was no elevator in the late-nineteenth-century han, and I had to walk up seven floors to reach a covered corridor surrounding a chapel. At one end, a group of young men and women were singing hymns, stopping now and then to talk, then resuming. They were rehearsing. At the other end, a priest with honey-coloured hair and beard was conversing with some women in Russian. He walked towards me.

"How may I help you?" Father Kallinikos spoke fluent Greek, having spent time in the Russian monastery of St Panteleimon at Mount Athos, the peninsula in Northern Greece, which since the 10th century has been an autonomous monastic community, with monasteries of all Orthodox nations. He invited me to look around, promising he would join me after attending to the parish ladies. St Panteleimon is interesting as a Russian outpost for its bizarre rooftop location and its view. The blue-green domes of the chapels of the other two Russian rooftop monasteries, St Andrew and the abandoned Prophet Elijah, are clearly visible from the covered veranda. So is the Galata Tower.

The three monasteries are dependencies of St Panteleimon in Athos. The huge buildings topped by the chapels, only a few yards from Galata's embankment, were built in the late nineteenth century as hostels for Russian pilgrims on their way to Athos or the Holy Land. They once housed hundreds of White Russians; now they shelter Anatolian immigrants.

Father Kallinikos approached me with a cup of hot tea. "We Russians use large cups, not the minuscule glasses of the Turks." The young men and women rehearsing belonged to the church choir. "There are many Russians in Istanbul today, several thousand. But very few attend regularly. Of course, every Sunday the chapel is packed. But it's the same people who

ADMI
SHIP SUPPL

show up… Unfortunately, this last Russian tide has won itself a bad reputation."

The other Russian chapel, St Andrew, is smaller but more impressive. Its bright blue walls are covered in icons and frescoes in the typical style of Russian iconography, where colour and form is freed from the stylistic rigidity of the Byzantine tradition. But the chapel's highlight is its guardian, Madame Alyeksandra. I'd never seen an elderly hunchback with such shiny blue eyes.

"Couldn't you have come a bit earlier?" she mumbled. "I was about to rest." I apologised for my unexpected arrival. "So we have the same name… Where are you from?" she asked unlocking the chapel's door. "I'm Greek," I said. "How nice. Sightseeing?" she asked, giggling, in well-articulated Greek. "You speak lovely Greek," I exclaimed. "Now, isn't that normal?" she said. "Do I look like a peasant? Don't tell me you didn't expect me to speak it, for Christ's sake. I've lived here all my life. Any idea how many Greek friends I had? I speak Russian, Turkish, Greek and French, because I grew up in the Constantinople of the past, where people were educated, cosmopolitan, polite, refined…" She was out of breath.

I spent some time looking at the frescoes and icons, while Madame Alyeksandra waited impatiently by the door. "Can I take your photograph?" I asked. "Nooo!" she squeaked, hiding her face in her hands. "Are you mad? In these clothes? Put that thing down!" She turned her back to me and hid in the corner. "Come on, dear grandma, don't be upset," I said.

"I'm not grandma," she rellied. "I'm Mademoiselle Alyeksandra. Enough. Time to rest."

As she was locking the door I made my last try. 'Dear Mademoiselle, I'm sorry to have disturbed you. May I ask, are you one of the White Russians that…"

"Aaah!" she broke in. "What's all this? Are you trying to guess my age? What does my age have to do with you? Am I to be taxed for my years? Off you go. Come some other day if you want stories."

After moving to Istanbul I spent more time with Madame Alyeksandra, who was "born to a Russian family in Constantinople shortly before the Great War and the Revolution".

The ruined rooftop chapel of Haghia Triada seen from the "French Arcade", Galata

PART TWO

Asia and the outskirts

Old districts of the Asian shore: glimpsing Europe from "across"

Covered romance in Üsküdar: admiring the panorama of Europe opposite

A quick glance at Istanbul's cinema directory suffices to give an idea of the city's uniqueness. The directory is split into "European shore" and "Asian shore." No other city spreads on two continents. In no other city do people cross continents in an everyday commute from home to work. Separated by the Bosphorus, one of the world's most scenic waterways, and the Propontis (Sea of Marmara), one of the word's smallest seas, Europe and Asia glance at each other from a short distance. They join forces at the mouth of the Black Sea to form what, by virtue of its position at that junction, was always destined to be a world city.

Hearing of a city spread on two continents stimulates the imagination. Yet the first encounter with Istanbul's topography always surpasses one's expectations. Its profound impression on the senses of the traveller is never to be forgotten. The city owes much of its magic to its scenic perspectives, themselves achieved by its fragmentation into three chunks of land (two in Europe, one in Asia) separated by three bodies of water – a topography as complex as it is scenic. Situated right on the meeting point of Europe and Asia, of the Mediterranean and the Black Seas, Istanbul couldn't possibly have had a better setting.

I was lucky: my first ever sight of Istanbul was from the deck of a cruise ship, and I will always recall that day's vivid images. We crossed the Dardanelles as the sun was rising, and sailed down a Marmara Sea as calm as a lake of olive oil. By the time we reached the Princes' Islands it was evening, and the sunset found us the moment the ship entered the mouth of the Golden Horn. The panorama made me fall for the city before even setting foot in it, as had happened to many travellers before me. "It is at the point where the Marmara meets the Golden Horn and the Bosphorus that God and Man, nature and art, have placed or created, in unison, the most marvellous spectacle human eyes may see," de Lamartine wrote, expressing reflections and feelings that have overtaken many other travellers before and after him.

For the traveller not lucky enough to make the same entrance, a similar – albeit more brief

The famous tulip-shaped glasses used to serve tea on the commuter ferries

– sensation is achieved by simply hopping on one of the city ferries doing the Europe-Asia commute. The most obvious routes are from Eminönü or Karaköy to Üsküdar or Kadiköy, and from Beşiktaş to Kadiköy. These ferry rides I take for pleasure every now and then, with the sole purpose of enjoying the views. The ferry ritual involves drinking tea, in the little tulip-shaped glasses emblematic of Turkish tea culture, and maybe eating a simit bread roll. All this on deck, of course, as long as the weather permits, to indulge in the "dolce far niente".

My journey sometimes starts in the Art Nouveau terminal of Beşiktaş. From its café on the first floor one may contemplate the entry to the Bosphorus, the Tower of Leander, the

The Tower of Leander (Maiden's Tower) outside Üsküdar

Asian shore opposite and the movement of tankers and other large ships up and down the strait. It is a place that tourists have not discovered; only seamen and workers from the ferries sit there to play backgammon and sip tea. I plan the ferry crossing so as to catch the sunset on board when returning to the European shore. The line of minarets and domes of the Old City appear as black silhouettes against an orange fire, and the first lights of Europe start to flicker timidly. In all my wanderings around the globe, I have seen nothing more scenic than this view of waterways and hills dotted with monuments on all sides.

These boat rides – for less than two euros, tea and simit included – are the reason for the frequency of my inter-continental crossings. This of course doesn't mean that there are no delights on the Asian shore. Most of the Asian shore is devoid of monuments in the strict sense, which is why foreigners hardly ever make it there. It is also true that endless kilometres south of Kadiköy are urban sprawl, the best planned, cleanest and possibly most affluent in Istanbul, but without much charm. Nevertheless, there are some unspoilt old villages on the Asian shore of the Bosphorus, quaint and "undiscovered" by the crowds of yuppies that have disfigured Europe's Bosphorus villages. And there are the historic neighbourhoods of Üsküdar and Kadikoy, which are definitely worth an exploration.

"Two cities, which in no way resemble each other, stretch on the hills of Asia. Üsküdar, with its Asian aspect, is like an Asian extension of Stamboul [the Old City]. Kadıköy's brand new houses stretch on a promontory..." Bertrand Bareilles' observation in the early twentieth century still holds true. There is little in common between the two cities today, now neighbourhoods of the megalopolis. Their only common feature is that they rival the Sultanahmet area in antiquity. In the north, Üsküdar lies under the Çamlıca hills. Dotted with mosques, it lives under the shadow of their minarets. Kadiköy, in the south, has always been cosmopolitan and affluent, and until the 1960s its old nucleus retained a non-Muslim majority. It seems that the bay at Hadarpaşa separates two worlds, as does the Galata Bridge: Islam, poverty, veils and baggy shalwar trousers in the north; bohemians, artists, cafés and bars, churches and expensive private schools in the south.

Üsküdar was my destination on my first ever boat trip in Istanbul. I wanted a chance to take a closer peek at the Tower of Leander, known in Turkish as Kız Kulesi. One of the city's most romantic symbols, the tower rises at the point where the waters of the Marmara meet those of the Bosphorus, on a rock close to the Asian shore. It is connected with several myths. One is narrated by Ovidius, the Latin poet: Hero, a priestess at the temple of Aphrodite in Sestos, a town of the Dardanelles, falls in love with Leandros, a youth from the town of Abydos, on the opposite shore of the strait. Leandros crosses the Dardanelles every night to meet with his love, but one night during a storm he drowns. Hero commits suicide by falling into the strait. The European readers later "transported" the legend to the Bosphorus, and placed Hero's temple on the rock where the tower rises. Despite the inaccuracy, the tower became known as "Tower of Leander" to the Christians.

The Turks, on the other hand, connect the tower to another legend, according to which a sultan had a much cherished daughter, whom a fortune teller predicted would die because of a snake bite. The terrified Sultan had his beloved daughter shut in the tower, hoping that no snake could reach the tower, surrounded by sea. Yet a snake did bite her, hidden in a basket of grapes she was sent. From this story stems the Turkish name Kız Kulesi, meaning "Tower of the Maiden".

Legends aside, the first time that the rock where the tower stands appeared in history was when the Athenians founded a customs office there, having taken control of the Bosphorus during the Peloponnesian War. It is generally accepted that the first building on the rock, built by Manuel Comnenus (1143-1180), gave way to a tower by Mehmet the Conqueror. The tower was rebuilt several times, and the present structure probably dates from Mahmut II (1808-1839). Its most striking characteristic is the baroque dome with the long flag mast, which makes an elegant silhouette. Until recently it was used as a lighthouse and it's now been converted into a restaurant. But over and above all these practical uses, it's always been a symbol of eternal love.

The hills of Üsküdar rise above the port in a very appealing spectacle. Hills and coast are adorned with a symmetry of mosques. None is beautiful inside, but their exteriors combine to form the dreamy silhouette of an oriental quarter. Üsküdar appears in pictures from the last century as an aggregate of wooden houses and silent streets. Amorphous concrete engulfs the mosques today. My friends hate the area. "It shelters zealots and morons," one said, after my many attempts to convince him to accompany me. He meant that the borough is a centre of both the religious and the fascist "Grey Wolves".

Üsküdar is no other than the ancient Hrysoupolis, which became Scutarium in Roman times, a military term surviving in English as

pp 252-253: Sunset over the Old City as seen from a ferry approaching Europe

"squadron". Its first name ("Golden City" in Greek) is said to derive from the golden colour its houses radiated in the sunset. They still do reflect the dying sun, making that explanation very convincing. A more materialistic explanation ascribes the name to the fact that the town controlled the straits and taxed all ships crossing.

In Byzantine times, the settlements on the Asian shore were not considered part of Constantinople, but were autonomous. Hrysoupolis was captured by the Turks in 1352, 101 years before Constantinople fell, and rapidly became a Turkish town. Yet the hills above always retained large Greek and Armenian populations. Many Armenians remain today in the hills, whose quarters, dotted with churches, are much more middle class than Üsküdar. The latter, now mostly in the hands of Anatolian migrants, is said to conserve the village-like atmosphere of an old Istanbul Muslim neighbourhood, where good neighbourly relations are of primary importance and the local imam is a figure of unchallenged authority.

Once, touring the hills above Üsküdar, I came across the complex of an Armenian church and school. Workers were busy painting in the latter and an elegant woman was giving instructions. They were renovating for the coming school year. The woman instructing was Madame Elise (let us give her that name); she was the headmistress.

"I would like some information on the community," I said. She spoke perfect French, as all urban Armenians of her generation do, and she was fairly competent in English. But not Greek. "I do understand of course, we had so many Greek neighbours in the past. But I can't speak it any more." She took me to her office and offered me tea. Dotted around the walls hung portraits of the Great Leader (Atatürk), his quotes and address to "Turkish Youth". "We have to have them, it is mandatory," she said.

"There are about 4000 Armenians in the periphery, judging from the number of families registered with the parishes," she said. "But there are many not registered. Our school has 200 students; most are Gregorian, a few Armenian Catholics." I asked if the students speak to one another in Armenian. "Sadly, they mostly speak in Turkish," she said. "It all depends on the family. The strictest do not speak Turkish at home, but most do. Our aim is to make students as fluent in Armenian as possible." She said that all social science courses must be given in Turkish.

"So history is taught in Turkish, from Turkish books. And needless to say, you can't touch on the 1915 genocide." She became nervous. "Everybody has private knowledge... There's no need to discuss it in class. We live here. It's better to pretend to forget." She was thoughtful for some minutes. "Their books, their teachers are trying to turn our children against our very identity," she said scornfully. As I was taking notes, she leapt forward. "You won't use my name, will you?"

On their way from Europe to Kadıköy, ferries first stop at Haydarpaşa, where a magnificent chateau-like railway station captivates one's attention. Built in 1909, Haydarpaşa station, terminal of all trains to and from Asia Minor, was Kaiser Wilhelm's present to Abdul Hamid. At the time, French company Collas et Michel had won a concession for the construction, repair and management of the Empire's lighthouses, Anglo-French capital controlled the Ottoman Bank and Russia had secured for herself, through the Treaty of Küçük Kaynarcı (1774), the role of the Protector of the Sultan's Orthodox subjects. The Germans belatedly decided to join the race for "peeling the Ottoman artichoke." Bismarck's Germany, aiming to become an energy giant, took part in the scramble with a plan to build a railway connecting Constantinople to the oil fields of Mesopotamia – the Baghdad railway. The Germans won the concession and the railway, planned to deliver Mesopotamia's oil to the Germans, became an inseparable part of the Eastern Question,

Deutsche Bank financed the building of Haydarpaşa, which gave a very different message to the Sirkeci station. Haydarpaşa symbolises not the dreamy world of the Orient, but the empire's modernisation. The railway never reached Baghdad, and the plan turned sour as the Great War erupted. The railway route traversed largely Armenian-populated territories and the Germans encouraged the Young Turk junta to "cleanse" them of those Christians whose sympathies lay firmly with the Allies. The results are tragically well known, and the genocide is often regarded as German-inspired. The Haydarpaşa station is the most impressive relic of the German railway plan, also reflected in the name of the Asian shore's largest avenue, Bağdat Caddesi (Baghdad Street). Like the Eminönü branch of Deutsche Bank and the Reich's massive embassy in Pera, it is a relic of German imperialism in the Orient.

From the sea, Kadıköy holds no appeal. And yet the streets in the old centre of what was once Chalkedon are full of charms that most visitors never see. A tourist here is a rarity. I don't remember having ever encountered one, apart from the occasional Israeli visiting the beautiful synagogue lost in the backstreets of the Yeldeğirmen district.

Famous all over the Christian world, the name Chalkedon is synonymous with the

Fourth Ecumenical Council and the crystallisation of Christian dogma. Emperor Marcian dictated that the Fourth Ecumenical Council, originally convened in Nicaea, be transferred to Chalkedon, a small town of Bithynia opposite Constantinople. He was resolved to preside over it, since acrimonious theological debates of the time threatened his realm's unity. "Heretic" beliefs were thought to conceal challenges to imperial authority. Like many of his successors, Marcian would take an active part in purging them. In 421, in Chalkedon's cathedral of Haghia Euphemia, the Council excommunicated the Monophysites, those Christians who held that Jesus did not have two natures, a human and a divine, but only one – a divine.

In the theocratic Byzantine Empire, excommunications, massacres, exile and revolts on religious grounds were commonplace. The most notable religious crisis ever was Iconoclasm (730-842), when the influence of rising Islam and its prohibition of images shook the very ideological foundations of the Eastern Church. But before and after Iconoclasm, recurrent dogmatic disputes and their bloody quelling by Constantinople led many provinces to revolt. The empire often sank into chaos similar to that of central Europe during the Reformation and the religious wars. Byzantine provinces such as Egypt, Syria and Phoenicia, adhering to

The Ottoman boat terminal, Haydarpaşa

"heretic" creeds that Constantinople had purged, rebelled and welcomed the Muslims, who had promised to replace Constantinople's dogmatic tyranny with tolerance.

Theologian Gregory of Nyssa wittily summarised the dogmatic hysteria of his age: "Everything, streets, squares, crossroads, is full of those speaking unintelligibly. I ask how many oboli I owe, they answer philosophising on the born and the unborn. I wish to know the price of bread, I am told that 'the Father is greater than the Son'. I ask if my bath is ready, I am told that 'The Son was made out of nothing'."

But Chalkedon existed centuries before religious hysteria won it world fame. On the narrow peninsula occupied by the present districts of Kadıköy and Moda, colonists from Megara settled in the sixth century BC. Pitton de Tournefort claimed the selection of the site was foolish: the historic peninsula of Constantinople opposite, with the Golden Horn providing one of the best natural harbours in the world, was the obvious choice. Ignoring it, the Megarians had to construct two artificial ports. Tournefort narrates the legend: when Byzas, founder of Byzantium, asked the oracle at Delphi where to build his colony, he was told to settle "opposite the land of the blind". This led him to the sight of present Saray Burnu. Tournefort, in turn, charged the settlers of Chalkedon with blindness.

What Tournefort did not take into account was that the Golden Horn, although a perfect natural port, required a large metropolis built around it to control it; the Byzantines managed to safeguard it only after fortifying the Galata shore opposite their capital. The charge of blindness is rather unfair.

Chalkedon lived most of its post-ecumenical council existence in obscurity. Captured and destroyed by the Seljuks several times, it fell to the Ottomans in 1350, more than a century before Constantinople. The Ottomans used its walls and many of its edifices as building material. The city was never colonised by Muslims and was mostly deserted until Constantinople itself fell and became the Ottomans' new capital. Engravings drawn by some of the last visitors to Byzantine Constantinople, such as the Italian Buondelmonti, depict Chalkedon as a sad set of ruins. The place later took on the Turkish name Kadıköy, which translates as "village of the judge" but is most probably an adaptation from Chalkedon.

Haghia Ephemia, the venue of the legendary council, must have disappeared long before the Ottoman conquest. "This miserable village of 700-800 souls conserves nothing of its past but for its name, still in use among the Greeks," Tournefort wrote. The name of the historic church was still used for the local parish, which Tournefort visited: "There is no sign that the Church of Haghia Euphemia was the one now in use by the Greeks, since Euagros informs us that it was situated in the town's outskirts. And Monsieur de Nointel, the Ambassador of France... assures me that the ruins of the historic church are about a mile away from the borough, and that he had seen a plaque there commemorating the Council".

The present Haghia Euphemia is a nineteenth-century church whose elegant belfry has a laden dome and characteristic French windows. It stands on a crossroads in the heart of old Kadıköy, a warren of narrow streets with a few surviving Belle Époque houses. The church, hidden behind a high wall, is worth a visit. It survived the 1955 vandalisms and preserves an impressive gilded iconostasis and marble columns mimicking the Byzantine style. It is dedicated to the first saint born in the region, who was martyred for her faith in 303, before the foundation of Constantine's New Rome.

On a second crossroads down Muvakithane Sok (where Haghia Euphemia is) is the Armenian Gregorian church of Surp Takavor, distinguished by its campanile with the conical domes, typical of the classical Armenian line. Around the two churches squeeze Kadıköy's antique shops, music stores (selling old vinyl records) and bookstores, some of which have stocks of very old European books. Here is also Kadıköy's most famous patisserie, Baylan, owned by an elderly Greek, Monsieur Harry, who studied the art of confectionery in Vienna in the 1930s. The café is a city legend. Originally on the Grande Rue de Péra, it later moved to Karaköy Square and opened a branch in Kadıköy. For decades Baylan has been a meeting place for the intelligentsia and art world.

Most people flock there today for the famous coupe grillée, a caramel ice-cream topped with caramelised nuts. This is Monsieur Harry's creation. I love coupe grillée, but for me the real attraction is Monsieur Harry himself. He is one of the last representatives of that class who were fluent in Greek, Turkish and at least two other foreign tongues, and who have seen and lived in Istanbul as it was: a cosmopolitan metropolis. Harry travels regularly to Paris or Vienna and often holidays in Greece.

Conversely, the vast majority of Constantinopolitans who remain in the city are poor, both materially and culturally. "Everyone who had an opportunity to leave did so," an elderly Constantinopolitan now living in Athens had told me. "Those left behind are either the most desperate, who had nowhere to go or were too poor to even attempt to migrate, or a very few rich people who did not want to leave their businesses. These people do not represent us," he said. "They hardly even speak Greek, let alone French, which we were all fluent in. And most have never been abroad. If they have, it was only to Greece. They don't know what is means to be a Constantinopolitan." Harry, who has seen and done much, does. His stories about the city (and about the Vienna of the 1930s) have made me leave my Pera home for Asia more than once.

An empress' diadem: the Bosphorus

Yalıs on the Yeniköy waterfront

It has been called a water snake, a garland, the diadem of an imperial capital, and has given inspiration to poets, writers and painters through the centuries. The Bosphorus, a narrow sea corridor uniting the Marmara and Black Seas and separating Europe and Asia, follows a sinuous 32-kilometre course northbound from the city to the Black Sea (Euxenus Pontus to the Greeks). Its shores are littered with palaces, castles, churches and mansions, while its Turkish name, Istanbul Boğazı (the Istanbul Strait), emphasises that it is an inseparable part of the city. Most of its residents cannot imagine the city without the Bosphorus, and for many – locals and foreigners alike – the first images Istanbul brings to mind are the Bosphorus panoramas.

Bosphorus is a Greek word, meaning "crossing of the ox". Behind the not-so-romantic etymology hides a Greek legend. This is hardly unexpected, since the strait played an important role in the migrations and the commercial life of the Greeks, who settled in the area from the first millennium BC. The legend goes that Zeus had fallen for Io, a priestess of Hera and daughter of the king of Argos. The eternally deceived wife of the Greek god turned her priestess into a cow and sent a fly to bite her and make her run continuously. The idea was to prevent Zeus from catching her and returning her to her human form. The fleeing cow crossed the narrow strait, thus naming it, and fled to Asia. In case you are wondering, Io was pursued by the biting fly all the way to Egypt where Zeus caught up with her, turned her into a human again and had a son with her – one more in the string of infidelities Hera had to bear with.

To both residents and visitors the Bosphorus is first and foremost a succession of scenic landscapes, "perhaps unparalleled in the world", as the English writer and traveller Julia Pardoe wrote in 1836. Yet the strait is also of prime strategic and economic importance, and has been so since antiquity. Situated north of the Sea of Marmara, (the "Propontis" of the Ancient Greeks – "precursor of the Pontus"), the Bosphorus combines with the Dardanelles (the Hellespont) in the south of that water basin to form a long water avenue connecting the Mediterranean and Black Seas, collectively known as "The Straits". Each of these waterways has more than one name in Greek; one derives from mythology, the other from the region's pre-Greek inhabitants.

Over the last three millennia, competition for control of this water avenue has pitted all the great powers of the time against one another. The struggle of the Greeks for economic penetration in the Black Sea basin led to the legend of Jason and the Argonauts. Later, the straits became a battleground between the Greeks and the Persians, between Athens and Sparta, the Byzantines and the Italian city states, the Ottomans and the Russians. The Crimean War united those who wanted to prevent a Russian takeover of the straits and entry to the Mediterranean; the Gallipoli campaign in the Great War was an Anglo-French plan to seize them.

Every time I sit by the Bosphorus, I recall Turkish writer Orhan Pamuk's short story *The Boy who Watched Ships Go By*. The Nobel Laureate author writes of the sensations the incessant parade of all sorts of vessels – from tankers to a Soviet warship – produced on his childhood imagination, as he watched from the window of his Cihangir home. To grasp the economic and strategic importance hidden behind the beauty of the Bosphorus, one need on-

The aesthetics of this monument in Beşiktaş do not do justice to Atatürk, the leader who saved Turkey from Islamic obscurantism

ly spend an hour monitoring the incessant traffic along its route. Walking or driving along the Old City's Marmara shore, one sees hundreds of vessels queuing to enter the waterway, so important for international navigation.

The Istanbul municipality has inaugurated a new system of monitoring traffic and ensuring safety; modern lighthouses stand on all the promontories along the strait. Accidents are now few and far between, but the notorious Bosphorus currents and the congestion did produce many tragedies in the past. Julia Pardoe mentions that ships often crashed on the parterres of the seaside mansions, and sometimes on the mansions themselves. She describes an incident when a ship ended up in the living room of an Armenian banker. And Pamuk remembers how crowds ran "to watch the Bosphorus burn" as two tankers collided to produce an explosion and fire.

The strait is excellent for fishing, especially during the change of seasons, when it is crossed by migratory species. A "true" Istanbulite is supposed to know the seasons when these species are available, something neither I nor my native Istanbulite partner have mastered – nor any of my friends, for that matter. The Bosphorus fills the plates in the seaside restaurants along its shores. Its boat-taverns serving fish grills, stuffed mussels and fried squid are a peculiarity of Istanbul. There were dozens of them in the past but they have dwindled in number after much pressure from restaurant owners and to the dismay of many Istanbulites. The street vendors selling fried or grilled bonito in sandwiches luckily remain.

It is the serene beauty of the waters and forested hills of the Bosphorus, destined to produce romantic and positive thoughts, that draw me to the channel every now and then. As I imagine is the case for many other people of all sorts of backgrounds and dispositions, the Bosphorus is my panacea. Its sight, be it in the daytime or in the night, under any sort of weather, is a killer of all gloom and stress, a balsam to the soul and the senses. Even if the effect of delight is doomed to fade as one is forced back to reality, a Bosphorus walk or boat ride is an easy and often necessary escape, so that one may face the inevitable return to one's troubles rejuvenated.

A Bosphorus cruise is a luxury I indulge in once in a while, and is not to be missed by any visitor to the city. For only four euros the municipal ferries do the proper Bosphorus cruise, going all the way to the fortress of Anadolu Kavağı near the mouth of the Black Sea and back. They depart from Eminönü and reach Anadolu Kavağı after slightly more than an hour and a half. I always hop on them on weekdays, since

the horrendous crowds on weekends spoil the fun.

During the trip perspectives of this marvellous topography succeed one another as the boat follows the twists and turns of the strait. It is true that the massive building of recent decades has much deformed the panorama. In the faded coloured photographs of a 1960s tourist guide that I unearthed in a bookstore a thick green carpet covers the hills and descends to the very water, intercepted here and there by the villages on the shore. Very few buildings – schools or palaces – were perched on the forested hills at the time. Today, a concrete sprawl has replaced the dense forests in many of the valleys behind the first row of hills on the shore. Despite the supposedly strict regulations, even some of the latter asphyxiate under a profusion of concrete villas.

The concrete mass occasionally peeps from behind the hills, and the skyscrapers of Maslak and the forest of antennas on the Büyük Çamlıca are ugly scars visible from miles away – trash that humans have dumped on nature's beautiful tableau. "To be seen in all its beauty, the Bosphorus should be looked upon by moonlight," Julia Pardoe wrote. She speaks of the star-studded sky and the moonlight, of the "holy quiet" of the evening which lend to the Bosphorus "a mysterious indistinctness which doubles its attraction". This is all the more true today, when the magic veils of darkness also serve the purpose of concealing the ugliness added to the perspective since Pardoe's time, transforming the phalanxes of concrete boxes and the characterless villas into flickering lights reflected on the waters.

The ferry exits the Golden Horn and takes a northbound turn into the Bosphorus. The 1,560-metre-long suspended bridge, named The Bosphorus Bridge or simply The First Bridge, dominates the lower end of the channel and the panoramas from the junction of Istanbul's three waterways. It was inaugurated in 1973 and followed by a second one further up the strait. People either love or hate it, depending on their perception of whether it adds to or spoils the scenery. My conclusion is that the bridge is the only creation of modern architecture that has added to the city's beauty. It's a monumental but elegant gate towering over the Bosphorus currents and the thousands of vessels they carry, a Colossus of Rhodes of modern times. Sadly, one cannot stroll on it and admire the magnificence that spreads on all sides below. For years it's been the favourite venue for suicides, so the police have sealed off the bridge to pedestrians to discourage potential jumpers.

What everybody agrees on is that the First Bridge has become emblematic of Istanbul, em-

An excursion boat passes in front of Anadolu Kavağı

WWW.SUKRUTUR.COM
REZ : 0532 467 39 59

bodying the horrible banality of a "city bridging two continents". The phrase is a horrible banality not only because of its repetition in thousands of guides and leaflets, but also because it promotes a coy image concealing the truth: Constantinople and later Istanbul, as well as Turkey today, are places where East and West, different people and different ideologies, waged relentless war on each other. In recent years, deep ideological divides have threatened the country's social unity: followers of Atatürk and his vision of secular modernity clash with Islamists, liberal internationalists clash with xenophobic traditionalists. The assertion that the bridge symbolises how the city reconciles East and West is a gross misrepresentation. You simply have to ask the zealots of Çarşamba and the Europeanising bourgeoisie of Nişantaşı what they think of each other to realise that the balance some like to see is an illusion.

Entering the strait, the quarters of Pera appear as layers of apartment blocks neatly ascending the hills. One realises how intimate Istanbul's connection to the sea is – the city is turned to face it. Sea surrounds it on all sides, and its hilly topography guarantees that not only the houses by the shore have good views of the water. The poet Paul the Silentiary said in an epigram that "a room with a good view is a safer possession than virtue". It is reasonable to assume he was referring to a sea view. He was a contemporary of Emperor Justinian, who passed a decree forbidding building that would obstruct the view of the sea – "one of the greatest pleasures of this Royal City" according to the emperor. The decree prohibits the construction of houses within 30 metres of the shore. Many other decrees would pile up over the Byzantine centuries to ensure, among other things, that the views enjoyed from the top floors of buildings would not be obstructed by additions to those already in front of them. Sea views are still much sought after, making any villa, apartment or house offering them a valuable asset. In Istanbul, the prime criterion for evaluating real estate is whether it enjoys a sea view, and how unobstructed that is.

The thirst for panoramas made Byzantine aristocrats build their mansions atop hills, and drew the emperors to Blachernae. Yet Byzantine Constantinople was confined to its triangular peninsula and hidden behind massive walls. It was the Ottoman city that spread on the Pera hills beyond the Galata walls, and along the Bosphorus. By the seventeenth century the strait would become the prime holidaymaking area for the pashas, the Phanariots and the Christian merchants of the capital. Ottomans developed a new and even more intimate relationship with the sea embodied in the *yalı*, a type of timber mansion built on the waterfront, which became a symbol of their capital city. This relationship was a very possessive one. Well-to-do pashas and Christian merchants who owned a *yali* enjoyed impressive views of the waters, but their mansion cut the shore off for everybody else. The ideal was for the Bosphorus panorama to enter their living rooms through large windows and be enjoyed from their very sofas.

The avenues along the Bosphorus shores are a recent addition, brought about by the near extinction of the *yalı*-owning classes by the Republic. Until early last century roads ran through or behind the villages, whose buildings came down to the shore to be 'licked by the water'. The word *yali* is said to come from the Turkish word *yalamak* (to lick), although its derivation from the Greek word *aigialos* (shore) is more plausible. Most *yalı* had their own landing dock and boat shelter, where the owners were rowed to from a pier downtown. From the ferry one may spot the few wooden *yalı* surviving here and there; many burnt down and most were replaced by concrete villas, given that the upkeep of wooden buildings is both costly and time consuming.

Transportation to and between the Bosphorus villages was carried out by boats until steam ferries were introduced in the mid nineteenth century. Thanks to the frequent steam ferries the localities became more accessible and many rich people started leaving the congested city and living permanently by the Bosphorus, whose villages gradually turned into suburbs. The urbanising trend of the late nineteenth century is reflected in the architecture along the canal: most of the surviving *yalı* are Art Nouveau. Most of the suburbs on the European shore and many on the Asian shore had a Christian (Greek and Armenian) majority well into the 1950s. The churches in most places are larger and grander than the small *mescit*, which catered to the few Muslims. Large Jewish communities resided in Ortaköy and Kuzguncuk, but today the Jews of the Bosphorus are concentrated in Yeniköy.

The colour of the channel's waters changes from season to season. Depending on the weather and the sky it ranges from azure to deep blue, from emerald to lapis, from dark blue to ash grey. Some claim to be able to forecast the weather by simply looking at the colour of the Bosphorus at a given time. "Poyraz (the north wind) is coming, it will be cold today, so don't lower the heating," Necla, my cleaning lady, says, claiming that the Bosphorus was turquoise last evening. "A turquoise Bosphorus means wind is coming from the north-east." It turns out she is right.

Cihan prepares the pills for his migraine as soon as the colour of the water warns him that Lodos, the south-west wind, is coming, and tries to stay indoors. It is a pity nobody can read in the Bosphorus an earthquake warning, to relieve Istanbulites of their greatest fear.

My observation on the Bosphorus waters is that they never take on that radiant blue of the Aegean that I was brought up with. Moreover, even when the sun shines brightly here its light never equals the clarity and intensity of the Aegean sun. In most of Greece the beauty of nature is wild, flamboyant, at times even blinding, and provokes a wild joy, some sort of ecstasy. Nature here is discreet, the colours are mild, and they inspire tenderness and serenity. They evoke romanticism rather than ecstatic joy. The vegetation is also very different as there are no pines and olive trees, but a dense carpet woven from all sorts of trees. Oaks, magnolias, chestnuts, beeches, fig trees, poplars, elms and lindens cover the hills and valleys, reaching the water.

The Bosphorus is at its most beautiful between April and May, when its Judas trees blossom, dressing the hills with shades of purple and pink. There is an urban legend that the colour of the Judas trees is no other than the *porphyra*, the imperial colour of Byzantium, reserved to members of the imperial family. According to the legend it became the imperial colour because Constantinople was founded when the Judas trees had blossomed… There is little credibility to the myth: violet-scarlet *porphyra* was a royal colour from early antiquity and was extracted from shells. But I like the myth for its attempt to link the beauties of the city to its history.

The ferry trip allows a quick glance at the strait's gems. The kitsch mass of Dolmabahçe Palace on the European shore is succeeded by much more elegant Çırağan, now a frightfully expensive hotel. Then comes the First Bridge, the right to walk on which I'm deprived of due to the sorrows and suicides of others. Right before it, on the European shore, the elegant line of a baroque mosque projecting on a platform marks the trendy suburb of Ortaköy. Standing on the Ortaköy waterfront one sees the mosque's slender minarets contrasting beautifully against the virile modern line of the bridge. A similar contrast is to be seen on the Asian shore opposite, where the other end of the bridge dwarfs Beylerbeyi, possibly Istanbul's most elegant Ottoman palace.

The ferry continues past Arnavutköy (Mega Revma in Greek), a beautiful and unspoilt formerly Greek village of the European shore. Arnavutköy's waterfront boasts the most amazing row of Art Nouveau *yalıs* on the Bosphorus,

Good Friday service in Haghios Georgios, the Greek church in Çengelköy

while its backstreets are a collection of timber houses with delicate woodwork. The suburb also boasts two other things – a stunning cathedral, Taksiarhes, whose dome rises behind the lines of wooden houses, and the most dangerous undercurrent in the strait. Its Greek name, meaning Great Current, serves as a warning. Arguably, the place is the best preserved suburb on the European shore, even though skyscrapers and cement have deformed the hills above it.

Kuleli Military School, a huge building with two identical towers on the Asian shore facing Arnavutköy, marks the vicinity of Çengelköy, one of the most picturesque and introvert Bosphorus settlements. Çengelköy's treasure is the Greek church of Haghios Georgios. Damaged during works for the enlargement of the main avenue, the church still enchants with its carved wooden iconostasis, one of the most beautiful of any Greek church I have ever visited. The walls of the premises hide a beautiful garden and graveyard, where the church's Epitaph procession takes place every Good Friday. I was so impressed by the stunning iconostasis and the friendliness of the parishioners when I visited last Easter that my anger at having missed the ferry to Prinkipo for the Epitaph procession there was quickly appeased. We finished the evening over grilled calamari with wine sauce in the Çengelköy Iskelesi restaurant on the waterfront – a surprising dish given that Turks never use wine in cooking, due to Islamic tradition.

Arnavutköy is succeeded by the gulf of Bebek, an undistinguished suburb of expensive cafés and boutiques. Bebek's redeeming feature is its seaside park and the Bosphorus (Boğaziçi) University on the hill above. Inaugurated as Robert College in 1863 to provide an American education in Constantinople, the university is a sight to see. Its attractive historic buildings would not be out of place on an Ivy League campus while no other university premises in the world could rival its vistas of the strait and the Rumeli Hisarı, whose walls are contingent to the northern end of the university.

Rumeli Hisarı (Fortress of Europe) and Anadolu Hisarı (Fortress of Asia Minor) face each other on one of the narrower points of the strait and have been transformed now from the fearsome military outposts they once were to major attractions of the Bosphorus. The first was built by Mehmet the Conqueror in 1452, as part of his plan to control the strait and take Constantinople. Anadolu Hisarı on the Asian shore had been built by Beyazit Yıldırım ("The Thunderbolt") in the late 1390s, again as an outpost to checker Byzantine power. Mehmet used both fortresses to block aid being shipped to Constantinople from the north during the

1453 siege. Today, Rumeli Hisarı is the venue for concerts on moonlit summer nights, and the coast in front of it is lined with some of the nicest tea houses and boat restaurants on the Bosphorus. Anadolu Hisarı is the centre of a quaint village of timber houses, giving an idea of what the Bosphorus suburbs looked like before the internal migrations and consequent massive construction of the last decades.

The ferry calls at Yeniköy, the most interesting European suburb after Arnavutköy. It appears from the ferry as a garland of *yalıs* reflected on the waters; on its hills the bell towers of its churches rise over the roofs. Yeniköy, the Greek settlement of Nihori, is the birthplace of the mother of Greek poet Cavafy, who dedicated a poem to the village "where nature smiles to the visitor" and praised its dense vegetation. Today, Yeniköy is an exclusive suburb with good restaurants and forested hills, and it still preserves some of the air of Ottoman Constantinople thanks to its timber houses, churches and tree-lined main street. But the Christian absence is striking. The Greeks make themselves seen only at Easter, when the resurrection mass draws crowds from all over the city to whichever of the suburb's three Greek churches is holding the service that year. I always attend with my Turkish and Greek friends. It is very encouraging that many Turks come to

An Antiochean woman guards the Greek church of Taksiarhes, Arnavutköy

these services joining their Greek friends and helping greatly to fill a church that would otherwise be half empty. Yet every time we leave the church with our lit candles, which custom dictates should reach our homes still alight to bless them, we provoke amazed stares and often questions that betray the genuine amaze-

ment of the district's residents. Greek customs are unfamiliar to the newcomers, and even the old ones do not remember them any more. The Greeks are a blurred memory of the past, having become something of a folklore.

A silence always falls on the crowds as the ferry approaches the end of the Bosphorus and the mouth of the Black Sea, a silence that betrays their awe. On the Asian shore, the Byzantine fortress that Turks have named Yoros Kalesi dominates the hill of Anadolu Kavağı, guarding the northern entrance to the Bosphorus. The latter, until recently a quaint fishing village, is now an aggregate of fish taverns and tourist shops, but nevertheless retains some charm. Climbing the steep hill to the fortress is worth the effort, both for the amazing view of the mouth of the Black Sea and for the building itself, which was built by the Byzantines but fell to the control of the Genoese in the last years of Byzantine rule. The insignia of the Palaeologi dynasty are still visible on its towers.

It was in the mouth of the Black Sea, so clearly visible from the fort, that the mythical Symplegades stood. According to the legend these were two moving stones that collided into and crashed any ship – and even bird – attempting to pass through to the Black Sea. The Argo, the 50-oar ship of Jason and the Argonauts, was the first to cross through the rocks, using the advice of the fortune teller Phineas. The Symplegades are the personification of the deadly currents of the Bosphorus, which posed so many troubles to Greek navigators at the time, clouding the stunning beauty of the strait with the fear of sudden death. Modern technology ensures that the passengers of today are spared this fear of dying in the currents. What remains is the magic of the passage and of the sunsets and moonlit nights of the Bosphorus admired from a deck.

The entry to the Black Sea seen from Anadolu Kavağı

The Princes' Islands: people, stories and feasts in an idyllic refuge

The ferry to the Princes's Islands reaching Prinkipo (Büyükada)

The princely name befits an exclusive resort. The island group, 15 kilometres south of Istanbul in the Marmara, has traditionally been a favourite refuge of the city's non-Muslim élites and expatriates. Four out of nine are inhabited – Proti (Kınalıada), Antigone (Burgazada), Halki (Heybeliada) and Prinkipo (Büyükada) – and are dotted with remnants of refinement: wooden mansions with ornately carved finishings, elegant hotels and seaside clubs. They are remembered as places of opulence and romanticism and associated with the merriness of the Belle Époque.

In spite of these happy memories, the name of the island group has a horrific origin. Owning a summerhouse on the islands was a matter of status in turn-of-the-century Constantinople and holidaying there a privilege, but the islands were a purgatory for Byzantine royalty. The

royals after who they were named did not arrive to relax in the idyllic setting much appreciated later. Victims of the intermittent and ruthless feuds between contenders for the throne they were exiled on the rocky and forested archipelago, often blinded or castrated, to spend the rest of their days interned in one of its numerous monasteries.

The list is long. Overthrown by Leo the Armenian, emperor Michael Rangave, his wife and four children were confined to different monasteries in Proti. Leo was himself murdered by agents of the emperor Michael Traulos on the church altar on Christmas Day, 820. His body was taken to Proti along with his wife and sons, who were castrated. One died during the operation, the other two went blind and deaf because of it. Emperor Romanos Lekapenos was exiled to Proti by his own children in 944. In 969, Empress Theofano followed. In 1068, Emperor Romanos Diogenes founded a monastery in Proti, not knowing that he himself would finish his days there, overthrown and blinded by Emperor Michael Doukas. Despite the splendour of its art, Byzantium was shot through with cruelty and corruption.

The Ottomans left the islanders unmolested. They granted special privileges to this Greek enclave, where both the permanent settlement of Turks, as well as the erection of mosques, was prohibited. Only Greeks resided here until the mid nineteenth century. As all Constantinopolitans, they were spared the hated child tax. The parochial island society had minimal contact with Constantinople, since the islands were hard to access. The only times they witnessed a massive influx of visitors was during the plague epidemics in Constantinople: rich pashas, Christian merchants and foreign delegates fled to the safety of the archipelago until the epidemic subsided

A French traveller, Frederic Lacroix, wrote of "a sort of democracy, where local Turkish lords are lenient. The inhabitants consist exclusively of Greek fishers, farmers and rowers." Voyagers stress that the islanders were spared not only from co-existence with Turks, but also from their visits. Charles McFarlane, a Briton visiting in 1828 at the final stages of the Greek Revolution, wrote of islanders singing patriotic anthems featuring its heroes and battles. The audacity greatly surprised him. "At such moments, it is hard to grasp that these Greeks are slaves..." He explains how the absence of Turkish settlers made the slanders feel freer and happier. The islands were the periphery of Constantinople where church bells were allowed.

Their metamorphosis from quaint fishing communities to resorts was the result of developments in sea transport. Until the 1840s, they

e rotting wooden mansion
the Danasses family, Prinkipo

were reached by rowing boats or sailboats, whose Greek rowers and captains were renowned for their skill. The pleasant excursion took several hours, however, and was only possible in the best of weather. In 1846, British-made steamboats considerably shortened the journey, ending the islands' isolation. A number of affluent non-Muslims, especially merchants, chose them as a summer retreat from Constantinople's humid heat and congestion. The islands were integrated into the capital, becoming its most exclusive "suburb", a local equivalent of the French Riviera. Holidaymakers and locals co-existed without much interaction.

Today, ferries to "The Islands", as Istanbulites refer to the group, depart from the quay by the Sirkeci train station. They take little more than an hour to reach Prinkipo (Büyükada), the most distant of the group. As with all ferry trips in Istanbul, the journey is half the fun. As the boat departs, many passengers head to the rear of the ship to admire Istanbul's panorama. On a good day, passengers sit on the deck suntanning and sipping tea from the tulip-shaped glasses, sometimes munching on a simit, the ubiquitous bread ring sprinkled with sesame (the same bread ring is a *koulouri* in Greek). It is customary to throw morsels of simit in the air and feed the clouds of seagulls, which always surround the ferries. The seagulls are pretty assertive in claiming what they think is owed to them: I have had my simit snatched more than once! Sometimes dolphins accompany the ferry. Dolphins once abounded in the Marmara, but their population has dwindled because of pollution.

As to human companions, crowds on the island ferries are always very mixed. From late spring, tourists board, heading mainly to Prinkipo (Büyükada). Greeks prefer Prinkipo and Halki, Israelis go solely to the former. Then there are the islanders themselves, some of whom commute to the city daily. One cannot escape noticing, especially on weekends, the large number of navy cadets. Turkey's naval academy has been stationed in Halki since 1850, and young cadets on their weekend leave board the boats looking awkward, their all-white uniforms contrasting sharply with their dark features.

Seen from afar, the islands appear like a string of rocks rising from the water. A closer look reveals that they are covered with dense vegetation. Pines dominate the thick green carpet spread over the hills. Swimming in the polluted Marmara is not advised, while most of the rocky beaches are unattractive. The best time to visit is spring, to enjoy the symphony of colours and smells.

The Princes' Islands are an oasis of tranquillity. No cars are allowed on them except a few police trucks and those of the municipality, collecting the garbage and distributing gas and water bottles to the few shops. One either has to walk, rent a bike or hop on one of the phaetons, a symbol of the archipelago. There are no shops apart from those catering to basic amenities. You come here in order to relax and meditate, and the islands have traditionally attracted writers and artists.

Until the 1950s, their towns spread like forests of leafless trees, with wooden buildings of a grey-brown colour. Many of the wooden mansions burnt down; concrete replaced most of the rest, which has altered the appearance of the towns. Today, white predominates.

The islands are the last enclave to have somewhat preserved the cosmopolitan feel of Ottoman Constantinople. Kınalı retains an Armenian majority, whilst Prinkipo is said to have a Jewish majority in summer time. Although the Greek majority of the three largest islands has been depleted, churches and monasteries still greatly outnumber mosques. Recent arrivals of Assyrian Christians and Alevites from Turkey's eastern provinces gave a new boost to the archipelago's cosmopolitanism.

Antigone, the second island to be reached from the city, used to be covered in pines until a disastrous fire in November 2003 wiped out the dense forest. Antigone nevertheless remains my favourite island, perhaps because it stays tranquil even in midsummer. The island's Turkish name, Burgaz, is a corruption of the Greek *pyrgos* (tower). In old lithographs a tower is depicted on the shore and another atop the hill, where a Byzantine monastery stood. There are no traces of either tower left.

The bicycle is an essential means of transport in Halki

Grave from the Prinkipo Greek cemetery

Antigone was the most Greek of the islands. There was no mosque here until 1953, when the few Muslims asked for one to mark the 500th anniversary of the Conquest. The overwhelmingly Greek character inspired the authorities in the past to raise a large metal Turkish flag on the hill above the town.

For me, Antigone is the island of Madame Keti. I met this elderly Greek lady by the jetty during my first visit. She was walking up and down, smoking a cigarette. I immediately understood she was Greek from her black clothes (Muslims don't wear black for mourning). Approaching, I asked whether it was possible to visit the church, an impressive eclectic cathedral mixing neo-Byzantine with neo-Gothic elements. She walked me there and made a phone call to Andreas, the priest.

Madame Keti was one of the last 15 or so Greeks permanently on Antigone. Most of the island's two to three thousand are new arrivals from the south-eastern provinces, especially from Erzincan. Many are Alevite; the islands' *cemevi* (Alevite shrine) is found here.

A mother of five, Keti was a typical Constantinopolitan Greek woman: merry, laughing all the time and extremely gossipy. And yet there was something that seemed to be weighing heavily on her. "My youngest daughter, Elisabeth, is the only one of my children who lives here. She is married to a Turk... He's a very good boy," she said almost apologetically. The couple have one daughter, Melissa.

"They're having problems," Keti said. "Mixed marriages are frowned upon; religion poses insoluble problems." Keti's husband was dead. "Elisabeth has always been determined and opinionated. She hid her relationship from us. When she spoke, it was to announce her coming marriage. It was such a shock to her father; he died the same night." Keti cried for a while. She told me her other children were living in Greece.

The priest arrived. A father of four, he looked young and attractive. Haghios Ioannes, erected in 1896, is one of Istanbul's largest churches. Andreas showed me around the

The Greek cemetery on the highest hill of Antigone

church, whose interior doesn't match its exterior splendour. He tolled the church bell every evening, and Madame Keti opened for those wishing to light candles.

I met Elisabeth at her shop, a convenience store by the port. Her dynamic character was immediately apparent. Talking with her revealed some of the problems Istanbul non-Muslims deal with. "There are so few of us left," she complained. "How could they expect me to find a Greek husband here?" She said she was happy with her choice; Ertan, her husband, was caring and respectful. "The only problem is with the state."

She told me that although Ertan was willing to have Melissa baptised, the state wouldn't allow it. "In Turkey, the child takes the father's religion by law," she said, adding that even the parents' consent made no difference to this. "If we're thinking of leaving, it's only because of this." Elisabeth didn't want her children registered as Muslim. "We had to christen Melissa secretly in Greece," she confided, voicing her concern that local society would give Ertan a hard time if they found out.

"I don't want to leave Antigone," she said, telling me of their difficulties. "They wouldn't accept Melissa into the Greek school on Prinkipo because her father is Muslim." Elisabeth had to take her daughter every morning to the Italian school in Şişli, north of Pera – a two-hour journey from the island. She felt resentment towards the local Greeks, who had ostracised her after the marriage. "I despise them, they only know how to gossip," she said. Meanwhile, Melissa and the priest's children were chasing each other and shouting in Greek nearby, unaware of Elisabeth's dilemmas.

Burgaz was the refuge of Sait Faik Abasiyanık, the famous Turkish storywriter. He lived with his mother in the villa built by the Greek merchant Spanoudis right opposite Haghios Ioannes from 1934 until his death in 1954. A sensitive, lonely person, he retreated to the parochial island community, living modestly among the fishermen. Their lifestyle, values and agonies are often the theme of his stories, in which minorities are dealt with affectionately. Sait Faik is also renowned for his love of animals. A homosexual, he must have found life almost impossible in the strict moral climate of his time. He died from cirrhosis at the age of 48, after having written some of the most moving pages of Turkish prose. The Spanoudis Villa is now a museum dedicated to him.

I revisited this community a year later, after settling in Istanbul. Madame Keti was more concerned than ever. "They're leaving," she almost whispered. Elisabeth and Ertan were moving to Greece, to look for better work and some peace of mind. "I'll be left alone," she said. The other news was that the priest had left his wife and moved in with a Greek lady in Pera. "Now I have to toll the bell every evening," Keti said. "But if I die, who will take over?"

On my third visit I ran into Elisabeth and Ertan, cheerfully sipping tea in a seaside café. They had established themselves in a border Greek town and were here on holiday. "I am not going deeper inside Greece; I don't want to feel cut off from Antigone. We return every holiday," Elisabeth said. They seemed happier than ever. A new member had joined the family, one-month–old Daphne. They had found work

A moment of contemplation on the deck of the islands' ferry outside Kınalı

in Greece and were not considering returning; they'd be coming and going, they said. But Madame Keti wasn't there. "She died suddenly, shortly after the great fire," Ertan said. Her death, the flight of the priest and Elisabeth and Melissa's departure had brought the number of permanent Greek residents down to 11.

I headed to the Greek cemetery at the top of Antigone's highest hill. It was a spring day, shortly after Easter. Although no trees had grown yet, the slopes were green, covered in thyme, lavender and flowers of all colours and scents. The walk offers panoramas over the town below and the island of Halki. It takes about 40 minutes to reach the hilltop. On the road, I picked some yellow and blue flowers to put on Keti's grave.

The cemetery is one of the archipelago's most idyllic spots. A wall surrounds the graves and the church of the Metamorphosis (Transfiguration). I knew Gülay, the guardian, from a previous visit. "Now the trees are burnt we freeze in winter. The air strikes from every direction," she said. Gülay comes from the Black Sea region and lives in the small house beside the church with her son. Her husband works in the town. Their only companions up here are a dog and a donkey. "My boy does the 40-minute walk to school every morning, returning every afternoon, always alone, often under rough weather. I am sure he'll be a runner one day!" she laughed.

The ruins of a Byzantine church, sole remnant of the monastery built here by Emperor Basil I in 865, stand on the hill.

The French adventurer Pierre Gilles mentions encountering a church and cistern here on his 1545 visit. The ruins surround a modest church of the 1860s dedicated to the Transfiguration. Here and there are scattered capitals and fragments of marble friezes, remains of the Byzantine edifice. Lines of graves follow, amidst a plethora of flowers.

From every corner of the cemetery one can glimpse the sea and the islands. The beauty and serenity of the place – breeze and views and scents – awakens feelings of happiness and placidity. I placed the flowers on Keti's grave. Who succeeded you in tolling the bell? I wondered. I had forgotten to ask Elisabeth. Maybe I unconsciously refrained from asking, afraid of hearing that the bell is now silent. Its sound was in a sense the requiem of Greek Antigone.

Halki is the group's second largest island in area and population. Traditionally a transition between parochial Antigone and social Prinkipo, it tried to catch up with the latter and was once dotted with elegant wooden mansions. Few survive; most fell victim to fires and neglect. Compared to its rival, depicted as a rude, vain, extravagant diva, Halki was traditionally described as a modest, shy virgin, quiet, discreet and intellectual.

To the outside world, Halki is known as the seat of the Orthodox seminary, situated in the monastery of Haghia Triada (Holy Trinity) on a hill above town. The seminary was closed by the Turkish state in 1971 after the military coup, when a new law was passed prohibiting private higher education. Its reopening has been a consistent Greek demand and another reason for friction between Greece and Turkey.

From Prinkipo, Halki appears as two hills united by a stretch of low ground. This silhou-

Demetres Mandacıoğlu, one of the las
Prinkipian Greek

ette gave the island its Turkish name, Heybeli, meaning "saddle–like". Indeed, the similarity to a saddle is striking. The Greek name derives from *halkos* (copper); there was a copper mine here from antiquity until the nineteenth century.

The monasteries found on all of Halki's hilltops flourished in Byzantine times; it was to one of them that Theodore Studites, the Iconodule abbot of the Studion monastery, was exiled by Iconoclast Leo the Armenian. Byzantine manuscripts were kept in many of them until the eighteenth century, but they were ruthlessly plundered by European travellers, ending up in many of Europe's large libraries. In the years leading up to the Greek Revolution, members of the Filiki Etaireia met secretly in Halki's monasteries.

The Ottoman naval academy, founded in 1773, was moved to Halki in 1824. The move, during the first years of the Greek Revolution, must have been intended as a warning to the archipelago's Greeks. The arrival of the academy was very much resented by locals, as it was accompanied by the first permanent Turkish settlers. Today, the navy maintains installations all over Heybeliada.

During my reconnaissance visit to the island I had travelled in the most unlikely company. Hopping on a ferry from Prinkipo, I ran into Zeki, a young naval officer living in Halki. He was interested in practising his English (I spoke no Turkish at the time) and I was interested in meeting a Turkish officer. He said the caretaker of the Greek cathedral of Haghios Nikolaos was his friend and suggested the three of us tour the island – an offer I couldn't refuse.

It turned out that Sabri, the caretaker, lived in the impressively austere building of the old Greek elementary school, now abandoned and in decay. He was a member of the Arabic-speaking Orthodox community of Antakya (Antioch). He was given the post because there was no Greek to take it: the few on Halki were all elderly.

Zeki rushed home to change into civilian clothes and then our tour began. A number of impressive wooden mansions of prominent Greek families line the northern end of the quay, just below the Haghia Triada hill. Before its construction in 1925, those mansions stood on the very waterfront – as did those along the Bosphorus – and had private anchorages and private beaches. The massive staircases leading to the latter survive.

Sabri opened up Haghios Nikolaos for us. Its massive iconostasis of white marble and the huge chandelier, brought over from Paris, reveal the aesthetic preferences of the haute bourgeoisie, who holidayed on Halki and who commissioned the cathedral.

Zeki joined us there. We hired a phaeton

and headed for the theological school in the grounds of the Haghia Triada monastery. Its gardens give glorious vistas over the archipelago. I was allowed to briefly admire the church, whose interior of sculpted wood is coated in gold leaf, and look at the spectacular library, with its thousands of old and precious volumes. The school was built in 1896 by the famous architect Pericles Fotiades along neo-Byzantine lines.

The monastery dates to Byzantine times. European travellers who visited all commented on the views and idyllic setting, and most mention the precious manuscripts housed in its library. Many were stolen or bought by the travellers and visiting ambassadors, and a few have found their way to Oxford's Bodleian Library. The theological school was opened on the premises in 1844, and continued to turn out clergy for the Orthodox Church until the Turkish authorities closed it.

The phaeton continued along the street, piercing the dense pine forest to reach what became my favourite spot on the island, the tiny shrine dedicated to St Spiridon. It is also known as "the Arsenios monastery" from the name of its founder. Dating from the nineteenth century, the wooden buildings of the shrine stand on top of a cliff in the south, lost amidst the pines. The wooden church is painted in a charmingly rustic style. All three of us sat in the courtyard, gazing at the view towards Prinkipo. Zeki, a native of Malatya in south central Anatolia, said that he felt he was in another country. I understood very well what he meant.

Prinkipo (Büyükada) is the most distant, the largest and the most famous island in the group. Greeks and Turks call it "The Island", and many agree that it is the prettiest of them all. Unbeatable in architectural and natural beauty, it can nevertheless become tedious on summer days when hordes of tourists and picnicking Anatolians from Istanbul's slums invade.

The streets around its town are bathed in the colours and smells of bougainvillea, oleander, mimosa, hibiscus, honeysuckle and jasmine. But the island's most outstanding feature is the Belle Époque wooden mansions, reminiscent of the late Ottoman capital's splendour. Prinkipo was a sort of Riviera, where the upper social strata of all Ottoman "millets" interacted in a refined environment, introducing customs and tastes very different to those of the islanders. As far back as 1862 Constantinopolitan Greek historian Scarlatos Vizantios accused the holidaymakers of destroying the island's serene and parochial atmosphere.

Prinkipo used to be a multi-ethnic microcosm in the summer, as the multitude of extant shrines betrays. An Armenian Catholic church, a Roman Catholic parish and a synagogue exist

alongside the many Greek shrines and a late-nineteenth-century mosque. The sumptuous villas bear the Greek, Armenian, Jewish or Levantine names of their original owners.

Today, Greeks and Armenians have dwindled, but Büyükada remains the hangout of Istanbul's Jews. Their presence dates back to the Belle Époque and rose dramatically after 1923, when many Greeks fled, fearing Turkish retributions after the Asia Minor defeat. Despite a dwindling of the community caused by immigration to Israel, Jews are the majority here in summertime – or so it is claimed. Judeo-Espanyol is widely spoken in the shady side streets.

Ever since I settled in Istanbul I have associated Prinkipo with Good Friday. The little church of the Panaghia Eleousa (Virgin the Helper) is the only one in Istanbul to hold an Epitaph Litany (procession). Situated on the Fayton Meydanı, the square where carriages await passengers, it is crowded every Good Friday not only with diaspora Prinkipians returning home to celebrate Easter, but also by many Greeks, either from Istanbul or Greece.

Hearing that the litany would be allowed to tour around town, as Greek custom dictates, brought me to Prinkipo on my first Easter in Istanbul. The procession hadn't been allowed for years. Arriving at the island I was greeted by a banner opposite the Art Nouveau boat terminal reading "Happy Easter to our Orthodox compatriots. Municipality of the Islands". Chants resounded from the main square. The phaeton drivers chatted nonchalantly and the surrounding streets were crowded with policemen talking on walkie-talkies. The mayor waited by the church door to welcome the faithful. It was a very emotional moment for all those returning as visitors to a city they had left decades ago with memories of the 1955 pogrom and the evictions and petty harassment of later years.

The most intriguing aspect of the litany is the reaction of local Turks towards it. I had realised before that Greeks are an item of curiosity, especially for the young or the Anatolian newcomers, who have had no experience of them. The Greek exodus has erased them from memory – the sound of their language, their customs, their foods. In the 1960s large parts of Istanbul were Greek-populated and Greek was heard all over the city, but most people wouldn't recognise it today or would mistake it for Spanish.

The spectacle repeats itself every year. As the litany leaves the church to take to the streets, the carriage drivers look on in a respectful silence. The children, bearing candles and effigies of saints, come first. The choir follows, with Greek women and girls from all over the city, then comes the crucifix and the priests, then the epitaph and about 50 to 60 faithful – a

Epitaph procession, Prinkipo

large congregation for an Istanbul Greek church. Among them on this occasion was myself with some German, American and Turkish friends. The police surround the procession, block all side streets to make way and occasionally talk on their walkie-talkies in low voices so as not to disrupt the chants.

The shopkeepers come to their doors and look on, interested and silent. People come to their windows to witness a spectacle as exotic to most as a Buddhist procession would be to the average Athenian. I once noticed a young woman stretching her mobile phone out of the window, then speaking to her friend on the line: "They're singing, can you hear?"

If Turks are curious, Greeks tend to be very emotional. Many of the elderly cry all along the litany. Someone uninformed about the community's fate may interpret these tears as religious zeal. But the tears are mostly for the past and present and for the uncertainty of the dwindling community's future. After parading along the backstreets and stopping in front of the sumptuous but closed off cathedral of St Demetrius, the litany returns to the church and as the faithful leave, the phaeton drivers say to them, "May God accept your prayers."

The Good Friday procession is very much a Greek affair, but Prinkipo's other major Christian festival draws thousands of Muslims from all over Turkey. On St George's Day (April 23), pilgrims flock to the monastery dedicated to the saint, which is on a hill outside the town. Many belong to the Alevite sect, a tolerant and syncretic branch of Islam. To outsiders, seeing Muslims venerate a Christian saint is probably a bewildering sight. Yet it is a very common one all over the Middle East. In Turkey, Syria and Egypt Muslims visit churches to pray to a saint they consider a miracle worker and to be blessed by the priests. St George is much revered by Muslims. The dragon slayer of the legend is seen as a hero, a fighter against evil, and is not necessarily associated with Christianity.

The Prinkipo pilgrimage is one of the most important in the region. The feast of St George coincides with a national holiday: April 23 commemorates the inauguration of Turkey's first National Assembly. This ensures massive participation. If you want to attend it's best to hop on the first boat to the island early in the morning. Yet there is such pandemonium, even on the 7am boat, that finding a seat is a hard task.

The festive atmosphere hits you the moment you set foot on the island. Outside the terminal, people distribute sweets: they are pilgrims of earlier years whose wishes came true and who want to express their gratitude. At the same time, street vendors sell candles, oil, handkerchiefs and cotton reels, as well as icons and keys. The objects appear unrelated to one another and devoid of any meaning. Yet all have a symbolic value lost in time. It is only after one reaches the bottom of the steep ascent to the monastery that one realises this pilgrimage of Muslims to a Christian shrine is essentially a pagan commemoration, reviving practices that predate both religions by millennia.

The monastery is on a steep hill out of town. It is easily reached by a phaeton from the square in front of the Greek church, but on April 23 the difficulty is getting hold of a phaeton. One may have to queue for more than an hour before one becomes available. Another option is to take a boat from the town to a beach close to the monastery. I myself have always opted for walking. It does take some time, but the walk takes you through scenic surroundings and is definitely more exciting than queuing for ages. I have never managed to calculate how long the walk from the ferry terminal to the foot of the hill takes. I always get distracted and make long pauses to admire and take photographs of the elegant mansions on both sides of the road.

At the base of St George's hill, street vendors sell pretty much the same as their competitors at the port. Extras here include miniatures of houses, keys and people and a multitude of offerings clearly labelled: for child, for marriage, for love, for house, for car, for success for university exam, for money, for luck. All wishes that pilgrims are likely to have are represented by some minuscule offering that they purchase and leave with the saint. Keys symbolise luck. Icons, dyed eggs and crosses are also sold. Most of the pilgrims are women of all ages and social classes, some veiled, others sporting the latest fashions, gypsy mothers with flocks of children, young Istanbul professionals, women from the slums and Arabic Christians from around Antioch.

It's normally a half-hour trek to reach the peak and the monastery, but on St George's day you may need well over two hours. If you were wondering why on earth all those cotton reels are sold, you get your answer as soon as you start ascending. Many pilgrims tie the thread on a branch at the lower end of the ascent and unwind it slowly on their way to the monastery. If the thread finishes along the road, they tie a new one and continue unwinding. Legends from Greek mythology crossed my mind when I first saw this practice. Since ancient Greece, cotton thread has represented life, and its unwinding from the reel symbolises the human being's journey through time. The cotton thread is the future, it is destiny, and the pilgrims unwind it murmuring prayers, wishes and chants to the powers that they believe determine our lives. On both sides of the road a wall of cotton thread is raised, resting on bushes.

The bushes are decorated with hundreds, maybe thousands, of knots from cloth and paper. The knots are traditionally fertility charms, and make the bushes look like primitive out-of-season Christmas trees. Each knot represents a wish of the pilgrim who tied it; sometimes the knots are simple strips of paper on which the pilgrims have scribbled their wishes and pleas to the saint. Reading them is revealing; most ask for "a good husband", a child or a house.

I have always been breathless on reaching the monastery, built in 963 when Nikephorus Phocas was emperor of Constantinople, according to tradition. The monastery is quite tiny, and the thousands of pilgrims have to wait patiently to enter. Upon entering, many women cover their heads, as if in a mosque. The monks by the door warn them not to remove their shoes. Inside the church the incense, the smell of candles and the murmur of prayers and thanksgiving transports the visitor to another dimension. The worshippers sit in front of the icons, kiss them and recite prayers. They wait patiently to be blessed by the priests, who place their heads under a cloth and recite a prayer. The icon of St George, believed to be miraculous, is covered with the silver offerings of the Greeks, representations of people or parts of the body. The more "modern" offerings are from the Anatolians, among them a profusion of watches, not always of precious metals.

"The fashion of dedicating watches to the saint is a recent one," explained a middle-aged Phanari Greek, now resident in Thessaloniki, who was helping with the reception of the pilgrims. "People are eager to offer the saint whatever they own of value. Greeks in the past offered their jewels, as Loxandra does in the novel. For many of the Anatolians, the watches are their most valuable possession." He said about 40,000 people visit the monastery during the year.

Prinkipian Greeks and Turks scorn the pagan customs of "those Anatolians" and condemn their ignorance of Greek traditions. "I am so frustrated at these silly customs they have imported. They just pollute the environs of the monastery," a Turkish woman at the islands' municipality building complained. Ironic comments abound on the Greek side. If you ask me, the pilgrimage is one of the most moving spectacles I've ever witnessed. I feel for these people, travelling often for days to reach the island, their devotion, their need for help and at the enthusiastic way in which they evoke the forces of good to assist them in their everyday lives. The pilgrims greet one another with the words, "May God accept your prayers." The kindness of these words moves me deeply.

Fertility charms by the monastery of St George, Prinkipo

Two boys training pigeons atop an old Greek house,
Kumkapı

The photographs in this book
are by Alexandros Massavetas

Editor: Julie Barrie
Design: Poppy Alexiou & Alexandra Drossou
Pre-press: Multimedia S.A.
Printing: Psyllidis Dimitris

Series Editor: John Psaropoulos